edition

CHARTING
SECRETS

Trade like a machine and finally beat the
markets using these bulletproof strategies

LOUISE BEDFORD

Wrightbooks

First published in 2013 by Wrightbooks
an imprint of John Wiley & Sons Australia, Ltd
42 McDougall St, Milton Qld 4064

Office also in Melbourne

Typeset in 12.5/14 pt Perpetua Std Regular

© Louise Bedford 2004, 2007, 2013

The moral rights of the author have been asserted

National Library of Australia Cataloguing-in-Publication data:

Author:	Bedford, Louise
Title:	Charting secrets: Trade like a machine and finally beat the markets using these bulletproof strategies / Louise Bedford
Edition:	Revised ed.
ISBN:	9781118543184 (pbk.)
Notes:	Includes index.
Subjects:	Stocks — Charts, diagrams etc.
	Stock price forecasting.
Dewey Number:	332.63228

Printed in Singapore by
C.O.S. Printers Pte Ltd

10 9 8 7 6 5 4 3 2 1

Disclaimer

Contents

Contents

10 System development secrets 255
There's more to trading than just diagnosing the trend. It's time you looked at your entire trading system and filled in some of the blanks so you can trade like a machine.

11 The short and the long of it 265
Markets have a habit of reversing trend and fouling up your plans of attaining a neat and easy profit. To last in this game, you need to make money when the market is going down as well as up. Keep reading as all will be revealed...

12 More psychology secrets 279
Sophisticated traders value their own psychology just as much they do their trading system. Underestimate the importance of your emotions and you'll shoot yourself in the foot.

Acknowledgements

A project like this just couldn't happen without loads of support. Without support, it's easy to give up on a whim. This is what stops a lot of people in their tracks when they're on the brink of success. As the years pass in my life, I've found this to be more accurate than ever.

I feel very fortunate in my life to have been cocooned in the warmth of so many special traders from my Mentor Program. There are too many people to mention, but you know who you are. You've given back so much to me, and I feel extremely grateful.

Thanks to Chris Tate (www.tradinggame.com.au) for being the best business partner I could ever imagine. Your ability to master complex trading systems and make them tradeable, even for terrified new traders, is just exceptional. You've nudged and prodded me to achieve more than I ever believed possible, put up with my whines, and given me a proverbial whack across the side of my head when I needed it most.

Finally, my husband, Chris Bedford, has been by my side for more than half my life, supported me in my ambitions, and stood strong when I needed it most.

As you're reading this book, I know your goal is to trade like a machine, safely and confidently, never doubting yourself, with no ego. To achieve this goal, make sure you surround yourself with people who believe in you. It's one of the key differences between traders who excel and those who never achieve the results they yearn for.

I'm a product of those who supported me, and those who were unreasonable friends (always challenging me to create and achieve more). Without that support, there's no way I'd be the person that I am today. I would have surrendered my ambitions, submitted, and hung my head, not believing I was worthy.

My story

Years ago I climbed up the corporate ladder to achieve the role of a national sales manager. I was having an absolute ball, revelling in my ambition, loving every minute of it. Everything that I had aimed for was beginning to come true. However, everything wasn't as picture-perfect as it appeared.

At night, I would lie in my bed, staring at the ceiling, my heart racing. In my gut, I knew I was working far too many hours a week. Even though my career was booming, I was fast beginning to lose touch with my family and friends. When I really thought hard about it I realised I was getting up before the sun came up to go somewhere that sucked the best hours out of my day, only to spit me out as a used, exhausted shell when it was night-time again. Maybe you can relate?

I yearned for a life where someone else wasn't yanking my strings as if I was a puppet. I craved freedom, but I just didn't dare to believe it would be possible. Everyone I knew seemed to have a job or a business that devoured their youth and their creativity, so their family only got to experience the leftovers. I didn't have anyone to follow. I sensed there was something better out there, but because I didn't have an example to copy, I just kept on my treadmill and ran faster.

Then, just as I was at a high point in my career, something hit me out of the blue.

It started as a little niggling, aching feeling in my right ring finger. I began to drop things and sometimes my hand would jerk uncontrollably. I would be ripped out of a deep sleep with hand and arm spasms so painful it felt like my arm was about to give birth.

To begin with, I consoled myself. 'It's OK,' I said. 'It's only one arm. I'll teach myself to do everything with my left hand.'

Isn't denial so quick to step onto the stage of our lives?

Then, my left hand started to spasm as well.

With a creeping sense of dread, I realised that something very, very serious was wrong with me.

Over a period of a couple of weeks, I lost the use of both of my arms. I'd wake up and hear groaning and then realise that it was me making strange sounds all because my hands hurt so much in my sleep. I'd scream when I tried to dress myself. I couldn't feed myself. I couldn't hug my husband. It was the most painful thing I've ever been through in my life (and frankly, given that I've since been through childbirth twice without drugs, I feel I'm in a position to judge pain).

I found that even simple tasks such as opening doors had become agonising. My performance at work began to suffer as I jumped on the health professional merry-go-round. From specialist to specialist I travelled. I was informed that it would take me several years to recover. Some of the less positive members of the medical industry did their best to obliterate any hope that I had of reaching a full recovery. I was told, 'you have to be realistic!' No-one could specifically state what was wrong with me, and they were all taking guesses. My diagnosis came years later — but at the time, the experts were of no use whatsoever.

My spirit was slowly being crushed. I fell into an abyss of blackness. I was completely vulnerable and terrified about what the future held.

The most basic physical functions were now daily challenges. I decided that I had to leave my corporate role. Frankly, they were glad to get rid of me. These days, loyalty to your employee just doesn't seem to register as being a worthy quality. Anyone who can't perform is shunned.

Life was looking bleak. I went from working more than 60 hours a week to struggling to feed myself. My self-esteem hit an all-time low. I had no idea how I would manage to eke out a living for myself, other than the faint glimmer of hope that trading represented.

I was already trading profitably before I left my career. However, things assumed a new urgency. I was petrified that I may never work again and amid this sense of rising panic, my trading plan began to write itself with a clarity that I had never managed in the past. (Sometimes when we have our backs to the wall, we can achieve things that we never dreamed were possible.)

My computer was set up at home so that I could review the Top 200 shares one by one. After 12 seconds of looking at a chart, the software would flick forward and bring up a new share without me needing to touch the keyboard. My broker's phone number was programmed into the speed dial setting on my phone so I could push the button with a pen in my mouth. I was in business.

I didn't need to be able to use my arms, I just needed to see my charts and follow my trading plan. Trading became my career. It more than replaced my income and allowed me to scrape back some of my damaged self-image. It gave me something to focus on rather than my own somewhat dire situation.

Several years later I still have the occasional problem with my hands and arms, but my situation is much improved. The focus that I applied to trading I have applied to physiotherapy, and I have regained my strength. Although I could now probably hold down a full-time job physically, I choose not to. The lifestyle that trading provides has well and truly surpassed my expectations.

I realise that you may be facing an even more critical situation on your journey towards effective trading. If it is not a health issue, maybe you are looking for a way out of the usual grind of daily survival or perhaps you have a dream that your life could be better in some way. Harness the power of your desire and convert it into hard work. Then I will feel that my struggle has not only benefited my family, but also other families whom I don't know and may never meet.

Christopher Morley is credited with saying, 'There is only one success — to be able to spend your life in your own way'. Isn't that the truth!

I'm here to tell you that you are allowed to live a life of fulfilment, where you feel successful and have achieved all that you desire. Don't let anyone tell you any differently. There's a lot of rubbish out there in society telling you that you have to work really hard, retire at 65, and give your entire soul away to an employer. But really, it's not the way it is. There's an easier, more fulfilling, more passionate way to live.

Trading profitably won't solve all of your problems, but it will take you on an incredible journey of self-discovery. It will open up some choices in your life. It will bring you face-to-face with who you really are. You may just have the raw, untapped trading talent within that will transform your life. You'll never know if you walk away ... If you put down this book right now, you'll be saying 'no' to freedom. Not just for you, but freedom for your family as well.

But, but...

Yes, I hear what you're saying—but isn't trading hard to do?

Well ... I don't want to sound completely blunt here ... but compared with what?

- Compared with working for a relative pittance, when you know in your gut that you deserve more?

- Compared with weaving through bumper-to-bumper traffic because you're 10 minutes late for work again?

- Compared with feeling so damn emotionally wrung out at having to face another 20 years of the same bulls#!t—when you can just smell what the markets could throw your way?

Trading my way is a walk in the park compared with THAT!

Yes, you'll need to focus. Yes, you'll need to sink yourself into learning effective trading habits. But, I will be right by your side. Listen to me and you can buy back your life.

So what has changed?

It's been several years since I wrote the first edition of *Charting Secrets*. However, when it came time to rewrite the book, I found that there really weren't all that many corrections of the principles that I conveyed to readers way back in 2004. You see, the rules of wealth creation never change. Ignore the rules and you'll eventually cop it. 'Idea of the week' is not for the sophisticated trader. If you have consistency and discipline with your trading you'll get the rewards.

However, some things are very, very different. No-one's job is safe anymore. The 'one career for life' is now a quaint, antiquated notion. Jobs that can be replaced by technology have been, the ratio of service people to their clients has dwindled critically, and it's almost impossible to get truly personalised service at all. Far out—I even have to run my own groceries through the scanner now (which never works and makes me swear as I turn bright red in the face with fury because I still haven't mastered the art).

Plus, because we are such a litigious bunch now, it's harder than ever to be an employer. Employers now end up burdened with so much bureaucratic red tape, compliance requirements and endless administration that some are even turning back to getting a job as a way to avoid the perils of being an entrepreneur.

We've seen the world plunged into the Global Financial Crisis, traders get skittish, brokerage companies go broke and steal their clients' money, and a great deal of sadness about the markets. Also, trading educators have emerged with little or no experience in trading, only to razzle-dazzle the seminar scene, and teach their course participants ridiculous methods that don't work. Some incorrectly quote me. Many steal my intellectual property and pass it off as their own, only vaguely understanding the principles behind what I'm conveying, and leading people astray with their lack of depth. Many people in this profession now seem to have a well-worn, dog-eared copy of many of my books on their bookshelf—which is just fine with me. I actually don't have an issue with having trained most of my so-called competitors. I do object when they incorrectly translate my works and bring their clients to the brink of financial oblivion. That to me is simply not on.

Many of these competitors have been driven out of business by ASIC (the Australian Securities & Investment Commission) and the ACCC (the Australian Competition & Consumer Commission). If you're not in Australia, I guarantee this pattern is repeating itself all over the world. Plus, often the truly unscrupulous fly under the radar. Others, who can't trade their way out of a financial black hole are hanging on in there, praying for the next boom. Because of their own lack of business and trading acumen they have resorted to practically selling their own furniture to try and pay their bills and stay in business.

This environment has created an era of distrust.

It's become more and more important to check out the longevity of your trading trainers, their success, and how people they've trained talk about them. Does your trainer have hundreds of testimonials from happy traders on their website? Do they stick with their traders for life? Can they show you success stories of people just like you achieving incredible levels of self-development as well as market returns? If not, then don't just walk away from them . . . run for cover!

You need this book now more than ever. At other times, this book might be justifiably considered a luxury or 'an option'. However, because of these global changes, I insist you now need to be actively, aggressively and earnestly digging everywhere you might dig, in search of a 'better way' of trading.

What it means to trade like a machine

Machines follow instructions. They're implacable, like robots. They don't deviate from their programming. They don't dwell on the past. Emotion and ego are foreign concepts to them. They keep on doing the same thing, over and over again, and don't get hung up on their results. Sure, sometimes their programming (or trading plan) needs to be adjusted. However, once that adjustment is made, the machine follows the new plan, never tiring, never changing a thing. Machines certainly never moan to their friends, throw hissy fits and quit in tantrums because it's no fun anymore. Like the Energizer Bunny, they just keep on going, and going and going . . .

These are exactly the qualities you need to cultivate as a trader. But don't make the mistake of thinking that you'll be able to do this alone.

Find someone you trust to help you achieve the results you deserve in the markets. When you do . . . you'll astound yourself with the results you'll achieve. It may even happen more quickly than you think. And just imagine, in a short while, instead of battling on and struggling to work out the hidden rules of wealth creation all by yourself, you'll feel safe and confident and be ready to trade like a dynamo. If you're serious about creating a better life for you and your family, I'll help you achieve your goal. Keep on reading to find out how . . .

Let's get started...

Once upon a time there was an intelligent guy with movie-star good looks. With only one year of sharemarket experience, he developed a bulletproof trading plan. At the age of 42, he left his job to become a full-time trader. In between tennis matches and golf games, he traded and traded. During his first six months, he beat the markets easily, and made twice his usual salary as a brain surgeon. He laughed heartily, his golden hair glistening in the sun. Next, he took an extended two-year holiday on his fabulous shiny yacht in the Mediterranean, with a harem of beautiful women half his age. By day they would bask in the sun and swim in the sea. By night they would drink cocktails and admire the perfect sunset before retiring to their cabins. Trading was so much easier than he had ever expected...

Quick reality check... this is a fairytale. This will not happen to you.

For some reason, the myth that trading is more like an exciting trip to the fun park than anything resembling work has circulated in our society. I hate to burst your bubble, but trading is a precise and somewhat boring activity. The rewards are fabulous for the favoured few who manage to master the basics. These clever traders discipline themselves to apply, and endlessly reapply, their trading system, and watch their bank balances multiply.

The rewards are fabulous for the favoured few who manage to master the basics.

People who make consistent profits in the markets tend to do the same old things again and again (and again). They may be boring, but they work. These methods, if you perfect them, have the lovely by-product of delivering money to your door by the truckload.

These days, there is so much information available in the field of trading. The number of books is overwhelming. If you made it your life ambition to read every book before you put a cent into a stock, you would never put on your first trade. There are probably more books on this topic than there are shares listed. No wonder you're confused!

If you are a sharemarket book junkie, can I give you a quick piece of advice?

STOP READING! START PRACTISING!

The majority of traders finish a book as if it were a novel. They consider it to be an interesting read, but what did they really learn? The only way to cement a concept is to use it. Drop everything (apart from this workbook, of course). Put all those half-finished books back on your bookshelf.

Throughout this workbook, I will present you with the principles that you will need to complete the exercises I have set. When I want you to use your new skills, I will challenge you to:

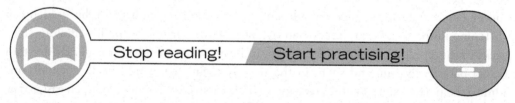

Stop reading! Start practising!

You will get a chance to impress me with how much you have learned, and establish a firm foundation of trading prowess before you continue learning about new concepts. I have included enough information to get you started charting if you're new to the markets, as well as some *Advanced strategies* for more experienced traders, which are highlighted in grey throughout *Charting Secrets*. In years to come when you require a quick reference about a particular charting topic, you will be able to read the relevant chapter without re-reading the entire book.

Educating yourself is the most effective way to gain knowledge. Turn off the TV program that enticingly tells you the All-Ords is moving up or down. For goodness sake, stop staring at that ticker that shows all of the share prices moving across the bottom of the computer or TV screen. It will only hypnotise you, not help you become a more proficient trader.

Take my word for it; you will be one step closer to becoming a better trader if you start to 'do', instead of just 'read'. You will learn more than you ever realised by putting pencil to paper. Seeing how much you have internalised, and then checking your knowledge with someone who has walked the minefield before you, is the best way to learn.

Have you dreamed of working only when you choose to, but as you drag yourself out of bed on yet another Monday — reality hits? Sick enough of this routine to do something about it?

If you're anything like me, you're the type of person who refuses to put up with a mediocre life! But yes, it is also scary out there. One area that scared me silly when I first started to get interested in the sharemarket was fundamental trading...

Fundamental versus technical analysis

Even though I predominantly refer to the 'sharemarket' in this book, keep in mind that I am encouraging you to cement your skills first, and then spread your wings to engage other markets. Whether you're trading the foreign exchange (FX) market, commodities, indices, or any other market, the principles I'm about to discuss will hold true.

In the investment field, there is often a tug of war between those with a fundamental viewpoint versus others with a technical perspective. *Fundamental analysis* seeks to detect which shares have a probability of increasing or decreasing in value based on announcements, company balance sheets and profit/loss details. However, even a surprisingly good track record does not necessarily ensure sharemarket success. It is perception that drives share price action. The emotions of the players in the market will ultimately create an uptrend or a downtrend. Positive announcements that are released to the press are often already factored into the share price, so even a strong profit result will not necessarily lead to a bullish reaction. Even if you use fundamental analysis in your investing, charting may help time your entry into a position. Personally, I found fundamental analysis confusing, boring and ambiguous. Luckily there is an alternative.

It is perception that drives share price action.

Developing skill with *charting* requires you to review actual price and volume action of a share to reach conclusions about the likely future direction. *Technical analysis* involves using formula and indicators, based on share price action, to estimate the likely future share price direction. The benefit of technical analysis and charting is that it crystallises the sentiment in the market by displaying price action in a visual format. Plus, if you get a large group of fundamental traders and chartists together in the same room, it's clear the most attractive group will be the technical analysts. Try it out for yourself. It's 100 per cent foolproof.

The good thing about charting is that specific trading rules can be developed. As you guessed, this book focuses on charting and technical analysis, as well as the individual techniques I use when I trade to create an income.

Can you do this?

When I started trading, it really was a case of learning by my own mistakes and banging my head against a lot of brick walls. Not only was this horribly expensive and time-consuming, but I also felt terribly alone and scared for a lot of the time. With my help, you'll never have to go through this yourself.

I firmly believe that anyone who really wants to become a good trader and beat the markets will be able to — given enough opportunities to practise his or her skills. Effective trading comes from mastering the basics. Any Olympic athlete will tell you that even naturally gifted competitors have to train relentlessly to perform at such high levels. There are also some initially non-gifted kids who end up at the Olympics because of their grit and determination. Trading favours anyone who is willing to put in the work required to succeed. Persistence, discipline and practise are the keys. Procrastination is your enemy.

There is hope — it's disguised as hard work though. By completing the exercises in this book, practising to recognise patterns as they occur, and being exposed to a vast number of charts, you will develop skill and confidence in share analysis. Once you've nailed these skills, you'll be able to apply them to any chart of any instrument from around the world.

Persistence, discipline and practise are the keys. Procrastination is your enemy.

This workbook is specifically designed so that you can test your knowledge in as close to real-life situations as you can get — the hard right edge of the chart. This is the area where history meets current reality. When the market opens at 10.00 am, everything you have learned will tend to blur into confusion. Your heart will race and your blood pressure will soar to new heights.

Overcoming these reactions requires confidence. My goal is to help you build that confidence by working through real-life examples.

I love this quote from Thomas Jefferson: 'Nothing can stop the man with the right mental attitude from achieving his goal; nothing on earth can help the man with the wrong mental attitude'.

To create a business-like profit, you must treat trading as a business, not a hobby. If the goal of trading well isn't one of your priorities, you will never derive a substantial income from the markets. The best investment that you can ever make is in yourself. If you look at successful people from all walks of life, you'll see that this philosophy acts as the common denominator. Trading follows this principle to the letter.

If the goal of trading well isn't one of your priorities, you will never derive a substantial income from the markets.

I am prepared to take you under my wing to guide your activity. However, the secrets within this book will only be revealed if you commit to completing the exercises. I can lead you to the essential principles behind the examples, but it will be up to you to discover their inherent wisdom for yourself.

So, how do you describe yourself to others when they ask the question: 'What do you do?' Is trading somewhere near the top of your priority list, or has it dropped way down to number 538? I can tell you now that the traders with determination and singleness of purpose will be the ones who come out on top in this game.

Get passionate about this. It is worthy of your attention.

Want to pinch the teachers' guide?

Did you ever feel tempted to peek at the 'teachers' guide' when you were at school so that you could know all of the answers? What a great short cut. The only problem with that approach is the moment you are given the answers, a little button in your brain activates to stop you from thinking. Most of the skirmish taking place in the sharemarket is within your own mind. Don't let yourself get lulled into reading this book the way you would any other—use your self-discipline to complete every exercise. Do this before you read my explanation.

If you are already familiar with a particular method, you are welcome to skim read that section, or skip it altogether. Just focus on the sections that you need the most development in. If you are already skilled in a particular area, you could even skip forward to the

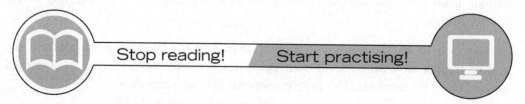

Stop reading!   Start practising!

symbol, and reinforce your skills before progressing. If you are uncertain about the meanings of any of the terms that I use, flick forward to the glossary (on page 317).

You should also consider that my explanations are just one possible way of interpreting the chart. Just because I feel that a particular trendline, for example, should be positioned just so, doesn't mean you are unable to disagree. There is no one right answer. Use my explanation to help you along, but if you vehemently disagree and can justify your decision, who is to say that your interpretation isn't equally as valid?

If you would like me to be your coach and your guide, then I ask that you make a commitment to me. Pick up a pencil and a ruler and be prepared to turn this publication into a smouldering heap of notes! By the time you've finished with it, I want to see comments, lines, descriptions and insights written down in the margins. If I meet you once you've completed this book, and your copy is not wrinkled, squashed or at least a little worse for wear, I will be secretly disappointed. If, by the final page, your book is not somewhat tattered, you will have missed the lessons that I am trying to convey.

I intend to rattle you with some of my views as well. You see, if you've already achieved everything you want in life, you simply don't need to change. However, the fact that you're reading this book tells me something terrific about you. You're willing to trust me to point out some things about the market and money that you haven't considered yet.

At the end of each chapter, I'm going to give you some ideas about how you can change your wealth mindset, so you can make room for cash to flow your way. Unfortunately, unless you work on your own level of self-development, you'll always achieve the same results. Since the Global Financial Crisis, this has become more important than ever. Working on your own psychology is absolutely essential. It's a heap of fun too. You're going to love it. I've called these sections 'Psychology Secrets', so make sure you pay close attention to those.

If you don't treat something with respect, it will slip away from your life. This holds true for people, emotions and money as well. Money flows to us or away from us entirely based on how we think about money.

I love this quote from Dr Maxwell Maltz from Psycho-Cybernetics: 'The self-image sets the boundaries of individual accomplishment. It defines what you can and cannot do. Expand the self-image and you expand the areas of the possible'. That's why psychology is so important for traders.

Know this—when alone, and in silence, the truly successful person doesn't rely on anyone else for motivation. This person can summon their own resources from within. A successful person self-motivates to achieve greatness.

That's where success is born. In the still quiet of the mind, without the pumping music of a seminar to conflict and confuse your true desires. Your time to shine begins as a tiny spark of light in the tranquil peace of your own thoughts. Rely on yourself for motivation, but look outward for inspiration.

You are either attracting or repelling money. There is no middle ground. And it begins with you. Your thoughts and feelings about money create either a fertile breeding ground, or a barren wasteland of a bank account.

Change your views about money, or your views will become your reality.

Your goal is to get to the point where your bulletproof trading plan will guide your every move with emotional detachment. By developing your trading skills, and your own individual psychology, you'll be miles ahead of 90 per cent of the other traders. So, enough throat-clearing. Let's get cracking!

Louise Bedford
Melbourne
March 2013
www.tradingsecrets.com.au

1

Chart and be sexy

Without a sound foundation, advanced charting principles will slip through your fingers. Plus, it's a well-known fact that chartists are damn sexy. Doubt me? I suggest you focus now and you'll soon reap the rewards.

IF THIS IS THE FIRST BOOK about technical analysis that you have ever picked up, you're going to need to grasp some of the basics before moving on. This chapter will provide you with a foundation for the exercises I have set out further down the line.

In the coming chapters, you will have the opportunity to see how I analyse a chart and to practise these skills for yourself. There is no one perfect answer, but to find out whether you are on the right track, you can turn to the 'Answers' section following each set of exercises or at the end of each chapter.

Will you promise me that you will not turn to the Answers section immediately? Resist the temptation to immediately flick forward. I want to give you a chance to fill out the review sections for yourself first. This approach is consistent throughout the book. I can guarantee that the people who do not immediately turn to the answers will benefit most in the long run.

We will start laying the groundwork for your charting career by looking at a few main concepts, the first of which is *weight of evidence*.

Weight of evidence

Imagine you're a private detective and you're working towards solving a crime. You wouldn't look at just one piece of evidence, would you? You'd look at several key pieces of evidence and then make up your mind. That would be the most logical way to progress.

Use the same method when looking at a chart. When several chart patterns and indicators point in the same direction, their signals are reinforced. If the weight of evidence of several indicators suggests that the share is uptrending, then the bulls have probably taken control of the market.

When several chart patterns and indicators point in the same direction, their signals are reinforced.

By using more than just one or two pieces of evidence that the share is trending in a particular direction, you are stacking the odds in your favour. The best chartists try to maintain complete objectivity and remove any emotion or gut-feel from their analysis.

There are hundreds of indicators to choose from. They don't all help your trading results. If you use 50 indicators, you'll probably just end up a quivering mess of nerves huddling in the corner. It's far better to choose a few judiciously. A method that I have found to help me do this is to separate the indicators into five categories.

The families

Indicators tend to fall into several distinct 'families'. I use at least one of the indicators from each family in order to form an opinion about the share price's likely direction. This is an ideal application of the weight of evidence theory. The families are:

- the line family

- the moving average family

- the momentum family

- the volume family

- the pattern family.

Throughout the coming chapters, we will explore each of these in turn. You will find some of these families simpler or easier to relate to than others. This is perfectly natural. You can start trading without fully grasping every aspect of charting (I certainly did!). Too much knowledge can paralyse you.

If you are familiar with the way charts are constructed and want to get into the meat of the book, turn to the next chapter, which commences on page 11, and we will begin our analysis using support and resistance lines, and trendlines. Keep reading if this is your introduction to charting or if you'd like a quick refresher on the way price action appears on a chart.

Chart construction

Your computer charting package can produce several different types of charts. We will look at each in turn below.

Bar charts

The individual building block of a bar chart is a single bar. Drawing a single bar requires an opening price, a high, a low and a closing price (see figure 1.1). The vertical line shows the high and low of that period. The two horizontal lines depict the open and the close. The open is the horizontal line on the left of the vertical line and the close is the horizontal line on the right of the vertical line.

Depending on what you ask your charting software package to produce, you may view an intra-day, a daily, a weekly or a monthly chart. On a daily chart, one bar will show the share price action for one day. If you look at a weekly chart, the open price will be the opening price at the start of the week and the closing price will be the final price recorded at the end of the week. The high and low will be the overall high for the week and the overall low for the week. In other words, whichever time period you utilise, the bar will show the activity for that session.

When many of these single period bars are plotted on a chart with the horizontal axis representing time and the vertical axis showing the share price, a traditional bar chart is created (see figure 1.2, overleaf). The inter-relationships of the bars show whether the share is generally going up in value (that is, bullish), or going down in value (that is, bearish). Periods of sideways progression are also evident.

Indicators may help you understand whether or not the predominant direction is likely to continue. You cannot predict the market direction. As legendary trader Jim

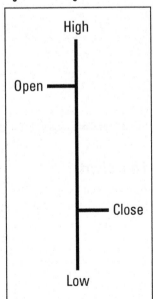

Figure 1.1: a single bar

High

Open —

Close

Low

Rogers, author of the bestseller *Adventure Capitalist,* says, 'Markets will rise higher than you think is possible and fall lower than you can possibly imagine'. The best that you can do is analyse the type of trend that existed in the past and take an educated guess that history will repeat itself. This is the main focus of technical analysts.

Crikey that little bar chart is an ugly thing, isn't it? It really doesn't call to my soul and give me an idea about the future direction of the price action. Don't worry. Once we get through this section, I'll introduce you to the beautiful and colourful candlestick chart. I know you'll fall in love with them. They're divine little creatures.

Figure 1.2: AGL daily—bar chart

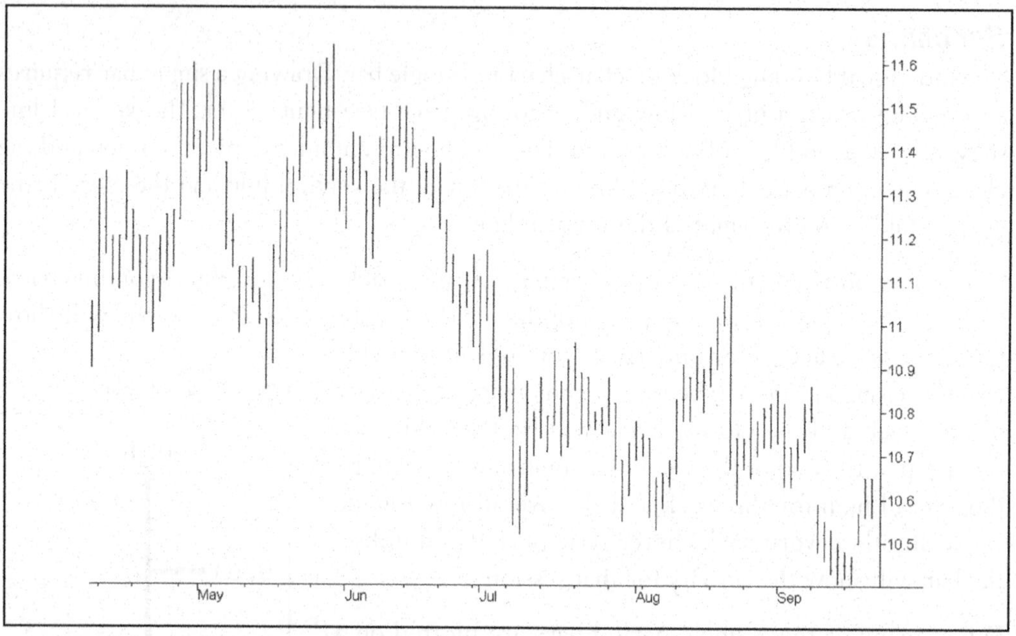

Source: SuperCharts version 4 by Omega Research © 1997.

Line charts

A line chart (see figure 1.3) connects the closing prices for each period, providing less information, but it is, perhaps, a simpler chart to interpret in comparison to the bar chart.

Figure 1.3: AGL daily—line chart

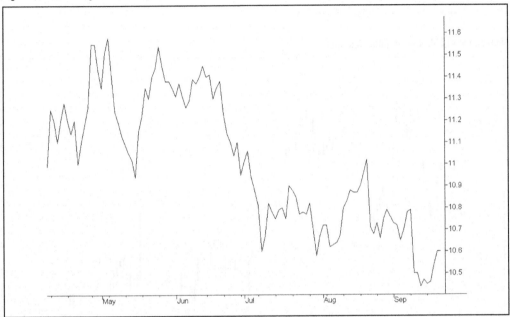

Source: SuperCharts version 4 by Omega Research © 1997.

Candlestick charts

A single candlestick represents the same data that you will find in a single bar, however, they look completely different. The origin of the name is obvious when looking at the chart (see figure 1.4, overleaf)—a candlestick chart looks like a series of candles with wicks at either end of the candle. In the next section we will explore the specific implications of each part of the candle.

The three charts shown in figure 1.2, figure 1.3 and figure 1.4 all represent the same information, and the same time scale; however, their graphic format ensures that each chart looks very different.

In my view, using a candlestick chart is clearly superior to using a bar chart or a line chart. I think that bar and line charts are ugly little characters. Bar charts are positively anorexic compared to the full-bodied candles, and line charts only show 25 per cent of the information shown in candlestick charts. (So, basically, candlestick charts are 75 per cent more intelligent than line charts.) I suggest that if you want to beat the markets, you should avoid these inferior types of charts altogether. There are many patterns that a candlestick chart displays that cannot be shown on a bar chart or a line chart. It may

5

take a bit of effort to learn how to interpret these types of charts, but it will give you an edge over other traders in the market.

Figure 1.4: AGL daily—candlestick chart

Source: SuperCharts version 4 by Omega Research © 1997.

It's important that you know up-front that I'm vastly biased when it comes to candlestick charts. I adore them, the way you'd adore any tool that has brought vast swags of money into your bank account. They're incredibly precious to me, and I have a feeling — by the end of this book — you'll be converted to my way of thinking.

I usually start with a weekly chart and then review charts of increasingly shorter time increments for the share that I am interested in trading. Any of the patterns we are discussing will be apparent on monthly, weekly, daily or intra-day charts. The word 'session' or 'period' means the time increment of that chart (for example, one period means one day on a daily chart).

...start with a weekly chart and then review charts of increasingly shorter time increments...

The markets are made up of people's emotions towards shares. If market participants predominantly feel fear that they will lose their capital or profits, the share price will ultimately decrease. If they mainly feel greed or hope, the share price will go up. A chart will show this interplay of emotion visually. It is one of the purest ways to analyse share price action.

6

Candlestick charting

The thick part of the candle is called the real body. This shows the range between the opening and the closing price (see figure 1.5). When the real body is white (or empty), it means that the close was higher than the opening price. When the real body is black (or filled in), the close was lower than the opening price. The colour of the candle depicts whether the candle is bearish or bullish. On a colour screen bullish candles are often shown in green and bearish candles in red.

The thin lines at either end of the real body are called the wicks, tails or shadows of the candle (regardless of whether they are above or below). The upper tail (the high for that period) is located above the candlestick's real body, and the lower tail (the low for that session) is located below the real body. The tails are usually considered to be of less importance than the real body, as they represent extraneous price fluctuations. The open and the close are considered to be the most emotionally charged points of the day and therefore they contain the highest level of significance in candlestick analysis.

Figure 1.5: definition of a candlestick

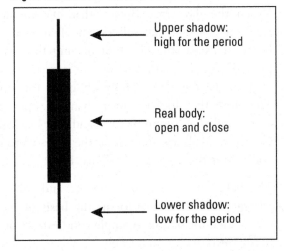

Figure 1.6: the white candle

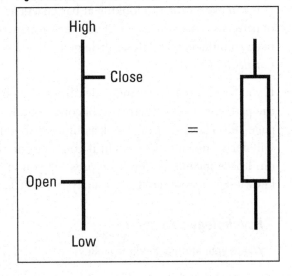

The white candle

When the day closes higher than it opened, this is a positive bullish sign. There is demand for the share and buyers are willing to pay higher and higher prices. The price is driven up as demand outstrips supply (see figure 1.6).

The black candle

When the day closes lower than its opening price, it is a sign that sellers have fear in their hearts. This has the effect of driving the share price down. The market sentiment is pessimistic, creating a far greater supply of shares for sale. Therefore the close is lower than the opening price, and the colour of the candle is black. A black candle clearly shows that the bears were in control for that period (see figure 1.7).

The bulls' and the bears' (buyers and sellers) struggle for dominance forms the basis of each candlestick formation. A single candlestick, or a group of candles, often has particular bullish or bearish significance.

Figure 1.7: the black candle

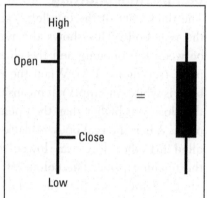

Once you get used to the way candlesticks can assist in your analysis, it is unlikely that you will ever return to looking at bar charts or line charts. Their unique graphic display of patterns can assist in identifying the reversal or continuation of trends. My trading has been so influenced by these little gems that I wrote a book on the topic — *The Secret of Candlestick Charting*.

If you haven't read my candlestick book or you'd like a basic understanding of some of the patterns that can help you become a more effective trader, turn to appendix A on page 287. The rest of this book assumes that you are familiar with these patterns, so you will derive much more benefit if you focus on these types of formations before reading on. I have included a few exercises for you in this appendix also. These will test your knowledge if your candlestick analysis is a little rusty.

Psychology secrets

What's your attitude towards money?

I know that we're talking a lot about the specifics of charting, and how to use technical analysis, but there is a deeper concept that I want you to be aware of before we go any further. Your views towards money may very well block your learning, unless you are determined to do some serious self-growth.

People's love affair with money has always fascinated me. Want to see normal people do completely bizarre things? Add some money and watch the games begin.

How about the friend who disappears after you loan them some money? What's going on there? Or the siblings who create merry hell at the reading of their father's will? Or the bloke with the secret bank account that he isn't telling his wife about? And then there's the girl who spends too much to impress people she doesn't like, with money she doesn't have.

See . . . it makes ordinary people just crack up!

So is money bad? Of course not. Then what the heck is happening?

Money, in and of itself, is meaningless . . . until we empower it. We give it meaning and it's our own thoughts and emotions around money that determine whether it's a positive or negative force in our lives.

I guarantee you this — change your views towards money and what it means to you, and you'll change your results as a trader.

When we realise that money is just a way of keeping score, and it's nothing more than a tool — we become detached from its power over us. We stop its control over our thoughts and our actions. Plus, ironically, this attitude paves the way for more of it to enter our lives.

Interestingly, some of the most greedy, money-hungry people I have ever met have barely any of the stuff.

So which comes first? The attitude about money or the money itself?

Having trained hundreds of successful traders, and seen them at every stage of their wealth development, I can definitely answer this one. The attitude towards money comes first. The way a trader thinks always precedes their actual share trading results.

In reality, some rich people are poor and some poor people are rich. It's just a matter of time until reality catches up with their mindset.

So, as you are reading this book, if I say some things about money that rattle you to your core, realise that I may have just touched a nerve. Recognise it and move on.

The best thing you can do to start altering your views towards money is to keep on reading.

Now that you've grasped some of the basics, let's begin our discussion of charting techniques. The next chapter focuses on the line family and will help develop your skills using these important tools.

2
The line reveals all... Well, almost...

Sometimes the simplest tools are the best. Just a few well-placed lines on a chart can tell you around 80 per cent of what you need to know about trend. Get ready to learn this essential skill...

IT'S AMAZING HOW MUCH INFORMATION one or two little lines can reveal about the direction of the share price. In this chapter we will have a look at the line family. This includes support and resistance lines, as well as trendlines. I will explain the principles behind these lines, provide an example, and give you a chance to practise your skills. By the end of this section of the workbook, you should confidently be able to draw in these lines to help you diagnose the share price direction. Let's start by looking at support and resistance lines.

Support and resistance

Support and resistance lines help you ascertain when a share is trading in a lateral band. Some analysts have suggested that this sideways movement can occur up to 70 per cent of the time. The support line can be seen along the base of a range of consolidation, and the resistance line can be seen along the top. They are horizontal lines that reflect the perimeter of sideways-moving share prices.

The share is basically bopping up and down, hitting its head on the resistance line and kicking against the floor to create a support line. It may be getting ready to break out of its confines. If the bulls win, the effect will be similar to a jack-in-the-box, and the break out will be upwards. If the bears are victorious, support will give way and the share will begin an avalanche.

If you think these lines aren't important, think again. If you're trapped in a sideways-moving share, you'll not only feel incredibly frustrated, but you'll be experiencing a significant opportunity cost. Plus, if the whole market is moving sideways, it's far better that you step aside and not trade, rather than try to enter new positions. Traders refer to this as being 'churned' by the markets. Not a very nice feeling at all.

For an example of how these lines appear, have a look at figure 2.1.

Drawing in support and resistance lines is an essential component of effective trading, and this will become clear as you progress through this workbook. To draw a valid support or resistance line,

Figure 2.1: support and resistance

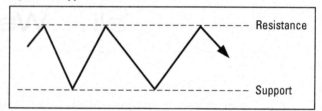

'they' say that it is important to connect at least two points of share price action for a tentative line, and three or more for a confirmed line. However, in real life 'they' won't be sitting beside you as you trade — so feel free to defy 'them' occasionally. A bit of rebellion never hurt anyone, so long as the weight of evidence is suggesting that the share is trending in a particular direction.

Why draw support and resistance lines?

There are several reasons for drawing these lines. You may want to see whether a share is actually trending, or just moving in a sideways band. Trying to trade a share that is going nowhere is always a frustrating endeavour. The unfortunate implication with a sideways-moving share is that your capital is tied up, preventing participation in other more lucrative opportunities. This opportunity cost is a frustrating consequence of being involved in non-trending shares. When using shares as a vehicle, a clear trend is necessary to benefit from and make substantial profits.

...a clear trend is necessary to benefit from and make substantial profits.

If a share is not trending, then just walk away. You will find many more opportunities. All you have to do is keep looking. When interviewed by Jack Schwager in *Market*

Wizards, James Rogers stated, 'Be very selective. Never trade for trading's sake. Have the patience to sit on your money until the high probability trade sets up exactly right'. This attitude will ensure your longevity in the markets and give you a chance to develop profitable strategies.

Another key reason for drawing in support and resistance lines is so that you will have an alternative entry trigger into a share that is already trending. Areas of lateral movement can represent a temporary pause prior to the share continuing upwards or downwards. Once the share breaks out of these areas of congestion, this can be a buy signal, or a sell signal. These lines can also form part of larger macro patterns (which are discussed in chapters 6 and 7) such as double tops or head and shoulders. If there is close overhead resistance, you may choose not to enter a position in that stock, as the profit potential may be limited.

Periods of temporary sideways consolidation are very healthy in a trending share. Marathon runners find the hardest part of the race is the uphill and downhill sections—the flat areas allow the runner to conserve energy and to prepare for sections of the course that are more difficult to manage. Shares behave in the same way.

To assess the strength of support and resistance, two factors should be considered. Firstly, the length of the consolidation is very important. The longer the period of consolidation, and the more times a support or resistance line is touched by share price action, the more these prices will be retained in the trader's memories. The other main concept is turnover. The higher the volume during the consolidation, the more investors have entered or exited at the support or resistance prices.

If you are not sure where you should draw in your lines, a quick rule of thumb is to draw a resistance line above a previous high price. All-time highs provide a level of resistance because traders tend not to enjoy buying at an all-time high. Also, if you draw a line just below a low price, this can be a proxy for a fully confirmed line of support. I realise that this does not comply with the previously mentioned 'three touches of the share price to confirm a valid line' concept—but it can work surprisingly well.

Marathon runners find the hardest part of the race is the uphill and downhill sections—the flat areas allow the runner to conserve energy…

I want to teach you the theory regarding these concepts, but also show you what I do in my own trading. Live trading doesn't always comply with the exact definitions I am presenting to you. For this reason, it is important to stay flexible in your approach.

Change of polarity

The change of polarity principle suggests that once prices break a significant resistance line, then this line should act as support for future trading activity. This will only occur if the uptrend is strong. When resistance becomes support, this is a very bullish sign. Figure 2.2 is an example of how change of polarity may appear on a chart.

The less a share pulls back, the stronger the trend.

Figure 2.2: change of polarity

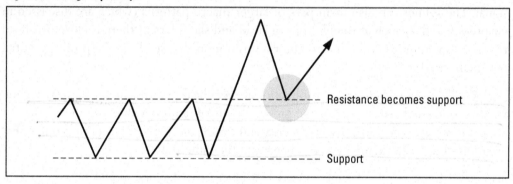

When the opposite happens and support becomes resistance, the bears have drawn a line in the sand that the bulls will have trouble crossing in the future. This is a sign of a downtrend that is likely to continue.

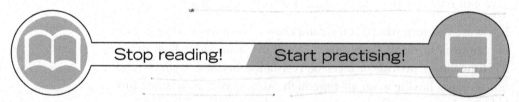

For each of the charts shown (figures 2.3 to 2.5), draw in where you would locate support and resistance. Once you have done this, circle any areas of the chart that show a change of polarity. Pick up your pencil and have a go.

The line reveals all…Well, almost…

Figure 2.3: CSL weekly

Source: SuperCharts version 4 by Omega Research © 1997.

Figure 2.4: EQI weekly

Source: SuperCharts version 4 by Omega Research © 1997.

Figure 2.5: NRT weekly

Source: SuperCharts version 4 by Omega Research © 1997.

Please do not turn to the answers yet. We have a bit further to go until you can see how clever you are by drawing the lines in the right place. Give yourself a quick pat on the back for resisting temptation. We still need to discuss uptrends and downtrends before you can check your charts against mine.

Uptrends

A trendline is one of the most basic tools that can help you ascertain whether or not a share is trending. These lines provide valuable clues regarding who is winning the war — the bulls or the bears.

An uptrend is apparent when prices on the chart consistently make higher lows. Each dip in share price action is followed by a subsequent trough that occurs at a higher price level. A trendline can be drawn on the chart to connect these low points. When there is sustained movement below this line, the uptrend is likely to be broken. When drawing a trendline, try to connect at least two low points for a tentative trendline, and three or more to confirm a trendline.

If you find that you have one or two extreme prices that do not conform to the general trending behaviour, disregard these when drawing in your trendlines. In statistics, extreme high and low values are called 'outliers' and are not included in the analysis. I suggest that you follow this same method.

You may also find that the share is creating a series of higher highs. This can reinforce the strength of the uptrend.

I'll get you started by showing you figure 2.6, but it's up to you after this.

Figure 2.6: BLD weekly

Source: SuperCharts version 4 by Omega Research © 1997.

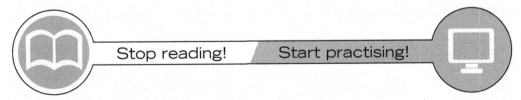

Turn back to pages 15 and 16 and have a look at the charts shown in figures 2.3 to 2.5. You should have already drawn in support and resistance lines on these charts. If you find that some of these shares are trending up, have a stab at drawing in diagonal lines connecting the lowest share prices. To do this, the line will need to be drawn underneath the majority of the share prices. Use a ruler to help you.

Once you've completed around 150 charts or so, the penny will finally drop.

Once you've completed around 150 charts or so, the penny will finally drop. When I tell people this in seminars, they always tend to laugh nervously, thinking that I'm joking. Nope, I'm serious. You need to apply yourself to this task if you expect to beat the markets. As stated by Aristotle, 'We are what we repeatedly do. Excellence, then, is not an act, but a habit'. Foster the right habits and your bank account will flourish.

You've done well. Keep reading to learn about downtrend lines, and wait just a bit longer before you check your answers.

Downtrends

A downtrend may be described as a share that makes consistently lower highs. A trendline can be drawn on the chart that connects the highest prices of a downtrend (at least two for a tentative downtrend or preferably three or more for a confirmed downtrend). This will result in a downward-sloping line drawn above the majority of the price action.

A lot of downtrends also display a series of lower lows. This is indicative of an enduring downtrend, so it is interesting to note when you analyse a share.

A downtrend indicates the bulls are waving the white flag of defeat to the bears. Every half-hearted push upwards in price is overcome by the force of downward momentum.

The downtrend will be broken when prices move above this downward-sloping line in a sustained upward direction. This will ideally be accompanied by higher volume levels relative to previous sessions. It is important that volume accompanies any upward movement after a prolonged downtrend. When a share increases in price on heavy relative volume, this is a sign that the bulls are exerting their dominance.

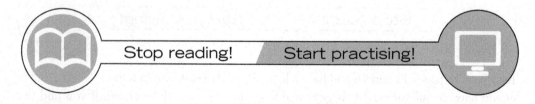
Stop reading! Start practising!

Have a look at figures 2.3 to 2.5 on pages 15 and 16. Draw any downtrend lines that are apparent.

Where to draw your lines

When beginners learn about the power of candlesticks and charts, the following question usually springs to their minds: 'Where do I draw in my trendlines and support/resistance lines? Do I draw in a resistance line above the shadows or above the real bodies?'

In my view, trend or support/resistance lines should be drawn at the level where the most points of the candle touch (see figure 2.7). For example, if the highs of several candles' shadows touch the $12.00 level, feel free to draw in a resistance line at that price. If there are a greater number of real bodies that would be connected by drawing in a line, then create a resistance line at this point. It would also be valid to draw a support/resistance line or trendline that touches a combination of real body and shadow extremes.

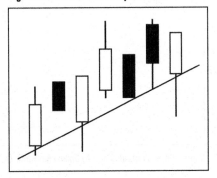

Figure 2.7: where to draw your lines

Draw in trend or support/resistance lines at a logical price level that will benefit your analysis.

Make sure that you have drawn in downtrend and uptrend lines on the relevant charts shown in figures 2.3 to 2.5 on pages 15 and 16. Once you've completed this task, continue reading to see how I have used lines to help me diagnose the trend. The suggested answers to figures 2.3 to 2.5 are shown in figures 2.8 to 2.10 on pages 20 and 21.

Suggested answers

Before you have a look at the charts that I have analysed here, I just want to remind you that if your chart doesn't look exactly like mine, you may not actually be 'wrong'. You may just see the chart in a different light. That's part of the beauty of charting. We don't all see the world in the same way. Don't kick yourself and throw this workbook across the room in a temper tantrum—just explore an alternative way of seeing the price action.

Figure 2.8: CSL weekly

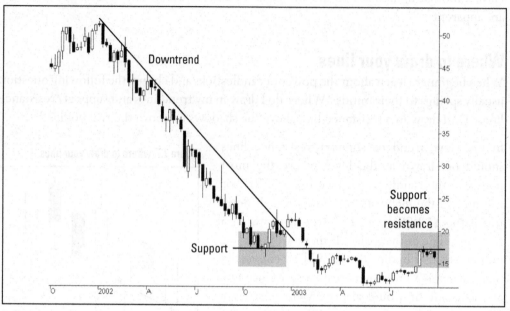

Source: SuperCharts version 4 by Omega Research © 1997.

Figure 2.9: EQI weekly

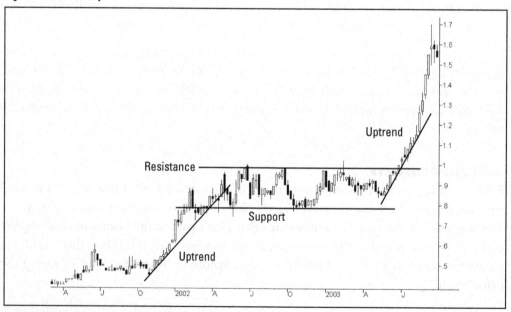

Source: SuperCharts version 4 by Omega Research © 1997.

Figure 2.10: NRT weekly

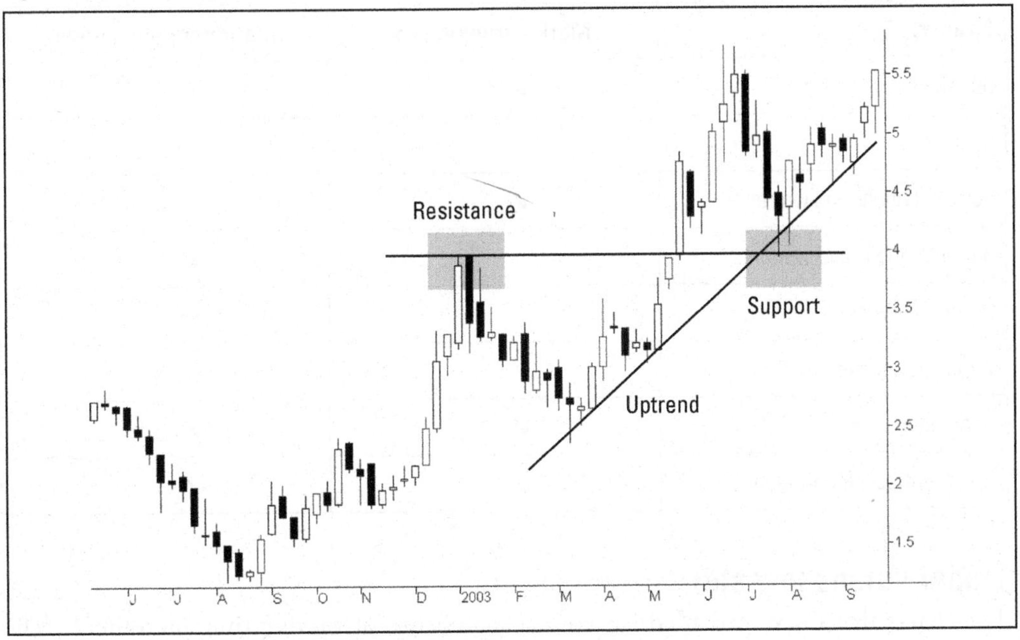

Source: SuperCharts version 4 by Omega Research © 1997.

Once you've compared your charts with mine, keep reading to understand some other important information about trading bear markets.

Why are downtrends important?

I get equally as excited when I detect a downtrend as when I find an uptrend. If this seems a bit strange to you, perhaps you are not familiar with some of the different instruments (for example, CFDs which are contracts for difference, options, futures, short selling) that you can use to capitalise on various trend directions and beat the markets. Have a look at table 2.1. This provides a summary of the different strategies that you can use to capitalise on various trend directions. Once you become more proficient at analysing share price direction, you may want to trade other instruments such as options. If the sharemarket is still new to you, I suggest that you stick with shares until you have gained some confidence. Use table 2.1 as a reference point when completing the rest of the workbook.

Table 2.1: strategies

Strategy	Market trending up	Market trending down
Buy shares	✓	
Short sell		✓
Buy call options and warrants	✓	
Buy put options and warrants		✓
Write call options		✓
Write put options	✓	
Trade futures	✓	✓
Trade contracts for difference	✓	✓

Trader versus investor

The charts that I have provided for you to analyse are of varying time increments. The skills you are cementing will be suitable when viewing any chart. Your trading style, position sizing and money management may have to alter, but the analytical skills will stay the same, regardless of your investment duration.

You will need to decide whether you fit the profile of an investor or a trader. Investors typically have a longer term view, but must be prepared to endure the inevitable downslide in share prices that the market periodically experiences. If you are more inclined to be an investor, you may prefer to use weekly and monthly charts.

Successful traders have a defined set of rules to exit the market promptly at the first sign of a downtrend. This requires additional monitoring and effort, but the rewards are well worth it. Traders tend to use a combination of weekly, daily and intra-day charts.

Lining it all up

You'll notice that most of the charts in this chapter are weekly. This is because it is important to analyse the medium to longer term direction before you look at a chart of a smaller time increment. Plus, I've used charts that are not exactly current on purpose. I'm hoping that by the time you look at these charts, if you've traded some of those shares before reading this book, you will have forgotten what the price action looked like. That way you can stay objective while you're looking at the charts I've prepared for you.

…analyse the medium to longer term direction before you look at a chart of a smaller time increment.

 Stop reading! Start practising!

If you've paid attention to this workbook so far, you'll be ready to link a lot of these concepts to gain a bigger picture of the share price action. Have a look at figures 2.11 to 2.15 on pages 24 to 26. Some of these shares are uptrending, some are downtrending, and others are just busy treading water, going sideways. Draw in uptrend or downtrend lines — whichever you feel are the most appropriate. If you are finding this to be a difficult task, I suggest that you hold this workbook away from you, at arm's length, and squint at the chart. If you think it's going up, draw in a line under the price action. If it's heading down, draw in a line above the price action. Mark in support and resistance lines, and circle any areas of change of polarity. In other words, use all of the tools in the line family to help you establish share price direction.

Once you've had a chance to draw in the appropriate lines and circle areas that show a change of polarity, keep reading to see how I have analysed these charts. The answers to figures 2.11 to 2.15 are contained in figures 2.16 to 2.20 on pages 26 to 28.

Take your time — there is no rush.

Figure 2.11: FKP weekly

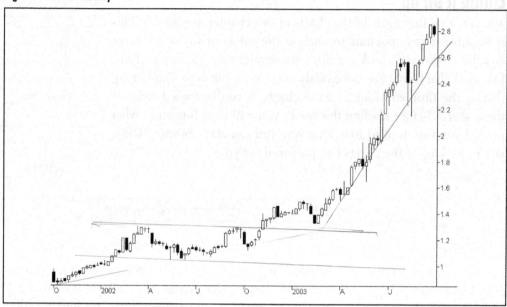

Source: SuperCharts version 4 by Omega Research © 1997.

Figure 2.12: GGL weekly

Source: SuperCharts version 4 by Omega Research © 1997.

Figure 2.13: GRD weekly

Source: SuperCharts version 4 by Omega Research © 1997.

Figure 2.14: HPX weekly

Source: SuperCharts version 4 by Omega Research © 1997.

Figure 2.15: HVN weekly

Source: SuperCharts version 4 by Omega Research © 1997.

Figure 2.16: FKP weekly

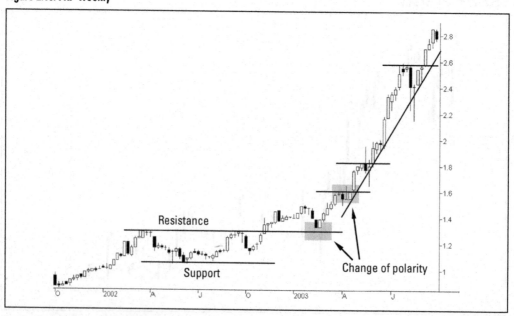

Source: SuperCharts version 4 by Omega Research © 1997.

Figure 2.17: GGL weekly

Figure 2.18: GRD weekly

Figure 2.19: HPX weekly

Source: SuperCharts version 4 by Omega Research © 1997.

Figure 2.20: HVN weekly

Source: SuperCharts version 4 by Omega Research © 1997.

While you have been completing these exercises, I can almost bet that you've been coming to some pretty major conclusions about trend direction. Just to check whether you've been concentrating, take a shot at filling in the following review section.

Review

1   Define an uptrend. Tell me in point form every piece of evidence that you can think of that suggests an uptrend is in place. If you come up with three potential entry points, that is 'average', four is 'good', and five and above is 'very clever'.

- HIGHER HIGHS .... HIGHER LOWS
- MORE WHITE CANDLES THAN BLACK
- HIGHER LOWS
- WHITE CANDLES ARE LARGER THAN BLACK
- POSSIBLY HIGER VOLUME

2   When a share is uptrending, is a support line stronger, or is a resistance line stronger? When a share is downtrending, is a support line stronger or is a resistance line stronger?

- SUPPORT LINE IS STRONGER WHEN TRENDING UP
- RESISTANCE IS STRONGER WHEN TRENDING DOWN

3   The goal of technical analysis is trend detection: true or false?

TRUE

4   In general, do uptrends or downtrends take longer to become apparent? Why do you think this would be?

UPTRENDS TAKE LONGER TO BECOME APPARENT BECAUSE INCREASE IN SHARE PRICES TAKE LONGER. DOWNTRENDS ARE QUICKER BECAUSE THEY ARE EMOTIONALLY BASED.

5   Why do we draw an uptrend line under the majority of the share price action? What are we waiting for?

WE DRAW A TRENDLINE TO IDENTIFY THE TREND BUT ALSO TO IDENTIFY IF TREND HAS CHANGED IF THE TREND LINE HAS BEEN VIOLATED

6   The more lines that you draw on a share chart the better: true or false?

…FALSE…

7   In an uptrend, what colour are the majority of the candlesticks? Why would this be?

GREEN OR WHITE, THE GREEN CANDLESTICK REPRESENTS A HIGHER PRICE THAN THE PREVIOUS DAYS CLOSE.

8   If the trend on a weekly chart is upwards, but the daily chart is displaying downtrending behaviour, does this mean that you should not buy that share? Justify your answer.

NO, IT JUST MEANS THAT THE SHORT TERM TREND IS DOWN IN A LONG TERM UPTREND

9   Have a look back through the charts you have analysed and the notes that you have made throughout this chapter. Review your findings and if there is anything that you would like to note as an insight, take some time to detail your thoughts below.

....

....

....

....

....

....

....

....

....

....

....

....

....

....

....

....

Review answers

1   Here are some of the possible uptrend definitions:

- The share displays a series of progressively higher lows.

- A trendline drawn below the share price action connecting these lows slopes upward from left to right.

- The share displays a series of higher highs.

- Each level of resistance is easily transcended, only to become a new level of support for future share price activity. (This is called change of polarity.)

- Horizontal lines to depict areas of support and resistance show the share price breaking upwards through resistance.

- Support holds strong and resistance is weak.

- Volume increases on upward movements and contracts during downward movements. (This will be covered in more detail in chapter 3.)

- Upward movements last longer than downward movements.

- The majority of the candles are white in colour.

- The white candles are generally longer than the black candles.

2   In an uptrend, resistance is weak and support is strong. In a downtrend, resistance is strong and support is weak.

3   True. The majority of good traders share the skill of trend trading. Technical analysis looks at chart patterns and uses indicators to help you analyse whether a share is trending upwards or downwards. And, we've already established that it's a super quick way to become sexy, overnight.

4   Uptrends take a lot longer to become apparent than downtrends. The bulls in the market tediously climb the stairs, while the bears tend to abseil down the cliff face. Shares seem to slowly move up in price but drop incredibly quickly. This is because the emotion of hope or greed is not usually as strong as the emotion of fear. Traders are more likely to sell out at the first sign of weakness. This can cause prices to tumble, whereas traders seem reticent to part with their hard-earned money and buy shares.

5   We draw in uptrend lines under the share price action so that we can watch for a trendline break. Once share prices drop below our uptrend line, we can assume that the uptrend is broken. If we only drew a line above the share prices to distinguish an uptrend, we would not be given a clear indication regarding when the downtrend has commenced.

6   False. The best technical analysts use very simple approaches to estimate share price direction. They are more likely to use only one or two lines to help them, rather than cover the chart in a manic spirographic frenzy.

7   Generally, in uptrends the candlesticks will display white bodies. This means that on a daily chart, the share opens in the morning and goes up throughout the day to close at a higher price. This is a bullish sign. It adds to the weight of evidence that an uptrend is in place.

8   If the weekly chart is trending up, and the daily chart is trending down, this means that the share is undergoing a form of counter-trend reversal. You could buy this share, but it may drop a little before continuing to trend upwards. The predominant trend is upwards as depicted by the weekly chart, so it is likely that this period of weakness will only be temporary.

Summary

- Draw in uptrend lines below the share price action.

- Draw in downtrend lines above the share price action.

- Watch for sideways movement. Draw in support below the share price action and resistance above.

- Be aware of change of polarity. If support becomes resistance, this is bearish. If resistance becomes support, this is bullish.

Psychology secrets

Can you feel yourself changing?

I'll bet you're a bit like me — I believe we all can change. We can even change our intelligence in specific areas. You see, studies have shown that those who believe that they can alter their behaviour and their habits to create a different outcome are happier people. They persist for longer. They score better on tests.

Those who think they can't change, and that intelligence is fixed, tend to quit at the first sign of trouble, and they don't stick around long enough to master a skill. I mean if you really believed that educating yourself about the markets wouldn't improve your results, then why would you bother?

You'd just take the easy way out. You'd play the 'blame game'. You'd make excuses.

Here's what it takes to change:

- Step 1: You must work out what you need to change.

- Step 2: You must commit to changing by writing down all of your reasons for the change and visualising your success.

- Step 3: You must take massive action to make sure the change happens, and sticks.

Whether you're giving up smoking, wanting to eat like a vegan, or wanting to adopt a life of celibacy, these three steps hold true. The same applies when a trader decides in their gut to make a real go of this trading game.

Decide what you want, visualise what will result in your life through achieving it, and then take massive action.

By reading this book, you've already begun to take massive action. It's great to see and I feel humbled by the trust you're placing in me to guide you.

Now that you have started to gain a level of confidence in drawing trendlines, let's add to your technical analysis skills. The implications of volume will be the next target of discussion.

3

Volume counts

I'm about to reveal secrets that few traders realise and even fewer use on a consistent basis.
Get this right and you're well on your way to achieving the results you deserve.

DURING MY UNIVERSITY DAYS, I was told of a study conducted in 1953 that involved Harvard business graduates. The study was designed to establish the common factors that caused graduates to ultimately succeed financially. Interestingly, 20 or so years after their degrees, 5 per cent of the graduates were earning 95 per cent of the total money earned by all the graduates. It was the same 5 per cent that had written down their goals and dreams all those years ago. Some even carried their personal mission statements in their wallets.

Do you want to be in the top 5 per cent of traders? Quick, grab a pen and paper and get writing. Underline parts of this workbook that resonate with you. Fill in every exercise, even if you are scared that you may not get the 'right' answer. Circle, highlight and dog-ear this book to get the best value. Re-read sections that initially seem confusing. It is not a race to finish. It would be far better to take your time and really internalise the lessons, rather than skim through it all in an afternoon. This display of discipline is one of the characteristics that separates professional traders from the unprofitable wannabes.

Earl Nightingale is quoted as saying, 'a time can come for each of us when more will happen to us in six months than transpired in the previous five years. Compound events in our lives can be compressed into remarkably short periods'.

This is 'The Phenomenon'. Your Phenomenon.

It's the payoff a trader gets after pouring their heart and soul into the markets. It is peak productivity time. Everything works. Doors swing open as if by magic. Income soars. You'll experience blockbuster trading.

If you haven't experienced this in your life already, success may be closer than you think.

I can't tell you how to turn on 'The Phenomenon'. But I can tell you a few factors that have to be present for it to occur:

- It will happen if you are open to it and geared-up for action.

- It seems to occur to people who have 'stepped up' in associating with other high performance people.

- It is often triggered with a single 'big break'.

Focusing on the lessons in this book could very well be your 'big break'. So don't lose concentration while I'm explaining these concepts. If you do, success might just slip through your fingers.

Why is volume important?

The best traders combine their knowledge of share price direction with an analysis of volume. Volume provides a measure of the strength of conviction of the bulls and the bears. By the end of this section of the workbook, you will be able to take an educated guess as to whether an uptrend or a downtrend is likely to continue.

To make money out of the sharemarket, you need to understand the psychology of the market participants. Charting helps to plot this psychology. If waves of greed and hope have spread through the majority of traders like ink into water, it makes sense that the share price will go up. If only a few traders are affected by a bullish news story, any share price increase will lack lustre and eventually falter. There is strength in numbers. You do not have to know the exact reasons behind the price movement, you just need to observe that it is occurring in order to profit from it. Volume can help you to understand whether the move is sustainable.

To make money out of the sharemarket, you need to understand the psychology of the market participants.

It doesn't matter 'why' the move is happening. It just has to be an observable, significant move in order to capitalise on the opportunity.

Reminiscences of a Stock Operator by Edwin Lefevre has been a very influential book. First published in 1923, it is a biography of terrific trader Jesse Livermore, who built his fortune and lost it several times. He stated:

> We know that prices move up and down. They always have and they always will. My theory is that behind these major movements is an irresistible force. That is all one needs to know. Don't be too curious about all the reasons behind price movements. You risk the danger of clouding your mind with non-essentials. Just recognise that the movement is there and take advantage of it by steering your speculative ship along with the tide. Do not argue with the condition, and most of all, do not try to combat it.

Let's look at some of the key points about the 'volume family' and how to use it effectively.

Overall volume

Overall volume refers to how many shares are traded each day. Why do you think it is important to trade in shares that have sufficient overall volume?

....

....

There are a few reasons it is essential to only trade shares which have sufficient overall volume. When I started trading, I remember buying a fairly large package of a speculative little company 'at market'. This effectively wiped out the queue of all of the sellers. I single-handedly managed to drive the price upwards during that day. Yes, for that moment in time, I was 'Queen of the Bulls'. This is a debatable title of honour, let me assure you. I created a volume spike in that unpopular, illiquid little share, all by myself. I bought so many shares I practically ended up buying the whole company!

It took me weeks to disentangle the position and exit. Since then I have made sure that I only buy a small percentage of the number of shares being traded on average per day. You don't want to control the market, and you definitely want to be able to get out of your positions. Without good levels of volume, you may not be able to exit from your position easily when you need to. This is why it is a good idea to only trade shares with a decent level of liquidity.

... I want the share that I am considering purchasing to trade at least every day.

As a minimum, I want the share that I am considering purchasing to trade at least every day. You can also apply a general overall volume rule. If you are in doubt as to whether the overall volume is sufficient, calculate the average daily volume over the past three months and never buy more than one-fifth of this amount. Some people apply a blanket ruling that if the share doesn't turn over 50 000 shares per day on average, they refuse to trade it. Rules like this will help you to engage appropriate trades and reject trades that will be potentially difficult to exit.

You probably won't have a problem with this when talking about shares like ANZ or CBA. The problem generally arises when you're trading outside the Top 100 shares by market capitalisation (the total number of shares issued, multiplied by the share price). Shares that have smaller market capitalisation can sometimes suffer from low overall volume.

Relative volume

Relative volume refers to whether volume is increasing or decreasing based on the past volume performance of the share. For example, a volume spike shows a higher relative volume in relation to the other levels of volume generally experienced by that particular instrument.

Have you ever seen a flock of raucous seagulls, all trying to scavenge the fish-and-chip leftovers at the beach? One seagull spies the chips and screeches, which encourages others to join the feast. Before you know it, you've got 50 of the little blighters, vying for your attention by making the most obscene racket possible.

Volume on a share chart is a bit like that. One or two traders jump into the share as the price increases. This catches the eye of a few more enthusiastic bullish traders. Suddenly, there is a heck of a din about that share in the media and in internet chat rooms. With excited screeches, more traders join the uptrend and momentum builds. This is what it takes to continue driving strength into a share price movement.

A potential trap

When I'm looking for volume to confirm the direction of a move, I seek more than just a one-day aberration in volume. If there is one particularly large volume spike, and the share is an optionable stock (one over which options can be traded), this may just represent the option spot month. (The spike in volume may reflect options on this stock expiring, so it is not a true indication regarding the effect of supply and demand.) This is much more likely if you look back over the history of the share and notice that this volume spike occurs every month, or on a quarterly basis.

Uptrend

To drive an uptrend, large numbers of traders must fling excessive amounts of money into a share. A lot of the software searches that technical analysts perform in order to find opportunities are volume-driven. Once volume increases beyond previously expected parameters, this acts as a beacon to dedicated chartists. Momentum gathers and more traders join the bullish rush of enthusiasm for that vehicle.

To drive an uptrend, large numbers of traders must fling excessive amounts of money into a share.

When volume increases as the share price rises, this suggests that traders have displayed a tendency to cash-in their profits. Almost immediately, they regret their decision and as the share price rises, they buy back in. This large turnover almost guarantees continual demand.

Wait for volume to confirm the direction of a trend, especially if you believe that you have identified a turning point in a downtrend. If volume is increasing simultaneously with the share price, then you are likely to be involved with a share that is trending up or beginning to trend upwards strongly. Also, look for temporary moves down in share price on light volume to confirm a strong uptrend. (These small corrections are called counter-trend reversals and represent a brief pause before the share continues its vigorous trending activity.) Moves downward on light volume suggest that the shareholders are hanging on tightly to their shares and are reticent to sell them to the eager buyers.

If a share price is increasing on low volume, this shows that there are only a few buyers who are driving the increase.

If a share price is increasing on low volume, this shows that there are only a few buyers who are driving the increase. These buyers will gobble up the available shares at these prices, and once they have been satiated, the uptrend will cease. Sellers panic, and begin to offer their shares at lower prices to induce more buyers to feast on the banquet. Sellers soon outnumber the buyers, and a sense of panic begins to inundate the market. A downtrend is initiated. As long as there are unenthusiastic buyers and fearful sellers, the downtrend will be maintained.

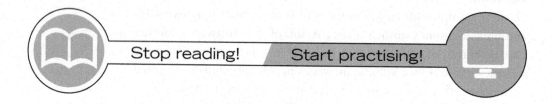

Stop reading!   Start practising!

Figure 3.1 shows an example of a strong move upwards in price. I actually bought this share on the basis of this price action. I want you to have a look at the point of breakout and list the many pieces of evidence that tell you that this move is likely to be sustainable. Remember to also draw from your knowledge of the line family to help you with your conclusions. If you know anything about moving averages, you can use this knowledge as well. This may whet your appetite for the topic of the next chapter.

Figure 3.1: AGX daily

Source: SuperCharts version 4 by Omega Research © 1997.

The breakout is likely to be sustainable based on these reasons:

- ABOVE 30 WK EMA
- MA IS TRENDING UP
- CONSOLIDATION WAS OVER A RELATIVELY LONG PERIOD
- LARGE SPIKE IN VOLUME
- BROKE RESISTANCE
- ONCE IT BROKE OUT, NO OTHER RESISTANCE.

Let's move forward in time and see if the breakout did continue. Figure 3.2 shows the eventual price move. The breakout was likely to be firm because there was a white candle on heavy relative volume breaking above a significant resistance line that coincided with an all-time high.

Figure 3.2: AGX daily

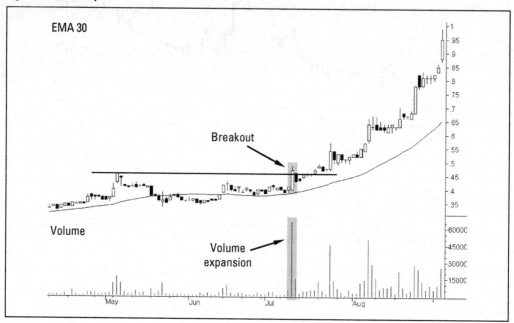

Source: SuperCharts version 4 by Omega Research © 1997.

Downtrend

If volume is increasing and the share price is dropping, then ripples of fear are flooding through the shareholders. More people are likely to react like the proverbial lemmings plummeting from a cliff and sell their shares.

Note, however, that even if there are only a few sellers and the share price is dropping precipitously, this is still a dire signal. For this reason, I consider volume to be more important to confirm an upward movement in comparison to a downward movement. Shares can fall from a great height under their own weight, without requiring much of a change in volume.

The emotion of fear is much more pervasive than the emotions of greed or hope. A sense of fear will spread very quickly throughout a market. It only takes one small stone to begin a landslide. It only takes one seller at a price below the current market value to create a selling frenzy. Learn to recognise the signals that indicate that a bear market has begun.

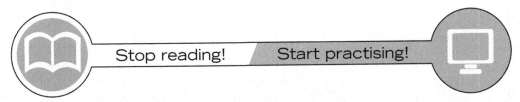

Let's have a look at an example of a strong move downwards in price (figure 3.3, overleaf). I have used a 30-week moving average on this chart. A 30-week moving average takes the closing prices of the last 30 weeks and averages them. Don't worry if you are not familiar with moving averages — we will be having a closer look at these very shortly. Examine the point of breakout and list as many pieces of evidence as you can find that tell you this downward move is likely to be sustainable.

Figure 3.3: CSL weekly

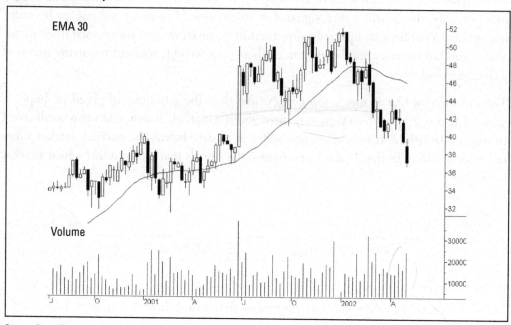

Source: SuperCharts version 4 by Omega Research © 1997.

The breakout is likely to be sustainable based on these reasons:

- BELOW THE 30 WEEK EMA
- BROKE MAJOR SUPPORT
- VOLUME IS INCREASING
- LARGE BLACK CANDLES

Let's move forward in time and see if the breakout did continue. Figure 3.4 shows the eventual price move.

Figure 3.4: CSL weekly

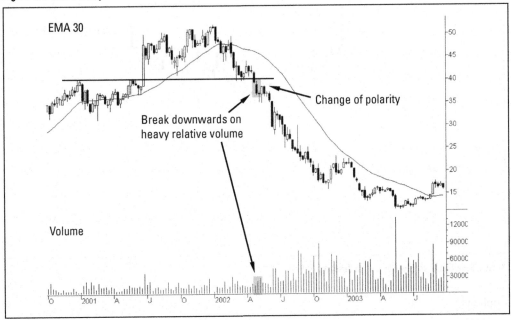

This share broke downwards past a significant support level, initiated by a black candle on heavy relative volume. It had already begun to trend downwards as indicated by the lower highs.

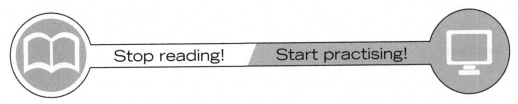

Stop reading!   Start practising!

Have a look at the following charts (figures 3.5 to 3.7). I want you to use your knowledge of each of the families discussed so far to assist you. Complete the pros and cons list to enhance your trend-detection skills. On the weight of the evidence you have collected, decide whether you have located an uptrend or a downtrend.

Figure 3.5: ZIM weekly

Source: SuperCharts version 4 by Omega Research © 1997.

Uptrend

Pros:	Cons:

Downtrend

Pros:	Cons:

Figure 3.6: UTB weekly

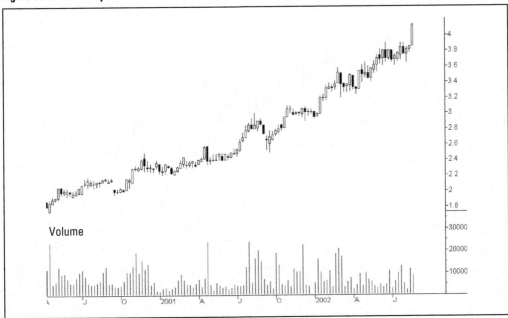

Source: SuperCharts version 4 by Omega Research © 1997.

Uptrend

Pros:	Cons:

Downtrend

Pros:	Cons:

Figure 3.7: TEM daily

Source: SuperCharts version 4 by Omega Research © 1997.

Uptrend

Pros:	Cons:

Downtrend

Pros:	Cons:

Once you have finished analysing these charts you can have a look at how these trades would have ended up had you entered a position (figures 3.8 to 3.10).

Answers

Figure 3.8: ZIM weekly

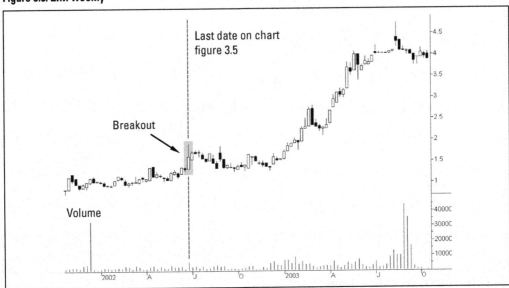

Source: SuperCharts version 4 by Omega Research © 1997.

Figure 3.9: UTB weekly

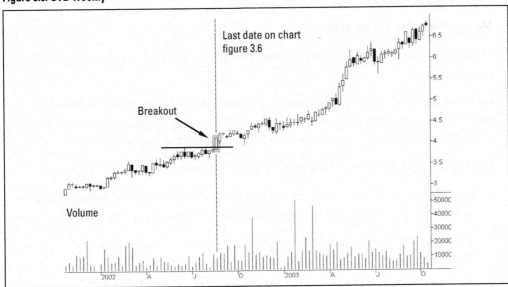

Source: SuperCharts version 4 by Omega Research © 1997.

Figure 3.10: TEM Daily

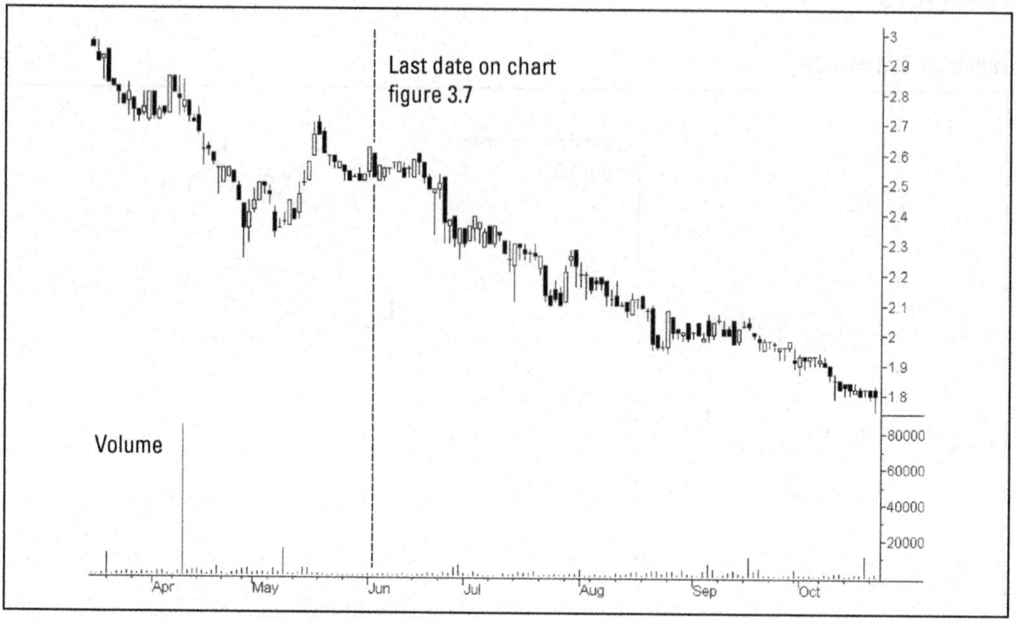

Source: SuperCharts version 4 by Omega Research © 1997.

Psychology secrets

Money ideas—are you out of balance?

I want you to have a think about—*when does money go from being a positive to a negative force in our lives?*

Here are my views on this. They may not exactly mirror your own, but I feel this is an important concept for traders to look at. You see, unless you fully question your own money mindset, you could end up sabotaging yourself down the track.

I feel you're out of balance with your views about money if:

* You allow it to become an obsession and it's one of the last things you think about before going to sleep, and the first thing you think of when you wake up.

* You judge the integrity and calibre of the people you meet by their bank account, their clothes or the car they drive.

* You judge your self-worth by your bank account, your clothes or the car you drive.

- Your sense of self is seriously compromised when you either make a lot more money, or lose a lot of money.

- You are more concerned with money than you are with your health, your relationships, your engagement in new projects or your enjoyment of a nice night out.

- You let it negatively impact your most meaningful relationships.

- You let money become more important than principles.

I'm not for one minute suggesting that there is any problem with being seriously financially wealthy, if that's your goal. However, I am saying that your views about money can sometimes get out of kilter and damage your emotional wellbeing and your relationships.

Unfortunately for some traders, the more frantic they feel about money, the more their aggression increases. Aggressive traders seek revenge and take out their frustrations by entering inappropriate positions, and dramatically increasing their position size when they are losing. The market will not reward your audacity if you hysterically yell, 'Double or nothing!' at your computer screen. Determine what raises your level of *aggressability*, before you are experiencing that situation. (It is so a word! It's in the glossary, so it must be a word!)

So...how do your views about money affect you? Take a few moments to have a think about it.

A quick word of encouragement

The fact is, being a trader and writing some thought-provoking comments for you in this book is a blessing. I fully realise that my life is structured around my own personal core values and the things I really like to do with my time.

I feel grateful.

So where are these little thoughts leading to?

You see, we live in an age of entitlement where the majority of people expect to win, and often give up at the first sign of a struggle. They seem to think that all they need to do is take that first step, and success will be assured.

However, you and I know that this isn't the case. The first step, while hard to make, is simply that...it's just the first step. To really excel, you must continue to push forward.

And that's what I'm here to help you to do. To keep on walking when you feel weak. To keep on pushing when you feel like stopping. To keep on striving when it would just be easier to settle back down onto a nice, soft couch.

A lesser person takes the easier option.

It's only 'courageous' if you face your fears and keep moving forward.

With the beginning of your sparkling, opportunity-filled career as a trader—more than anything, I wish for you courage. Courage to face your fears and take that next step...and the next step...and the next step. Persist until you understand. Educate yourself until it becomes clear for you.

You're going to love what I have in store for you in the chapters that are coming up. Keep on reading and all will be revealed...

Summary

It may help you to have a look at the following summary tables to cement the central principles related to volume.

If the medium-term price action trend is upwards, let's have a look at the meaning behind short-term price fluctuations (table 3.1).

Table 3.1: probability of medium-term uptrend continuation

Short-term price direction	Volume	Probability of uptrend continuation
Up	Up	Strong
Up	Down	Weak
Down	Up	Weak
Down	Down	Strong

For example, if the short-term price movement is upwards, and volume expands, then the medium-term trend is likely to continue upwards. If there is a counter-trend reversal that shows the price decline, but volume goes up, this means that the bears are threatening the medium-term uptrend.

Let's look at a summary of volume characteristics during a downtrend. If the medium-term price action trend is downwards, table 3.2 summarises the meaning behind short-term price fluctuations.

Table 3.2: probability of medium-term downtrend continuation

Short-term price direction	Volume	Probability of downtrend continuation
Up	Up	Weak
Up	Down	Strong
Down	Up	Strong
Down	Down	Moderate

For example, if the short-term price movement is upwards, and volume expands, this means that the medium-term downtrend is more likely to reverse. If the share drops and the volume increases, this is a sign that the downtrend is quite entrenched.

You're doing beautifully with following these examples. What you're doing takes self-discipline, and that's why not everyone can apply themselves to this the way you are doing right now. You see, when you focus your self-discipline on a single purpose, like sun shining through a magnifying glass, you will succeed. It's just a matter of time.

The next chapter will introduce you to a set of indicators that can help build a composite picture of share price behaviour. Moving averages are one of the simplest indicators to understand and use. They have stood the test of time and helped countless traders develop their skills with trend detection.

4

Moving averages rock!

If I had to choose just one indicator to analyse a chart, a moving average would be my absolute first choice. You're about to learn the secrets of the moving average so you can apply them and excel in the markets...

JUST BEFORE WE HAVE A CHAT about how to use moving averages, I want to remind you about why you want to become a trader in the first place. Sometimes, in the midst of a lot of technical detail, your reasons for studying can get a little bit lost. Don't let that happen to you. I thought you'd like to know... *Eleven things they didn't tell me about being a trader:*

1   When you're a full-time trader, filling in your day with non-trading activities so that you don't tinker with your plan is harder than you'd think.

2   Finding other traders who understand where you're at is critical to your success.

3   Handling the profits is just as hard as handling the losses.

4   Over time you begin to become unemployable. Eventually you won't want any other job.

5   Trading with your back to the wall out of desperation usually doesn't work. You have to be at peace within yourself to learn the lessons the market is trying to teach you.

6   Trading Plan + Time + Support = Trading Success.

7   Sometimes non-traders will irritate the beegeebeez out of you because they'll think you're a gambler, unemployed, irresponsible or a stuck-up mole with too much money. Luckily, you and I know that trading is a noble profession where we live by our wits and get paid in direct proportion to our levels of discipline.

8   Your relatives won't respect or understand what you do, but when there's a crisis that money can fix — you'll be the first person they run to.

9   You'll need to find a deeper meaning in your life than just earning money.

10 The extra face-to-face time you spend with your family and the people you CHOOSE to be with is the most incredible gift trading can provide.

11 The choices that this way of life opens up simply can't be understood by the outside world.

Now that I've got that off my chest, let's have a chat about our first really cool family of indicators — moving averages.

Moving averages are truly the darlings of all the indicators. Technical analysts love them. A moving average takes the sum of the closing prices and averages it across a particular period. This indicator plots points that form a line designed to smooth out the fluctuations present when looking at the share price action. Essentially it provides an expression of the trend after stripping out the short-term turbulence. By the end of this chapter, you will confidently be able to interpret moving averages.

Share prices and moving averages

The location of the share price in relation to the moving average can provide important trading information. Have a look at figure 4.1. Observe where the share price is positioned in relation to the moving average. Can you determine whether to be a bull or a bear based on this information?

It may become apparent that when the share prices are located above the moving average, this is a bullish sign. Think about the meaning behind this. When share prices are above the moving average, this suggests that current prices are performing better than they have in the past. In effect, if the share prices were being rated as a high school student, they would have achieved a 'B' grade when they had been averaging only 'C's in the past.

Figure 4.1: ASX weekly

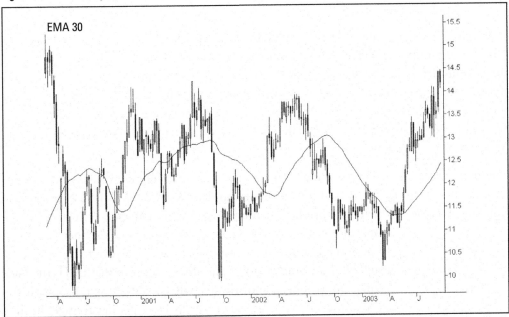

Source: SuperCharts version 4 by Omega Research © 1997.

To continue this analogy, you would expect that a student who had managed to go from a C grade up to a B would be capable of continuing his or her hard work, wouldn't you? The student may even hit an A grade, based on his or her track record of recent improvement. When share prices are above a moving average, based on the share's history, it is now outperforming its historical behaviour. It is more likely to continue to achieve at this higher level, which is why a share price positioned above a moving average is a bullish sign.

Conversely, when the share prices are located below the moving average, this is a bearish sign. What this is telling you is that the share has slipped from, say, a C to a D grade and has been underperforming its historical behaviour. Obviously this would not be a positive sign if you were looking at a high school student's marks, so it is not a bullish signal when looking at a share's behaviour.

Which time period to use

In general, if you are a long-term trader, you should apply long-term moving averages to your chart. If you are a short-term trader, you will need to use short-term moving averages. There is no point in using a 60-week moving average if you are a short-term options trader with an average hold time of four days. You are simply not matching the tool with the outcome you are expecting. It would be like using a tomahawk to put the finishing touches on a rare diamond.

If you are already trading and have some idea about how long you generally hold a share, take this figure and double it. For example, if you are a medium-term trader and tend to hold your shares for 12 weeks, you could try a 24-week moving average. If you are looking to apply a second moving average to compare its effectiveness, take your average hold time and halve it. You would then apply a 6-week moving average to the share chart. These are only suggestions. You will need to experiment with moving averages of different time durations.

There is no magic setting for using a moving average that will give you the best results at all times. Although we would love someone to discover the NMA (the Nostradamas Moving Average), which will predict turning points with 100 per cent accuracy, it simply doesn't exist. As a rule of thumb, I suggest that you use a 30-period moving average until you attune your eye to the impact of using different time periods. This does not mean that this is the ideal setting! Interestingly, your results will not deviate significantly if you use a 28-period, a 30-period or a 32-period moving average. In all of the charts in this book, unless I stipulate otherwise, I use a 30-period moving average.

> There is no magic setting for using a moving average that will give you the best results at all times.

If you are looking to try a shorter term moving average, use a 15-period moving average. When using a daily chart, the 15-period moving average will average the closing prices of the last 15 days. When using a weekly chart, the 15-period moving average will average the closing prices for the last 15 weeks. If you decide to use both the 15-period and 30-period moving average on the same chart, then you can experiment with looking for intersecting lines (golden and dead crosses) between these two moving averages.

Golden and dead crosses

Moving average lines that intersect have very important implications. A *golden cross* is where an indicator, or another moving average, crosses up through a moving average. This is a bullish sign. A shorter term moving average will hug the share price action more closely than a longer term moving average. So when a shorter term moving average crosses up through a longer term moving average, it will form a golden cross.

A *dead cross* is where an indicator, or another moving average, crosses down through a moving average. When a shorter term moving average crosses down through a longer term moving average, a dead cross will form. This means that the bears have just poked their noses out of the cave. A golden cross and dead cross are shown in figure 4.2.

Figure 4.2: golden cross and dead cross

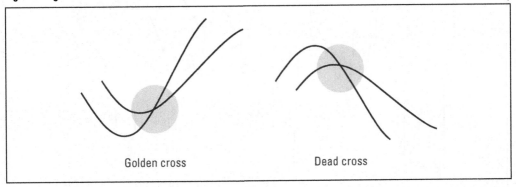

Golden cross   Dead cross

It is also important to note that moving averages tend not to be as effective if the share is trending sideways, unless the sideways movement represents a very wide range. This would suggest that it is best to draw in your support and resistance lines and trendlines before looking at the moving average for guidance.

An example

Figure 4.3 (overleaf) shows a 30-week *exponential moving average* (EMA) and a 15-week exponential moving average on a weekly chart of the ASX. An exponential moving average weights the most recent periods of share price action more heavily in comparison to the older periods. Notice where the golden cross and the dead cross occur. The golden cross is formed when the 15-week moving average crosses up through the 30-week moving average. This is a bullish sign. The dead cross is formed when the 15-week moving average crosses down through the 30-week moving average. This is a bearish sign. Also notice the location of the prices in comparison to the moving average line. When the prices are located above the moving average, this is bullish. When the prices are located below the moving average, this is bearish.

Figure 4.3: ASX weekly

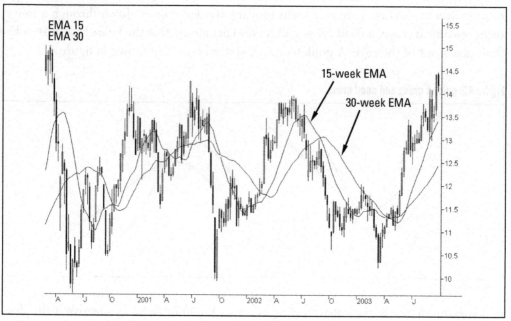

Source: SuperCharts version 4 by Omega Research © 1997.

Some analysts like to cover their chart with moving averages of up to 10 different timeframes. They find this to be a very effective way to conduct their own analysis. This is known as the multiple moving average technique. I tend to think that taking a longer term moving average and a shorter term moving average can derive the same result. The choice, however, is up to you. Given that charting is the study of price and volume action, the use of a great number of indicators can take you too far away from the raw data. I would prefer to see you use just a few tools, and use them well, rather than become obsessed with dozens of squiggly lines.

It is important to note that if the share price darts away from a moving average, it is very likely that a pullback will occur. A counter-reaction will usually make the price and the moving average converge. This helps to explain why dramatic price movements are quite difficult to maintain. Prices tend to revert to the mean over time.

Self-fulfilling prophecy?

Now that you're starting to understand a little more about indicators and share price action, you may be wondering whether the interpretation of these tools results in a self-fulfilling prophecy. Logically, as more people understand how to use technical analysis, it would seem that this would drive strength into the observable trend. If this is the case, then it would make sense for you to educate yourself as much as you can about trend analysis so that you can cash in on this herd mentality.

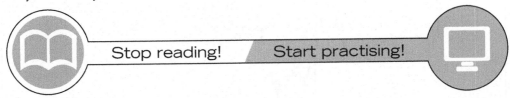

Stop reading!   Start practising!

You may need to set aside 15 minutes to complete these exercises. Remember that, as Winston Churchill stated, 'The man who can master his time can master nearly anything'.

Have a look at the following charts (figures 4.4 to 4.6). Think about your knowledge of the line family. Draw in trendlines as well as support and resistance lines. Now consider what you have learned about the moving average family. Circle any golden crosses or dead crosses. (I have used a 15-period and 30-period exponential moving average on these charts.) Consider whether the share price is located above or below the moving average. Based on this analysis, state whether you are bullish or bearish. If I have included volume on the chart, use this to validate your argument. List every piece of evidence that you can detect to support your view.

If you come up with three pieces of evidence, that is 'average', four is 'good', and five and above is 'very clever'.

Figure 4.4: BBG daily

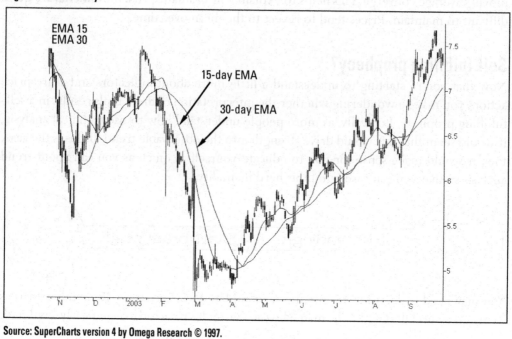

EMA 15
EMA 30

15-day EMA

30-day EMA

Source: SuperCharts version 4 by Omega Research © 1997.

....

....

....

....

....

....

....

....

....

Figure 4.5: BCA weekly

Source: SuperCharts version 4 by Omega Research © 1997.

....

....

....

....

....

....

....

....

....

Figure 4.6: BEN daily

Source: SuperCharts version 4 by Omega Research © 1997.

....

....

....

....

....

....

....

Suggested answers

Now that you have had a chance to combine your knowledge of the line family, the volume family and the moving average family, you are welcome to compare your answers with mine. Figures 4.7 to 4.9 show you how I have analysed the charts.

Figure 4.7: BBG daily

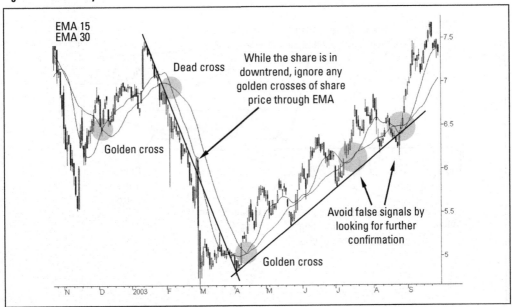

Source: SuperCharts version 4 by Omega Research © 1997.

Figure 4.8: BCA weekly

Source: SuperCharts version 4 by Omega Research © 1997.

Figure 4.9: BEN daily

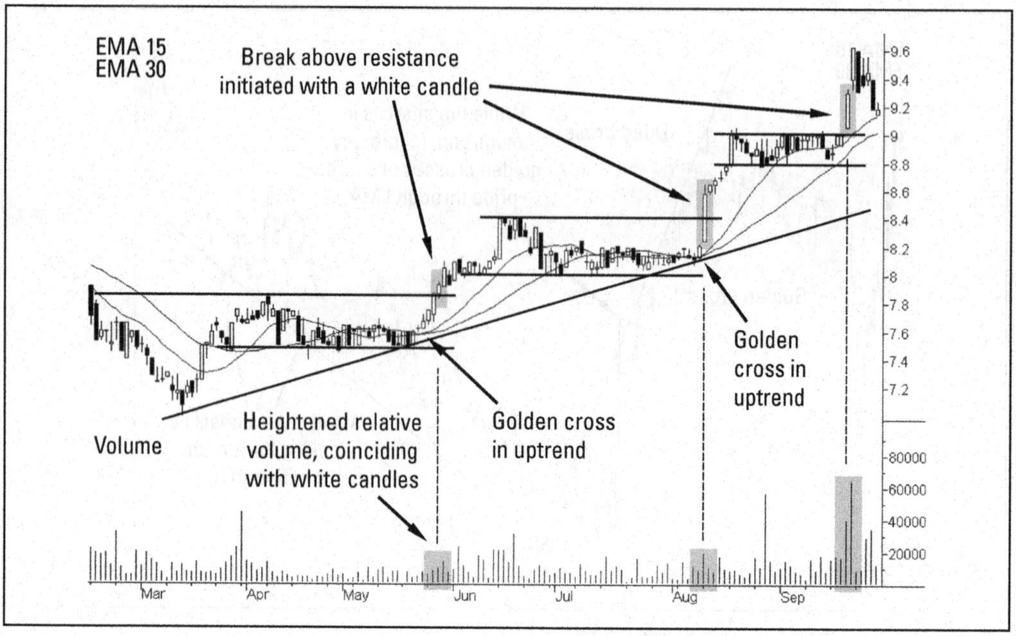

Source: SuperCharts version 4 by Omega Research © 1997.

Types of moving averages

There are several types of moving averages with a variety of complicated names such as weighted moving average, displaced moving average and exponential moving average. For the time being, I suggest that you stick with an exponential moving average. It won't make a lot of difference in the long run which one you use, but for the sake of consistency, I'll be using exponential moving averages throughout this book.

Make it a rule never to buy a share that is trading below its 30-week moving average. It is likely to be in downtrend. Even if you are a short-term trader, it is prudent to check that the overall weekly trend is upward. You will conduct higher probability trades by trading in the direction of the overall trend.

Make it a rule never to buy a share that is trading below its 30-week moving average.

If you are considering *short selling, trading CFDs, writing call options* or *buying put options*, you will want to find downtrending shares to increase the probability of making a successful trade. These strategies are explored further in chapter 11. I suggest that you start by checking the weekly chart. If the instrument that you are seeking to trade shows price action below the 30-week exponential moving average, you're more likely to have correctly detected a downtrend.

These rules will restrict your search to shares that are broadly showing trending behaviour in the direction that will most likely lead to profit. Obviously you will need to look more closely to time your entry and develop specific trading strategies.

Keep on focusing on what I'm telling you about the markets. I can guarantee you that there are people dumber, less good looking, and with fewer brain cells than you making money in the markets right now.

Psychology secrets

The age of overload

We're living in the 'age of the overload'. We end up overwhelmed, hooked up intravenously to emails, mobile phones and Facebook—pressing send/receive like some demented rat awaiting a pellet—convinced that our lives will dissolve if we step away from our desks.

If you really analysed your time, you may be surprised at how little 'peak productivity' you achieve throughout your day. Unplug. Get some time to yourself. Solitude without interruptions is precious. Reading where you have some time to think about the content is essential. Carve out some time for yourself and really think about the ideas I'm handing you on a platter. Pretty soon those confused concepts flittering around like butterflies will all begin to fly in formation for you.

Ralph Waldo Emerson said: 'The ancestor of every action is thought'. Napoleon Hill of the famous *Think and Grow Rich* said: 'You have absolute control over but one thing—your thoughts. This divine prerogative is the sole means by which you may control your destiny. If you fail to control your mind, you will control nothing else. Your mind is your spiritual estate. What you hold in your mind today will shape your experiences of tomorrow'.

Set aside an hour just to let your thoughts amble. I dare you. Do it this week. Put it in your diary. Now.

Summary

- A golden cross is formed when the shorter term moving average crosses up through the longer term moving average. This is a bullish sign.

- When the prices are located above the moving average, this is bullish.

- A dead cross is formed when the shorter term moving average crosses down through the longer term moving average. This is a bearish sign.

- When the prices are located below the moving average, this is bearish.

Your entire aim is to develop a scientific process for analysing signals, and not let your emotions dictate your trading habits. You need to define your signal in words so that another trader unfamiliar with your technique can duplicate your strategy. If it cannot be duplicated, it's not a system.

The next chapter will cover momentum indicators. Indicators under this banner help traders to establish whether prices are increasing or declining at a faster or slower pace.

5

My momentous
momentum mistake

*WARNING: I have a love/hate relationship with momentum indicators. Love them
or hate them, use them wisely and you'll establish whether a trend is likely to continue or slow
down. Handy information to get your hands on...*

YOU'VE DONE BEAUTIFULLY putting all of the pieces of this puzzle together so far. You realise
what you're creating here don't you? You're in the process of nailing the time-tested
trading principles that will help you trade confidently and safely, for your entire life.
You see, even though time ticks along, the markets are still made up of the same laws of
supply and demand. So once you really understand these concepts, no-one will ever be
able to take this knowledge away from you.

One thing that I've perfected is how to take traders from just starting out to being
incredibly profitable, professional traders. So keep on following along because I want to
see you become successful as quickly as possible.

Let's have a chat about the next family of indicators—momentum indicators.

Momentum refers to the rate of change of a price trend. Indicators from this family
measure the strength of potential moves. They can keep you out of an undesirable trade
by detecting when a trend is weak and is likely to reverse in the near term. They also
work well when used to limit the choices of a long list of potential trades. You can use

momentum indicators to weed out lower probability trades and leave you with a short list of shares that are likely to experience enduring trends.

In order to complete the exercises in this part of the workbook, you will need to read through a fair whack of preparatory information. Once you've got a solid foundation on how these indicators function, you can test your knowledge at the end of the chapter. My aim is to help you understand the implications of momentum indicators and how to use them to define when a trend is running out of puff.

What do momentum indicators measure?

The Relative Strength Indicator (RSI), Rate of Change (ROC) and the Stochastic (STO) are all momentum indicators and there are many more. When people's maximum level of pain or fear has been hit, a trend will change. Momentum indicators track this sentiment and provide a quantifiable method of evaluating it.

This is one area that brings the rocket scientists out of their closets. They will do their best to add complexity. Complexity doesn't mean that you will trade more proficiently. Let's see if I can explain the concept behind momentum simply...

Imagine you are about to shoot an elastic band across the room at your workmate. He has been particularly annoying and you have decided to aim for maximum sting factor. When you start drawing out the elastic band, it stretches easily and you don't have to exert much muscle to get it to extend. Near the limit of its extension though, you may find it a little more difficult, because the elastic band is getting close to its tolerance limit. At this point of maximum stretch the elastic band is now cutting painfully into your finger, so you release it. Snapping back to its original size, the band flies across the room and clips your target satisfyingly on the ear as you turn to gaze innocently out the window.

Momentum indicators look at the speed of the progression of the share price action and estimate when a turning point is likely.

When a trend is in play, sometimes it can become overextended and reach the point of maximum extension. In this tenuous position, it is unlikely that the trend will be able to continue in the same direction—just as the elastic band cannot continue past a certain point. At this moment, your momentum indicator will give you a signal that the trend is about to end and the share is likely to pull back to a more comfortable price level. Momentum indicators look at the speed of the progression of the share price action and estimate when a turning point is likely.

At the maximum level of stretch in a trend, the momentum indicator will provide either an *overbought* or an *oversold* signal. An overbought signal suggests that the uptrend is overstretched and a downtrend is likely to begin shortly. An oversold signal suggests that the downtrend is overextended and it is likely the share will soon begin an uptrend.

In his book *Trading for a Living*, Dr Alexander Elder states:

> **The market is like a manic–depressive person. When he reaches the height of mania, he is ready to calm down, and when he reaches the bottom of his depression, his mood is ready to improve.**

This accurately describes what momentum indicators are aiming to estimate.

Indexed momentum indicators

To help apply an objective measure regarding the maximum level of extension, some momentum indicators have pre-determined overbought and oversold lines. Examples include the Relative Strength Index (RSI) indicator, Rate of Change (ROC) and the Stochastic (STO) indicator. These are called *indexed momentum indicators*. For example, on a scale of 0 to 100, when looking at the RSI indicator, 30 signifies an oversold condition, and 70 represents an overbought condition. Other momentum indicators may not display these lines, but require the analyst to make a decision based on whether the indicator has reached a historic high or a historic low (see figure 5.1).

Figure 5.1: momentum indicators

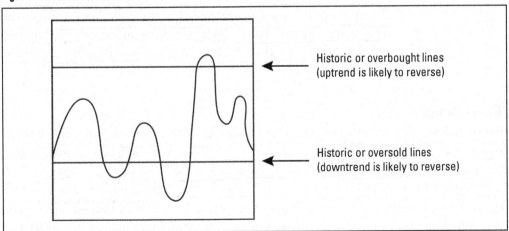

Historic or overbought lines
(uptrend is likely to reverse)

Historic or oversold lines
(downtrend is likely to reverse)

Interpreting momentum indicators

Let me offer you some encouragement. Even if you only trade with candlesticks, lines, volume and moving averages, you can still be a perfectly adequate trader. If you are finding the interpretation of momentum indicators to be hard yakka, you are welcome to leave it until you have gathered a bit more trading experience. Just skip forward until you find a part of the workbook where you feel more comfortable. I actually didn't use these indicators for the first few years of trading, and I still ended up being a reasonably good trader.

If you tend to like detail though, momentum indicators can help to refine your trading methods.

Bullish signs

If the indicator has been trending down and turns up, this is a buy signal. Oversold lines provide an objective measure of when a buy signal is likely to be strong. When the indicator crosses up through an oversold line, this suggests that the downtrend is likely to reverse. This is especially true if the indicator is at an all-time low. This is called the historic low and is likely to represent a major turning point.

In general, it is a bullish sign if the momentum line on the weekly chart is rising, and the momentum line on the daily chart is rising. This is even more significant at historically low levels. Note that if the medium- to long-term trend is upwards, a top reversal momentum indication may just mean a temporary downswing, rather than

If the indicator has been trending down and turns up, this is a buy signal.

a complete medium-term change of direction. All shares need a chance to pull back for a little while to give them a chance to relax before they continue their pursuit of higher prices. This ebb and flow in the trend direction is a natural and healthy sign of an enduring uptrend.

Bearish signs

If the indicator has been trending up and then turns down at any time, this may be considered a sell signal. When the indicator crosses down through an overbought line, this clearly suggests that the uptrend is likely to reverse. This is especially true if the indicator was at an all-time high when it turned downward. Remember that top reversal signals usually require a lighter weight of evidence to inspire a bearish share price reaction. Therefore, any downward movement of a momentum indicator is important to note. This is especially so if the share is already in a medium-term downtrend. Traders who are implementing a technical indicator stop-loss system may use this to exit their bullish positions.

In general, it is a bearish sign if the momentum lines on the weekly and daily charts are declining. This is even more significant at historically high levels. If the share is in a long-term downtrend, be aware that a bullish momentum signal may only represent a temporary counter-trend reversal. Almost all downtrends show small, lacklustre bullish recoveries from time to time. The bulls suddenly have false hope that an uptrend is about to begin. However, the downtrend is likely to continue, especially if all other indicators suggest a bearish direction will prevail.

Timing

Watch for actual changes in share price action to confirm these signals, rather than trusting the momentum indicator in isolation. Momentum indicators tend to tell us that the trend is going to change at some time in the future. They do not tell us when the trend is actually going to reverse, or how strong the reversal will be. This is a key point to note. There are very few traders who can successfully trade using these types of indicators alone. Believe me, I've tried!

Momentum indicators tend to tell us that the trend is going to change... They do not tell us when the trend is actually going to reverse, or how strong the reversal will be.

Ready to hear about my mistake?

Many years ago, when I first came into contact with momentum indicators, I decided to pile five of them onto the one chart. Sure, I could barely see the price action, or the volume, but far out—I thought I was a technical analysis champion. Who needed 'weight of evidence' when, frankly, I had those sexy looking momentum indicators all telling me the same story.

Then, I waited for exactly the right options trade to come along. I pounced, and sunk myself into it up to my neck...

And that, my friend, was the move that preceded my biggest ever trading loss in one day.

Since then, I've learned not to be so enraptured with a particular trading method that my good sense flies out the window. Learn from my mistake so you don't shoot yourself in the foot. Your goal is to trade like a machine. Apply weight of evidence or you'll suffer the consequences.

Consolidation and momentum indicators

If the share breaks upward from a consolidation range, the momentum indicator is likely to show signs of the share becoming overbought. This is because most momentum indicators are designed to register a change in the range of prices represented over the past several periods. Contrary to popular interpretations of this indicator family, this will often signify the beginning of a new uptrend, or the continuation of the existing uptrend. Often this propulsion into overbought territory after a range of consolidation is a positive, bullish signal. This is a widely misunderstood fact regarding momentum indicators. Usually an overbought area is a region that shows that an uptrend is running out of puff. After a period of price action consolidation, an overbought momentum indicator is likely to indicate that the uptrend is probably going to continue (see figure 5.2).

Histograms

Some momentum indicators are displayed as *histograms* at the bottom of your share chart. The type of momentum indicators that we have discussed so far are called *oscillators*. Oscillators take on the appearance of a squiggly line (for want of a better description). You can see an example of a histogram at the bottom of figure 5.2. This type of display lends itself to the study of divergence. You can look at divergence when using the RSI, the STO or the ROC, but there is a histogram momentum indicator that I find to be particularly useful called the MACD (or Moving Average Convergence Divergence).

You can use a histogram type of momentum indicator in conjunction with an oscillator momentum indicator, as shown in figure 5.2. Stop at two types of momentum indicators, though. Resist the urge to think that the more momentum indicators you use, the better your analysis will be.

This is a daily price chart of the Bendigo Bank share price. You can see that the most recent price action displays a higher high, but the MACD histogram shows a lower high. It's a great example of divergence.

Figure 5.2: BEN daily

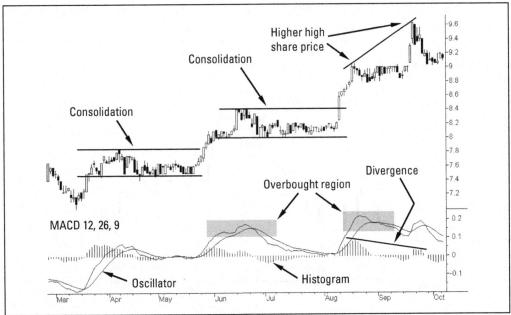

Source: SuperCharts version 4 by Omega Research © 1997.

Divergence

To help me explain this concept, I have enlisted the help of skilled trader and author of *The Art of Trading*, Chris Tate (www.tradinggame.com.au). Chris uses momentum indicators very effectively, so I appreciate his assistance.

There are several types of divergences, but the basic concept behind them all is the same. *Divergence* means that the share chart is forming higher and higher prices, but the momentum indicator is failing to make higher peaks. This is most easily visible when using a histogram. The same argument applies to a share that is making consistently lower lows, but the histogram is showing a higher low. Divergence suggests that the defined trend of the share price is likely to be weak and therefore unsustainable. Remember that this is only a likely event and it is good practice to check your suspicions with the actual share price action, rather than reacting on the basis of the momentum indicator alone.

> *Divergence suggests that the defined trend of the share price is likely to be weak and therefore unsustainable.*

Chris states: 'Traders who use oscillators such as RSI, the MACD oscillator or Stochastic will have noticed that there are instances when the oscillator does not confirm the price action. For example, consider the chart below (figure 5.3).

Figure 5.3: CAA weekly

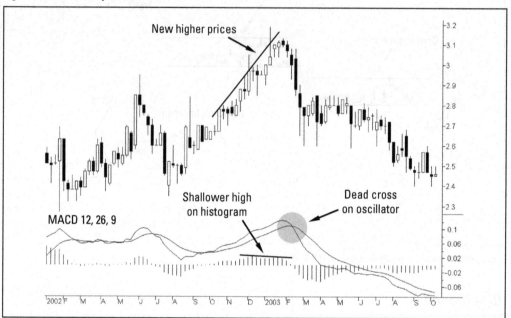

Source: SuperCharts version 4 by Omega Research © 1997.

'In this example, the price is making a series of new highs, whereas the MACD histogram has made a shallower high. The MACD oscillator also shows movement into the overbought area and has produced a dead cross signal. (As you know, this is usually a bearish sign.) Ordinarily we would interpret price making a new high as being a bullish signal but the failure of the oscillator to confirm this move introduces an element of doubt into our decision-making. In most instances we would like the oscillator, the histogram and price to be moving in the same direction with the same velocity.

'I need to sound a note of caution. True divergences are a rare phenomenon, they do not occur once a week. Powerful divergences may only occur a few times every year, so spending your life looking for divergences would simply be a waste of time. Likewise, applying a battery of oscillators to a chart in the vain hope that one might show a divergence is also a fruitless exercise.

'If you are diligent about looking at price action, when divergences occur they will be obvious to you.'

Divergence types

There are several types of divergence that can occur on a chart. As long as you understand the basic concept behind divergence, you do not have to memorise each type. However, it is still interesting to note each of the following possible variations:

Type 1 bullish   Price reaches a new low but the momentum indicator tracks to a shallower low.

Type 1 bearish   Price reaches a new high but the momentum indicator tracks to a lower high.

Type 2 bullish   Price makes a double bottom and the momentum indicator tracks to a shallower low.

Type 2 bearish   Price makes a double top and the momentum indicator makes a lower high.

If you are uncertain about the meanings of double top and double bottom, we will be covering these macro patterns in detail in chapter 6.

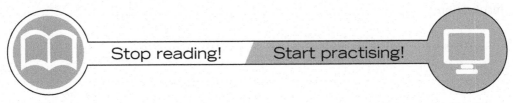

Have a look at the following charts (figures 5.4 to 5.6). Some of them show divergence and others don't. Use your trend analysis skills to define the direction of the trend and make notes to justify your answer. Identify whether any form of divergence is apparent. The answers to these exercises are covered in figures 5.7 to 5.9 on pages 83 to 85.

Figure 5.4: CDO weekly

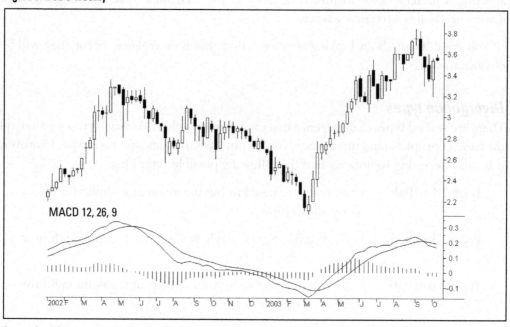

MACD 12, 26, 9

Source: SuperCharts version 4 by Omega Research © 1997.

Trend direction: ....

Likelihood of trend continuation: ....

Justification: ....

....

....

....

....

....

....

....

Figure 5.5: CLH weekly

Source: SuperCharts version 4 by Omega Research © 1997.

Trend direction: ....

Likelihood of trend continuation: ....

Justification: ....

....

....

....

....

....

....

....

Figure 5.6: LNN daily

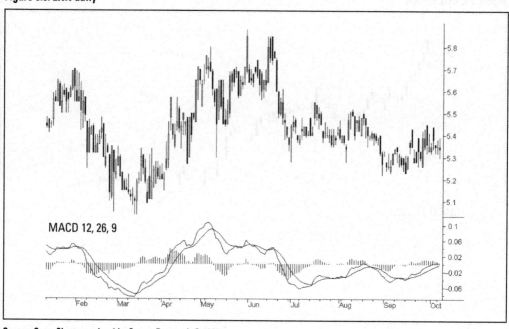

MACD 12, 26, 9

Source: SuperCharts version 4 by Omega Research © 1997.

Trend direction: ....

Likelihood of trend continuation: ....

Justification: ....

....

....

....

....

....

....

....

....

Answers

Figure 5.7: CDO weekly

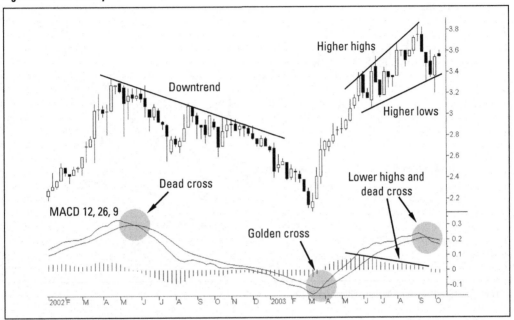

Source: SuperCharts version 4 by Omega Research © 1997.

Trend direction: Up—higher highs and higher lows.

Likelihood of trend continuation: Moderate.

Justification: Even though the share price appears to be trending upward, the future direction is likely to display sideways or downward movement. The share is making higher highs, but the histogram shows evidence of divergence as it displays shallower highs. The oscillator has also produced a dead cross at an overbought level, which is another a bearish sign.

Figure 5.8: CLH weekly

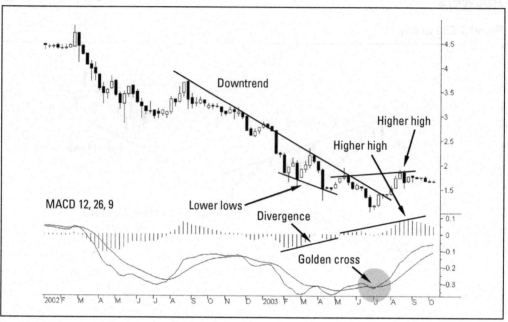

Source: SuperCharts version 4 by Omega Research © 1997.

Trend direction: Sideways recovery from a significant downtrend.

Likelihood of trend continuation: High.

Justification: The share is in a recovery phase after a significant sweep downward. There is evidence of divergence towards the end of this downtrend. Even though the share price action displayed lower lows, the histogram showed a shallower low. This should have tipped you off that the downtrend was likely to reverse. In the most recent share price action there are no signs of divergence with the histogram, and the oscillator has produced a golden cross. Combined with a recent higher high price, this is a tentative bullish sign. More confirmation would be required for you to become a definite bull. Another higher low in the share price would be preferable, as well as a break through the $2.00 mark (which represents a resistance level).

Figure 5.9: LNN daily

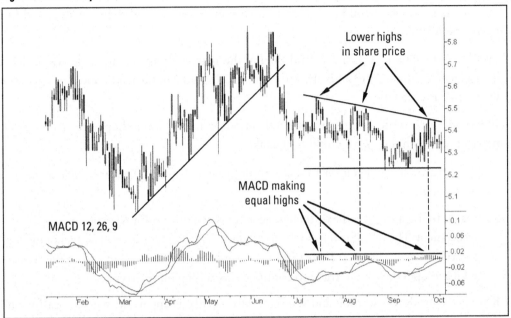

Source: SuperCharts version 4 by Omega Research © 1997.

Trend direction: Weak downtrend.

Likelihood of trend continuation: Uncertain. The share price has made lower highs, but the momentum indicator has made equal highs during the same time period. This could be interpreted as weak divergence.

Justification: This share does not appear to display consistent trending behaviour. If I don't understand the share trend, I will walk away and find another opportunity. Some shares just don't make a clear statement regarding their behaviour. Unless you can interpret the share price action easily, there is no point trading a muddy-looking trend. I can almost guarantee that you won't make money.

How to trade divergence

I asked Chris how he would progress in his trading if he noticed a divergence, and this is what he had to say.

'Firstly we may be in a position, and during the management of the trade we notice a divergence building. Alternatively, we could be considering a trade and notice that a divergence is present.

'If we are in a trade and notice that divergence is building, there are a couple of management techniques we could undertake:

1 Move our trailing stop closer to the current price. (Chapter 10 covers *stop losses* in more detail.)

2 Decide to use a staggered exit technique and lighten our position on price retracement. The use of candlesticks to highlight retracement is an ideal technique for this style of exit. The aim of this technique would be to remove profit from the trade and leave a portion of the trade to continue capitalising on the trend.

'If we are considering a trade and see that a divergence is apparent, we can opt for one of the following trading strategies:

1 Build a rule into our trading plan that says that we will not enter a trade when a divergence is present. Like all trading rules this one is not perfect and in running markets there is a possibility that price will continue to move in the anticipated direction despite the divergence.

2 Choose to employ a staged entry method. This is where you would buy a portion of the planned, ultimate package of shares you want to purchase. This can test the water before you dive in with a full position.'

Tate also told me that the same warning he gives about every technical indicator also applies to divergences. 'They are not the Holy Grail. They will not guarantee you success. The only thing that guarantees survival and, in turn, guarantees success is risk management.' (The topic of risk management will be covered in chapter 10.)

Momentum indicators can be incredibly complex. Always observe the price action and remember to apply weight of evidence, so you can confirm the likely future direction from a variety of sources.

Psychology secrets

Dealing with change

I know that a lot of people lost loads of money in the GFC (Global Financial Crisis). There were many lessons learned, but unfortunately, there were also some behaviours that have prevented traders who suffered a loss from moving on. It's tragic to watch.

People have become shell-shocked, and this has lead to indecision and confusion. It's not just traders who have been afflicted with this. It's also property investors.

The other day, I was having a chat with my friend Michael Yardney, my real estate mate, about this very topic. We were talking about change and how some people handle it well, while others struggle. Michael gave me a neat little method that he personally uses to handle change. Works like a charm.

Ask yourself these three questions:

1 What is the worst thing that could happen?

Could you die because of the change that's being forced on you? Could it be that you'll hurt or alienate one of your closest friends or relatives?

Spell it all out because by putting it down on paper, you rob it of its power.

Most change doesn't end up physically harming us...but our caveman brain feels like it will. Our fight or flight primitive mind reacts to threats as if we were about to get mauled by a sabre-toothed tiger.

In reality, most changes don't incur that level of extreme threat.

Then, ask yourself...

2 What is the best thing that could happen?

For example, if you've lost your job, you have a clean slate in front of you. You could find a much better job, recreate your life, develop new contacts, and perhaps even focus on developing your skills in a different arena.

(continued)

Psychology secrets (cont'd)

3 What's the most likely thing that will happen?

I'll bet there was some sort of middle ground, rather than the event creating a catastrophe in your life.

By asking yourself these three questions, it helps you remove the drama and get back to doing what's important—coping with the change and ensuring you're on track to use it as a springboard.

A lot of the emotional angst we feel in our lives is due to 'catastrophising' what is happening to us. If we apply a bit of 'real thinking' to our problem, we might just find that it's an opportunity in disguise.

Summary

- Momentum indicators look at the speed of the progression of the share price action and estimate when a turning point is likely.

- If the indicator has been trending down and turns up, this is a buy signal. Oversold lines provide an objective measure of when a buy signal is likely to be strong. When the indicator crosses up through an oversold line, this suggests that the downtrend is likely to reverse. This is especially true if the indicator is at an all-time low. This is called the historic low, and is likely to represent a major turning point.

- In general, it is a bullish sign if the momentum line on the weekly chart is rising, and the momentum line on the daily chart is rising. This is even more significant at historically low levels.

- If the indicator has been trending up and then turns down at any time, this may be considered a sell signal. When the indicator crosses down through an overbought line, it is a clear suggestion the uptrend is likely to reverse. This is especially true if the indicator was at an all-time high when it turned downward. Called a historic high, it is likely to represent a major turning point.

- In general, strong bearish behaviour is likely to be observed if the momentum line on a weekly and a daily chart is dropping.

- Watch out for divergences where the share price and the shape of the histogram are showing some form of dislocation. If a divergence is evident, this is a signal that the trend may be running out of puff.

If you found this chapter a little dry, the next chapter will refresh you so that you will be ready to star in a Norsca deodorant commercial, frolicking in the fiords of Finland. (Okay ... well, maybe it won't be quite that refreshing, but keep reading anyway to learn about some exciting macro reversal patterns.)

6

Finally nail macro reversal patterns

There's no doubt — I adore patterns. They give me an edge in the markets like no other. You're about to fall in love with them too ...

BEFORE I FELL IN LOVE WITH pattern-detection I was an unprofitable, unfocused trader who was about to quit. Then, all that changed. Patterns became my secret weapon. Once I started to understand the waves of money that flow into and out of the markets, and the psychology of the traders controlling that money, it was like a veil had been lifted. I was riveted. I studied charts like I was obsessed, imagining I could hear what individual traders were saying to themselves as they watched the same charts. I could feel their terror, and their greed. I could see where they were throwing money at a share in the hope that it would keep shooting skyward. I could imagine their shame as they barrelled out of their losers, heads bowed low, trying to think of how they'd explain their loss to their long-suffering spouse.

It was like watching a soap opera.

That ferocious curiosity for learning about patterns has never deserted me. So I hope that by the end of this chapter, you'll catch some of my enthusiasm for patterns and it will fuel your desire to learn more.

You see, the patterns made by the share price action are the footprints that show where the money is flowing. Just as an outback tracker uses signals to lead him to his quarry, you can track the footprints of the money trail and they will lead you to a profitable trade. Patterns will help you determine whether there is a build-up of interest in a share, or whether the share is likely to fall out of favour. Skill in this arena is a foundation of trading success. It is almost impossible to get a computer to recognise all of the subtle idiosyncrasies of pattern detection. For this reason, your own application of these concepts will get you much further than an electronic diagnosis of a chart.

The majority of these patterns do not require an exact definition. If you become too pedantic with the details, you will walk away from many profitable opportunities. You will sit on the sidelines, morosely watching trades pass you by. The principles behind the pattern formation, as well as the medium-term trend direction, are the keys to using charts effectively.

There are two distinct categories of patterns—*macro patterns* and *micro patterns*. Macro formations will help you assess the broad market conditions and trend. Micro patterns, such as candlestick patterns, will help you time your entry into a position. These patterns apply to all instruments, whether you're looking at an index, the FX markets, or a share—so it makes sense to focus on what I'm about to tell you.

In this chapter we will look at some of the major macro reversal patterns. These patterns signal a complete change in the existing trending nature of a share. I will discuss the location and psychology behind each formation, as well as the strategies you can use when you notice these patterns in the future. I will also cover some advanced strategies that are suitable if you are already an experienced trader. If you are new to charting, you may want to skim over the *Advanced strategies* section and return to it when you've gathered a bit more experience.

Chapter 7 explores macro continuation patterns. These are equally as important, as they suggest the share is experiencing a temporary pause prior to continuing its trending behaviour. These patterns may provide you with a belated entry trigger, just in case you missed the original signal. Alternatively, if you are already in the trade, you can take solace when they appear, and nip out to the pub to brag to your mates.

I have personally made money from trading every pattern we are about to discuss. These patterns occur frequently on Australian charts. Once you understand how they form they are easy to recognise. I have included an index of each of these patterns on page 327. This will act as a quick reference guide when you need to find a pattern description in a hurry at a later date.

Patterns in context

With any form of pattern detection, it is important that you take a step back and look at the bigger picture. To begin with, there are several phases we need to examine. By disregarding one of these stages, the predictability regarding the outcome of a pattern will be limited.

The phases I will be referring to are the *lead-up*, the *trigger* and the *confirmation* phases.

The *lead-up* to the appearance of a pattern must be examined in order to assess the potential strength of the reversal or continuation pattern. The lead-up phase consists of the activity of the preceding periods. For example, reversal patterns are only relevant if the share has already been trending, and will not be as appropriate for use while a share has been range trading. By range trading, I mean where the share prices remain predominantly between a horizontal support and resistance line.

The *trigger* phase is the actual appearance of the pattern itself. In macro patterns this may consist of several weeks of activity. Inexperienced traders who learn about the power of pattern detection are most likely to place too much emphasis on the importance of the trigger. If you look only at the trigger, and ignore the lead-up and confirmation phases, you will not receive the full benefit of pattern detection. Every phase is of equal importance.

Confirmation regarding the effectiveness of a pattern is an essential component of trend analysis. This phase involves the share price action directly after the appearance of the trigger. Some patterns (and some traders) require greater levels of confirmation than others. We will discuss which patterns require heightened levels of confirmation, as well as the strength of specific formations.

The amount of confirmation that you personally require will depend on your investment timeframe. Longer term traders can afford to wait for heightened levels of confirmation. Shorter term traders will sometimes need to act before the pattern is fully confirmed.

Let's kick off with some useful macro reversal patterns.

Double top

Double top patterns are characterised by a strong level of resistance that is touched on two separate occasions by subsequent price action. Basically, you are looking at two peaks in price action at approximately the same price level, separated in time. According to the strict definition of this pattern, the price variation at the two peaks should be within 3 to 4 per cent or less. However, I'm never one to go by the exact definitions in all cases. (If it looks like a duck and quacks like a duck . . . it's probably a duck.)

The peaks of the double top can be separated by a few weeks to a year and still be considered a valid double top pattern. For each of the patterns discussed, the peaks or troughs may not necessarily be exactly symmetrical. Real life rarely translates into perfectly formed patterns, so accept a degree of variation from the stylised diagram shown in figure 6.1.

Figure 6.1: double top

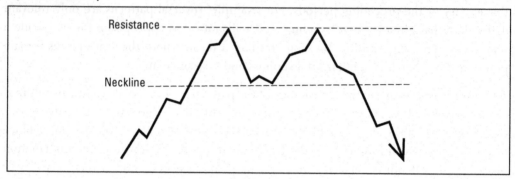

Location

Double tops can be seen on weekly, daily and even intra-day charts. The most valid double top patterns are derived from weekly charts over a medium-term timeframe.

The lead-up usually shows that the instrument has been in a sustained uptrend. This uptrend is often of an intermediate timeframe (three to six months or more). Support is formed at the 'neckline'. When support or the neckline is broken, the reversal pattern is confirmed. Trade in the direction of this break of support.

Trading below the valley of the pattern represents a break of the neckline. This means that the pattern has been confirmed. Usually this break of support will be initiated with a bearish black candle. If low relative volume coincides with this break of support, the strength of the decline may only be moderate.

If a double top forms in an existing downtrend, this can be considered a continuation pattern, and adds strength to the downward momentum. It reveals an unwillingness of buyers to purchase the share at higher prices. It reinforces the strength of the resistance line positioned at the peaks of the double top. Before buying this share, it may be wise to await activity above this seemingly impenetrable line of resistance.

Volume is usually higher during the formation of the second peak. The market is battling to decide whether the bulls or bears will arise victorious, and the increased volume depicts this struggle for supremacy.

The majority of these macro patterns has been around for many trading generations. Charles Dow first described a double top pattern in the *Wall Street Journal* on 20 July 1901.

Psychology

I have noticed that when looking at double top formations on a daily chart, if the tops are fairly close together and separated by quite a deep trough, the bearish reaction can be quite extreme. Falls in price of greater than 20 per cent are not uncommon. However, if the peaks are separated by a significant amount of time, the market's memory of the reticence to move to higher prices seems to be less distinct. For this reason, drops in price are not as vigorous. Regardless of how close the peaks are, remember to wait for a break of the neckline before acting. Don't try to pre-empt a double top. There would be nothing worse than if the other traders all gathered around pointing and staring at you for being a premature double top identifier. How embarrassing!

Early exits can be as damaging to your bank account as a late exit. Jesse Livermore stated:

> **After spending many years in Wall Street and after making and losing millions of dollars I want to tell you this: it was never my thinking that made the big money for me. It always was my sitting.**

Strategy

After you have completed your analysis, you will need to work out the most appropriate strategy to use. This involves deciding which type of vehicle is appropriate to make money from your observations; for example, shares, derivatives or futures. Each strategy needs to be firmly based on your analysis or you will be destined to lose money. Some markets will move more slowly, and so are 'easier' to trade. The returns to be expected from these markets are lower in comparison to more leveraged areas. Other markets are incredibly volatile and require a different method of monitoring in order to protect your capital, but the returns can be very impressive.

To obtain exceptional rewards you must be prepared to accept a higher level of risk.

There is no reward without risk. To obtain exceptional rewards you must be prepared to accept a higher level of risk.

If you are holding a share when a major top reversal forms, be sure to exit when your stop has been hit. Don't hang on, hoping that things will 'get better'. They won't!

Advanced strategies

Generally, one of the best methods to use when you notice the formation of a double top is to short sell the moment the pattern is confirmed. Short selling is where you can make money out of a downtrend by selling a share and then buying it back a lower price at a later date. You can achieve the same effect using a short CFD trade as well.

If you miss out on the first drop through the neckline, you can wait for a change of polarity to give you a second chance to enter (figure 6.2).

Traders who bought near the neckline may feel an overwhelming need to try and get out at their purchase price. This can explain why prices fall away after they have rebounded up to the neckline.

If you are aiming to use this change of polarity as a second chance to enter a position, waiting for a top reversal candlestick pattern can assist your timing. Bearish engulfing patterns and dark cloud covers are common patterns that mean the downtrend is likely to continue. If you're on the ball, you will have noticed that this 'second chance entry point' creates a peak that is at a lower level than the peaks of the double top pattern. This is consistent with the definition of a downtrend — the appearance of subsequent lower highs. Note that not all double top patterns will give you this second chance for a short selling entry (that is, a trade that profits from an enduring downtrend).

From an options perspective, once the double top is confirmed, the choices would be to enter a written call position, or a bought put position. Both of these strategies capitalise on a downtrending stock.

If you are planning to implement a pattern-based stop-loss method, you could position your short stop loss above the neckline. This would prevent you from getting stopped out prematurely if the share does re-test this price level before continuing to downtrend.

Figure 6.2: second chance entry

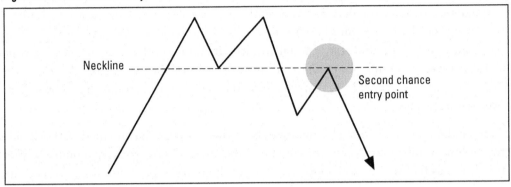

Neckline

Second chance
entry point

Example

Figure 6.3 shows you an example of how a double top pattern may appear in 'real life' as it is in the process of forming. Even though this example shows more than one defined trough, it will give you a perspective on how this formation can vary from the diagram in figure 6.1. In many cases the trough formed can show a rounded shape, or more than one touch of the neckline.

Figure 6.3: AMC weekly

Double top

Neckline

Source: SuperCharts version 4 by Omega Research © 1997.

Double top as a failed signal

If you notice a double top pattern that is in the process of forming, and you are planning on buying the share, it would be wise to wait and see whether the pattern is going to be confirmed before allocating capital towards it. Your purchase of the share can go ahead if there is trading above the level of resistance of the two peaks. Another way of looking at this principle is that you shouldn't enter into a trade that shows close overhead resistance.

Some traders act on the first closing price above the resistance line formed by the double top, as long as this occurs on heavy volume. Others may choose to await a pullback after the share has bullishly traded above the level of the double top. This change of polarity can give you another chance to have a stab at opening a long position. Trading above the two peaks means that the signal has failed and that trading long is an appropriate strategy (see figure 6.4).

Figure 6.4: failed signal

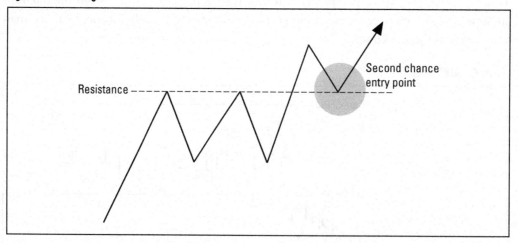

The less a share pulls back, the more bullish the future price action. Sometimes traders who await a pullback will miss the boat, so try to act on the initial breakout,

The less a share pulls back, the more bullish the future price action.

especially if you are a short-term trader. An appropriate pattern-based stop loss could be positioned just below the level of resistance. If the share collapses back into the range of trading under the resistance line, this would not suggest future bullish price action.

Double bottom

The double bottom pattern is characterised by a strong level of support that is touched on two separate occasions by the share price action before climbing again (see figure 6.5).

Figure 6.5: double bottom

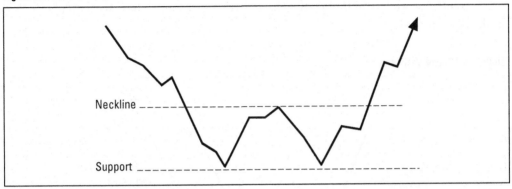

Location

This is a significant bottom reversal pattern. Resistance is formed at the neckline. When the share price closes above this level of resistance, particularly on heavy relative volume, the reversal pattern is confirmed. Trade in the direction of this break of resistance. If the level of support is broken, this suggests that the signal has failed. As with all patterns, a failed signal also provides a lot of information about trend direction. If a double bottom pattern fails, it is a very bearish sign.

If the two valleys of price action are close together, and the separating peak is quite high, the reaction of the share at the point of breakout is often extremely bullish. It is indicative of a very volatile share. Bottom-to-bottom price variation should be within 3 to 4 per cent to fulfil the exact definition. This can act as a guide. Remember though, if it has the appearance of a double bottom and leads to more predictable share price activity, it really doesn't matter how you define it—as long as you make money from it. The bottoms can be a few weeks apart, or up to six months or so.

The relative volume that coincides with the second valley is usually higher than the volume present during the formation of the first trough. This shows that the market is churning, trying to make up its mind whether to adopt a bullish outlook, or become bearish.

In many cases, after the bullish breakout past the neckline, the share price will come back down to rest on the previous level of resistance (which has now become support) as illustrated in figure 6.6. This is a healthy sign. The spring is compressing before propelling itself skyward. To suggest an enduring uptrend, it would be ideal if this compression occurred on low volume. This means that the shareholders intend to hang onto their precious little shares, even though they have dropped in value. They expect higher prices in the near future.

Figure 6.6: second chance entry

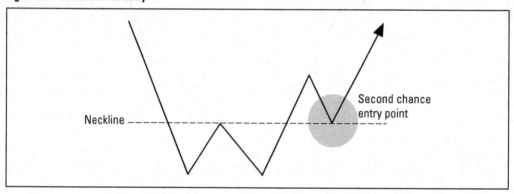

To trade this pullback effectively, you may consider waiting for a bottom candlestick reversal pattern. Examples include bullish engulfing patterns and piercing patterns. appendix A on page 287 discusses candlestick patterns in more detail.

Double bottoms can also form during an existing uptrend. See figure 6.7 for an example of how this type of pattern can provide a springboard for future share price activity.

Psychology

The market has tried to continue the existing downtrend on two significant occasions. When the neckline fails on heavy relative volume, it demonstrates that the market has become very bullish. The buyers outnumber the sellers and an uptrend is initiated.

Once the breakout has occurred, the market players often become subject to a *selective perception* bias. They notice the share more in their scans, in the newspaper and on the TV. They seem to see that company everywhere they look. This can drive strength into an uptrend, or a downtrend for that matter. Everything about the share is magnified. The management seems brilliant (or stupid), and the future direction of the company appears inspired (or completely moronic). Nothing is 'lukewarm' anymore. The selective perception bias can help explain why trends endure.

Figure 6.7: ADB weekly

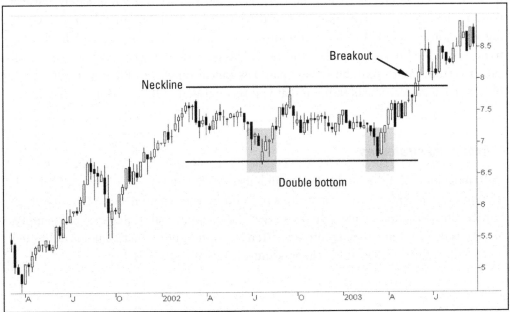

Source: SuperCharts version 4 by Omega Research © 1997.

A double bottom is, essentially, a re-test of a low price. The market is seeing whether prices will be supported at this level before ascending to a higher echelon of price activity. When there is trading above the neckline, it allows a higher level of support to form. This acts as a springboard for future price activity. For the bullish integrity of the market to continue, each level of support must be formed at a higher level.

Strategy

Waiting for the neckline to break upwards on a white, bullish candle with heavy volume could trigger you to buy the share. An appropriate pattern-based stop loss would be placed to exit a bought position if the share price closed below the neckline. This would keep you in the position if the share decides to pull back to this level before continuing to climb.

If the overall market is bearish, it is probably a good idea to wait for the pullback change of polarity to occur before opening a position. This will lead to heightened confirmation that the uptrend will endure. If the overall market is fairly buoyant, consider jumping into a long position at the first sign of a breakout. Breakouts are much more likely to hold when the whole market is whispering 'Buy, buy, buy!' to the participants.

If you try to trade one or two of these patterns and you are not immediately rewarded with a winning trade, don't just ignore the pattern completely in the future. George Soros elegantly stated: 'I'm blessed with an extremely poor memory, which allows me to deal with the future rather than the past'. This is good advice for every trader. It takes time to attune your eye to how these patterns appear on charts. Once you get the hang of it, when a pattern starts to form that you recognise, it will be love at first sight.

Advanced strategies

Confirmation of a double bottom could also act as a trigger to open a bought call option or warrant position, or write a put option. You would need to identify other indications to prompt you to choose between these potential strategies. For example, there is no point in entering into a written put option trade that contains unlimited risk unless the set up is ideal. The risk must justify the rewards.

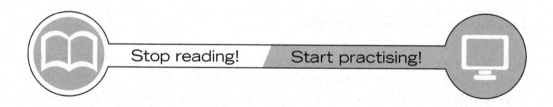

The GGL weekly chart in figure 6.8 provides an example of how a double bottom pattern looks on a chart. Identify it on the chart and think about how you would trade this.

Have a think about the insights you have gained from looking at macro patterns so far. Take some time to detail your thoughts here. Figure 6.9, on page 104, shows some suggestions.

Figure 6.8: GGL weekly

Source: SuperCharts version 4 by Omega Research © 1997.

....

....

....

....

....

....

....

....

....

Suggestions

Figure 6.9: GGL weekly

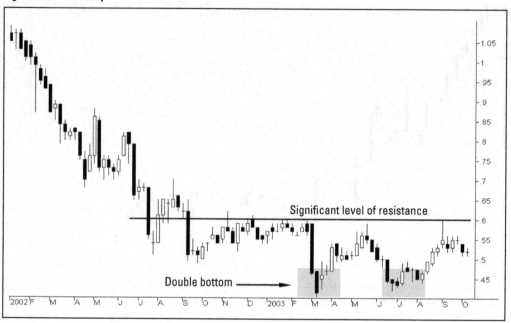

Source: SuperCharts version 4 by Omega Research © 1997.

There is a significant level of resistance at the 60¢ mark. I personally would have difficulty buying this share until I received confirmation that the share was trading above this level. I have just been caught out buying shares with close overhead resistance too many times to be sucked in again. I'd rather walk away until the share price action looked close to perfect, before making my move.

Triple top

Triple top patterns are characterised by a strong level of resistance that is touched by the price action on three separate occasions, before prices decline. Frequently this is at an all-time high of share price action. The highs should be well separated and clearly defined. It is common for these peaks to be quite sharp in appearance, whereas the troughs often take on a more rounded shape. Like the double top pattern, the triple top commonly displays this characteristic of a rounded valley (see figure 6.10).

Figure 6.10: triple top

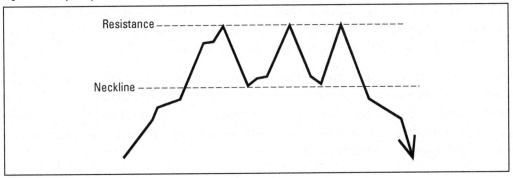

To qualify as a triple top pattern, the three peaks must be quite close to the same price level. Patterns don't always appear exactly as their definitions suggest. Minor variations are, of course, acceptable. If the central peak is higher than the other two, you have identified a head and shoulders pattern. (Head and shoulders patterns are generally traded using the same types of strategies, but it is useful to note, just in case you meet a technical analyst with a bad case of 'detailitis' at a dinner party. They're out there . . . take my word for it!)

Location

This is a significant top reversal pattern. Support is formed at the neckline where the lows of this pattern align. When support or the neckline is broken, the reversal pattern is confirmed. Trade in the direction of this break of support.

This is a pattern that shows a very high chance of experiencing a change in polarity. Prices will often experience a short rally back up to the neckline before falling away again.

Psychology

The bulls made a charge at the gate three times, only to be defeated. They have simply run out of energy. If the bulls have a quick splash of Gatorade, and manage to push share prices above the resistance level, this suggests that the pattern has failed. More companions are recruited to drive the price higher. The optimists come out of their dark cupboards and blink their eyes in the sunshine.

Strategy

These macro top reversal patterns show that a buy and hold strategy is not always the best course of action. A lot of people hold a share, wasting time while the market churns and shifts the stock restlessly from shareholder to shareholder.

Some traders insist on trying to capture the top and bottom of these peaks and troughs, and trade every move. This doesn't work. Trade with the broad trend and you will spend less on brokerage. It will also help increase your average hold time, increase your average profit, and improve your hit rate. If you're lucky, it may even make your pearly whites whiter and your breath minty fresh.

Advanced strategies

I am aware of only one method to make money out of non-trending shares, and that is to implement an option writing strategy. I personally would only use this strategy if the triple top represents a narrow trading range. If the trading range is too broad, and support and resistance are quite far apart, not even a written option will do you much good because you will have to position yourself too close to the price action to derive a substantial premium. This heightens your risk of being exercised.

A better idea may be to wait for a break of the neckline and short sell. An ideal trigger is a black candle closing below this line of support. A second chance for entry may be if the share rebounds up to the neckline and displays a candlestick top reversal pattern to justify a short entry. If you are already involved in a short position and you see a candlestick top reversal signify that a change of polarity is about to occur, you may choose to add to your position, or top up to a full position if you made a partial entry. A stop loss for your short position can be placed above the neckline. Trading above the neckline means that the share is not committed to a downward progression at this stage.

Other strategies include writing call options above the neckline once the pattern has been confirmed, using an appropriate CFD position, or buying put options or warrants.

Triple bottom

Triple bottom patterns show a strong level of support that is touched by the price action on three separate occasions. The overall trend in the lead-up phase has been downward. The lows of the triple bottom are often close to the lowest prices ever displayed by that instrument (see figure 6.11).

Figure 6.11: triple bottom

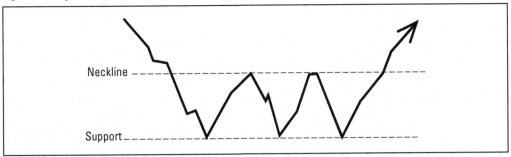

Location

This is a significant bottom reversal pattern. Resistance is formed at the neckline where the highs of this pattern align. When the share price closes above this level of resistance, particularly on heavy relative volume, the reversal pattern is confirmed. The support level acts as a trampoline before the prices propel upwards. Trade in the direction of this break of resistance.

Psychology

The market has tried to continue the existing downtrend on three occasions. It has struggled, without success, to close below the price shown at the level of support. When the neckline fails on heavy relative volume the market becomes very bullish. New buyers are attracted and existing shareholders add to their positions.

Strategy

Trade these patterns in the same way as a double bottom formation. Enter a long position when the share shows activity above the neckline and set a stop loss below the neckline to exit your position. (For a full definition of *long* and *short* see page 273). Don't be surprised if the share shows a change of polarity and drops back to this point of initial breakout before ascending again. A stop loss positioned below the expected point of pullback will keep you in a long trade, ready to profit as the uptrend unfolds.

The measure rule

I would like to introduce you to a rough rule of thumb that you can use to help estimate the strength of a move. This is especially valid after the appearance of any of the macro patterns that we have discussed so far. It is handy to be aware of the implications of this concept, even though this rule doesn't always apply exactly to all market moves.

The measure rule allows you to calculate the minimum price move expected after the appearance of a double or triple top, or a double or triple bottom pattern. It may help you to decide which share to trade if you are presented with a variety of opportunities. It is not infallible, but it beats the heck out of asking your brother-in-law's opinion.

To estimate how far the share price is likely to drop after the appearance of a double or triple top, have a look at the height of the formation. Take the highest high and the lowest low of the pattern, and subtract the height from the low. This will give you an idea how far the share price is likely to drop. For example, if the highest high of the pattern is $6.00, and the lowest low is $5.00, you could easily expect a share price decline of $1.00. As $5.00 would mark the neckline, it would be likely that the share price would drop at least to $4.00 (see figure 6.12).

The measure rule allows you to calculate the minimum price move expected...

Figure 6.12: measure rule — tops

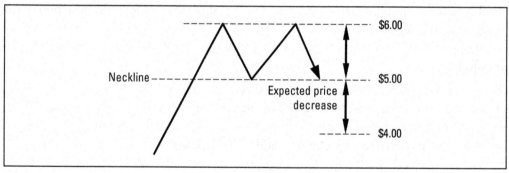

The converse is true for double and triple bottoms. Take the lowest price and the highest price of the trading range that form these patterns. The difference between these two prices will give you the expected price increase likely after the patterns have been confirmed (see figure 6.13).

Figure 6.13: measure rule — bottoms

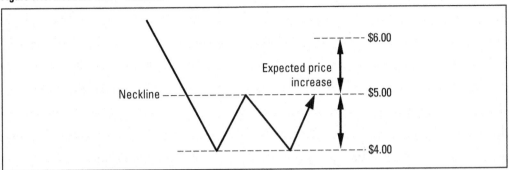

This concept helps to explain why the formation of a broader pattern often has a greater impact on subsequent share price activity. Taller ranges lead to more dramatic bullish or bearish effects. Any of the patterns that are subject to using a measure rule may help you determine whether it is worthwhile getting involved in a position in that share. Be aware that if the overall medium-term trend is established, this price target may represent a short period of consolidation before the predominant trend continues in the original direction.

Taller ranges lead to more dramatic bullish or bearish effects.

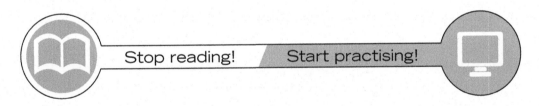

Have a look at the charts in figures 6.14 to 6.16. Identify the predominant macro patterns and where any changes in polarity occur. Summarise the major methods that you could use to make a profit from these opportunities. Draw on the chart the rough price move that would be expected as a result of these patterns forming. Suggested answers to these exercises are shown in figures 6.17 to 6.19 on pages 113 to 114.

Figure 6.14: NCM weekly

Source: SuperCharts version 4 by Omega Research © 1997.

....

....

....

....

....

....

....

....

....

Figure 6.15: ANN weekly

Source: SuperCharts version 4 by Omega Research © 1997.

Figure 6.16 shows the price action subsequent to figure 6.15. Have a look at this current share price behaviour. Would you be prepared to buy ANN based on this chart?

Figure 6.16: ANN weekly

Source: SuperCharts version 4 by Omega Research © 1997.

....

....

....

....

....

....

....

....

Answers

Figure 6.17: NCM weekly

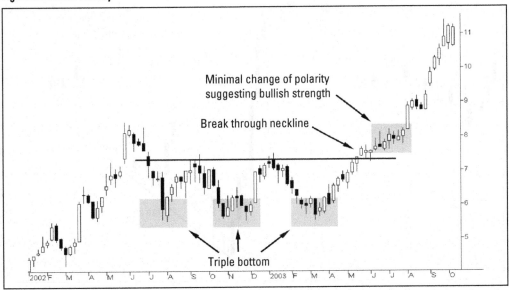

Source: SuperCharts version 4 by Omega Research © 1997.

Figure 6.18: ANN weekly

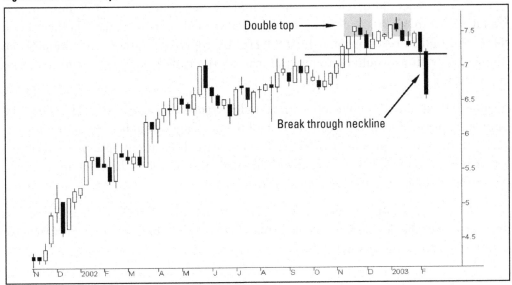

Source: SuperCharts version 4 by Omega Research © 1997.

Figure 6.19: ANN weekly

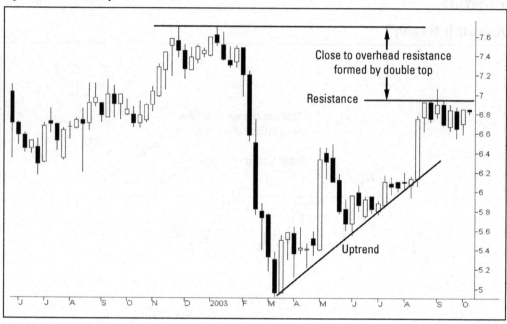

Source: SuperCharts version 4 by Omega Research © 1997.

Figure 6.17 shows that the triple bottom was confirmed with a break upwards through resistance, initiated by a white candle. The height of the triple bottom was about $5.50 to $7.30. According to the measure rule this increases the likelihood of a solid bullish reaction of at least $1.80. Appropriate strategies to capitalise on these observations would be to buy the share, buy a call option or warrant, or write a put option.

Figure 6.18 shows a double top with a trading range of around 50¢. Therefore the minimum price fall expected with a break of the neckline would be 50¢. To profit from these observations you could have short sold the share, bought put options or warrants, or written call options. If you were already in a share position at the break of the neckline, your stop loss should have triggered your exit.

In figure 6.19, because the current share price is quite close to the overhead resistance represented by the double top, it is likely that there may be a better opportunity to make a profit by purchasing another share.

Time for a break?

If you've been overloading your mind and your forehead is starting to get wrinkly with concentration, it's probably a good time to stand up and take a deep breath. Go and get yourself a nice cup of tea or coffee. Keep your motivation up so that you can continue to internalise what I am trying to convey. Don't just skim read if these concepts are unfamiliar to you — it will do you no good in the long run. Aim to really understand each concept before progressing. You may even choose to reread certain sections that did not initially seem clear. It's amazing what a second shot at understanding these principles will do for you.

Now let's move onto a few other valuable reversal patterns that can assist in improving your trading results.

Bullish and bearish V-reversals

The market violently and dramatically reverses its existing trend within a few periods. This is often accompanied by a significant increase in relative volume levels (see figure 6.20).

Figure 6.20: V-reversals

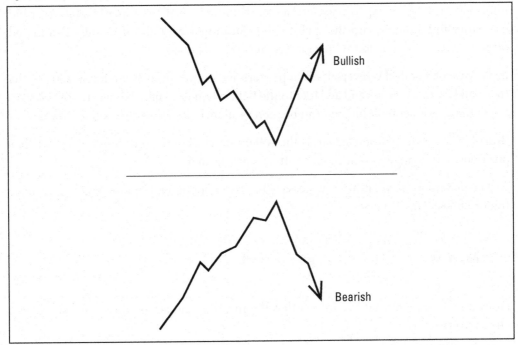

Location

Bullish V-reversals are bottom reversal patterns. I like to think of these patterns in a similar way to a depth charge. Once the share chart reaches a certain depth, the V-reversal activates and explodes upwards. You cannot tell in advance at what depth this will occur or how big the explosion will be, although an increase in volume would assist in adding bullish confirmation.

Bearish V-reversals are top reversal patterns. They can still provide a valid signal, even when they do not display an increase in volume. The share can drop from a great height with just a few sellers initiating the downward slide. Bearish V-reversals are like a big helium balloon — once the share floats up to a certain height, the balloon pops and the debris drops to the ground.

Timing is important, but very difficult to get right when trading these patterns. You want to capture the main thrust of the move, and not execute too late. Sometimes, by the time you notice a V-reversal pattern, the share has become so volatile it is like a bucking bronco.

Psychology

The market has violently altered its opinion of the value of the share, often initiated by a change in the fundamentals (company announcements, balance sheets and profit/loss information) of the company. Sometimes all that it takes is the whisper of a takeover bid, or a story in the news, and the sprint is on. An immediate sell-off or rally is initiated, often on heavy volume and with a fanfare of media reports.

In the case of a bullish V-reversal, often punters are so overjoyed at the initial activity that they will buy more shares and add fuel to the bullish bonfire. This is necessary for the share to continue to react bullishly, and can be seen as an increase in relative volume levels.

Bearish V-reversals epitomise fear as the sellers scramble over one another to exit their positions. The change in sentiment is often quite dramatic.

A certain amount of volatility is necessary to create opportunity in the market. Brilliant trader Dinesh Desai states:

> **We love volatility … for being on the right side of moving markets is what makes us money. A stagnant market means there's no opportunity for us to make money.**

However, too much volatility means that the market can flatten you before you have a chance to react.

Strategy

These types of patterns are notoriously difficult to trade. I suggest you wait for at least one higher low share price before attempting to trade in the direction of a bullish V-reversal. Medium-term traders could wait for a second higher low before entering.

This will provide a greater level of confirmation that the pattern will continue in the expected direction. Amateur traders are always trying to get in at the bottom of a trend and out at the top of a trend. This is impossible. Stop aiming for this goal. It will do you more harm than good. A stop loss can be placed below the V-reversal or below the closest low to protect your capital if the trend doesn't unfold as anticipated.

The dramatic price adjustment of a V-reversal will often create an increase in the volatility of the share.

Bearish V-reversals can use the same method by waiting for at least one or two lower high share prices before engaging a short trade. This increases the probability that you have correctly identified a downtrend. Using this method, a pattern-based stop can be positioned above the V-reversal for a wider stop, or above the closest low price for a tighter stop.

Advanced strategies

Instruments to trade in the bullish direction include the stock itself, a written put, or a bought call option or warrant. Bearish V-reversals may inspire you to write a call option, short sell, or buy a put option or warrant. Be aware that a bearish V-reversal pattern is not usually conducive to writing a covered call option. The small income you will receive from this action will usually be completely eroded by the loss of capital that you will experience as a result of owning the downtrending share.

The dramatic price adjustment of a V-reversal will often create an increase in the volatility of the share. This can have an impact on the pricing for options and warrants. The effect isn't always causal because option volatility is related to the standard deviation of the share price. However, in many cases, I have noted this type of pattern can affect volatility levels. The share has broken out of its predictable behaviour patterns. This can affect implied volatility levels of the option or warrant which can often boost the option and warrant prices quite dramatically. For this reason, bought derivative positions can become more expensive, and written positions instantly become a more attractive alternative.

(continued)

Advanced strategies (cont'd)

You may be involved in a written derivative position. If a V-reversal pattern occurs this would be contrary to your initial expectations. Suddenly you will find that it requires a lot more capital to exit your position. Unfortunately this by-product of an increase in volatility is very difficult to predict when you enter a position. It suggests that a *hard-dollar stop* is often more appropriate as an exit mechanism than direction alone. A hard-dollar stop can be effectively utilised for bought options and warrants, or futures. For example, when you've lost a maximum of 2 per cent of your allocated trading equity in any particular trade, exit that position immediately.

The golden rule of trading is: 'Keep your losses small and let your profits run'. Stop losses provide a sign that it is time to exit your position as the trade is no longer co-operating with your initial view. If you don't know how to set one, stop trading immediately! Every successful trader has determined an exit strategy prior to entering the trade (see chapter 10 for more discussion about stop losses). Figure 6.21 shows an example of a bullish V-reversal pattern.

Figure 6.21: CDO weekly

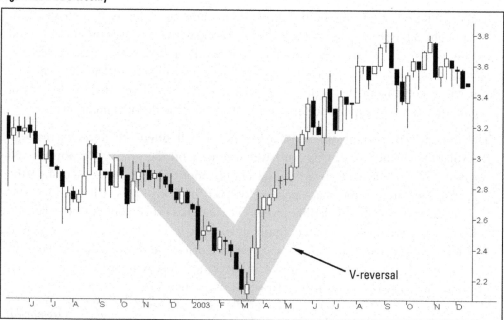

Source: SuperCharts version 4 by Omega Research © 1997.

V-reversal with a step

Some V-reversal patterns display a dramatic upswing and then a time of consolidation or sideways progression. Chris Tate has coined the phrase *V-reversal with a step* to describe this type of pattern. If a period of consolidation is in place, this provides a higher degree of certainty regarding the success of the V-reversal. If accompanied by heavy volume, the V-reversal with a step is distinguished from the more sinister *dead cat bounce* (which we will discuss shortly). The V-reversal with a step can also be seen as a top reversal pattern (see figure 6.22).

Figure 6.22: V-reversal with a step

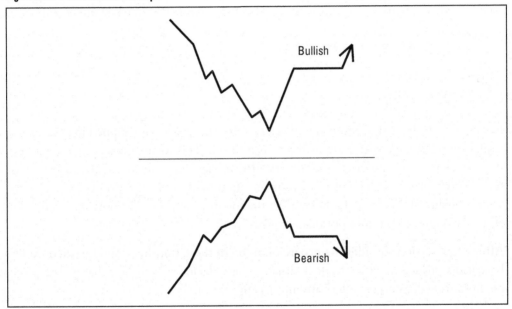

Especially in relation to a bullish bottom reversal this is a much more stable pattern than a typical V-reversal. It is less subject to altitude sickness. The period of consolidation gives the price action a chance to acclimatise before continuing, so it is not as likely to experience signal failure.

A stop can be placed below the area of consolidation that forms the step for long trades, or above the consolidation for short trades. This provides a tight pattern-based stop loss and can assist in lessening the damage if this formation does not end up reversing the overall trend.

Pattern detection is somewhat subjective. It can take quite a lot of practise to develop confidence. Remember to watch for signal failures as well as confirmations. This will provide you with two distinct opportunities for effective trading. With any of the patterns that we have discussed so far, if you observe closing prices above the top reversal pattern, it suggests that this signal has failed, so implement bullish strategies. If there is evidence of a failed signal with closing prices below the bottom reversal pattern, use bearish strategies to profit from your observations.

Psychology

Some traders will be caught like the proverbial 'rabbit in the headlights' and be completely stunned when a share reacts violently. In *The Disciplined Trader*, Mark Douglas states:

> **Fear will also limit your range of responses to any given situation. Many traders suffer considerably when they know exactly what they want to do but, when the moment arrives, find themselves completely immobilized.**

In the case of a bearish V-reversal with a step, after the share has dropped in price, some traders stay dazzled by the action and refuse to sell. This forms the step component of this pattern. These traders seem convinced that they can hold the share for the 'long term' and things will all be okay. (This is the equivalent of blocking your ears, screwing your eyes shut and yelling, 'La-la-la-la!' at the top of your voice. The horrible eventuality still exists. Ignoring it does not make it go away.)

After a few sessions of sideways progression, often these transfixed and terrified traders have had a chance to adjust to their situation, and decide to sell their shares. The prices begin to freefall as eager sellers attempt to appeal to belligerent buyers.

For bullish V-reversal patterns with a step, sometimes it can take a while for the current holders to absorb that a price rise has taken place. A churning of shares can occur, with very little price movement, before the share continues its bullish ascent.

Now that you're starting to grasp a few of the finer points of pattern detection, the key is not to get too cocky and try to predict market direction. You may believe you have the ability to pre-empt market moves because your intellect is so sharp it can slice cheese at a distance. If so, you may be in for a shock. There is a fine line between pattern recognition, and pre-empting market moves. As stated by trader Don Miller:

> **The minute the ego starts coming into our trading, it's disaster. The minute we start doing stuff that is more about building up our ego, the more likely it's going to show up in our results.**

Act only when the weight of evidence suggests you are in tune with the market. There is no place for gut feel when trading. There is a fine line between courage and stupidity.

Act only when the weight of evidence suggests you are in tune with the market.

Sometimes we get it right and our first impression leads us to make a brilliant snap decision. However, sometimes that snap decision lands us in hot water and can leave us with third-degree burns.

Example

The chart in figure 6.23 shows a V-reversal with a step, followed by a subsequent change of polarity.

Figure 6.23: ASB weekly

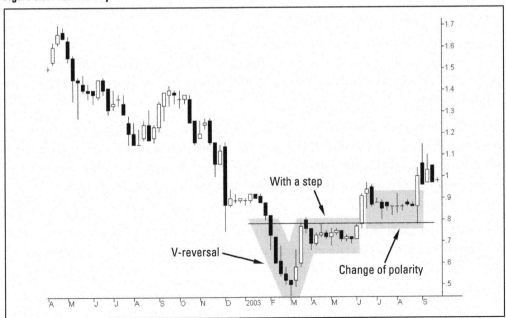

Source: SuperCharts version 4 by Omega Research © 1997.

Head and shoulders

During an existing uptrend, head and shoulder patterns are characterised by three (or more) peaks with the central peak being located at a higher position on the share chart than the first and third peaks (see figure 6.24).

Figure 6.24: head and shoulders

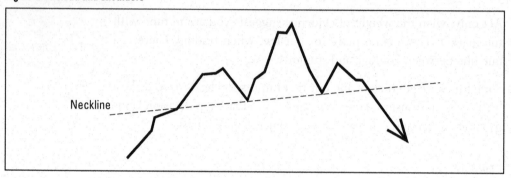

Location

This is a significant top reversal pattern. Support is formed at the neckline where the lows of this pattern align. When the neckline (support) is broken, the reversal pattern is confirmed. Trade in the direction of this break of support.

The break of the neckline usually coincides with the appearance of a bearish candle. As you could probably guess, this pattern often creates a small sucker's rally back to the point of the neckline—a characteristic shared with many top reversals, including the triple top pattern.

The head and shoulders pattern is usually formed over an intermediate period; for example, three to six months. If the neckline is downward sloping, it is said that the ultimate decline will be more significant. I personally have not found this to be accurate in the majority of cases, so I would suggest that you question this piece of technical analysis dogma.

This pattern is considered to be one of the most reliable macro top reversals. Thomas N. Bulkowski's *Encyclopaedia of Chart Patterns* suggests that they are up to 93 per cent reliable. They are also fairly easy to recognise.

If the shoulders of this formation are roughly symmetrical, this suggests the confirmation move will be voracious. Be prepared for a dramatic downslide.

Generally the volume is highest on the first shoulder with the next highest volume coinciding with the peak. The right shoulder shows the lowest relative volume. Trading above the central peak suggests signal failure and will trigger entry into a bullish trade.

Psychology

The market has tried to rally three significant times but failed. Price action above the highest peak means that the pattern is not confirmed and market sentiment has shifted to bullish.

It is actually possible for a formation which has multiple heads or shoulders to still qualify as a head and shoulders pattern (sounds like something out of a horror movie, doesn't it?). Most of the theories that we have covered in relation to the usual three-peaked head and shoulders pattern apply to these more complex versions.

Strategy

Because this pattern is usually so reliable, you do not have to wait for such stringent confirmation. When you notice that a share is in the process of forming a head and shoulders, this can act as an ideal set-up for a short sold position. An appropriate pattern-based stop loss for a short position could be located above the neckline.

Advanced strategies

Alternative choices would be to enter a written call option position, or a bought put option or warrant position. These trading strategies will capitalise on the existing downtrend. Waiting for the neckline to break and for share price activity to appear below the support of the neckline could act as a trigger.

If you find that you are capable of recognising the trigger, but you have difficulty acting, this is a psychological issue that will hold back your trading results. Recognise it and find ways to cope with it. Nathan Mayer Rothschild stated: 'It requires a great deal of boldness and a great deal of caution to make a great fortune'. Trading is not for those poor timid souls who are afraid of their own shadows. It takes courage to dive in, especially if you have faced a few losses and your ego has been cut down to size. Every trader in the world will face a moment of truth where he has the choice to quit, but only some will choose to continue.

Trading excellence involves making tough decisions. People who struggle with decisions tend to struggle in the trading arena. The key is to continually practise so that your skills become second nature and evolve into automatic reactions rather than requiring painful conscious effort.

(continued)

Advanced strategies (cont'd)

Paul Counsel from www.turtletrader.com states:

> Trading has everything to do with personal psychology, rules, systems, discipline, focus and skill. Like anything else that's skill based, once you start it takes time and practice to become skilful. *Ultimately trading is about making decisions between two choices, to buy or sell.* As simple as these two choices are, the variables that effect the decisions surrounding them can be as complex as the human mind can make them.

Example

Figure 6.25 is an example of a potential head and shoulders pattern in the process of forming. However, until it is confirmed by a break through the neckline, it cannot be fully defined as a head and shoulders.

Figure 6.25: WOW weekly

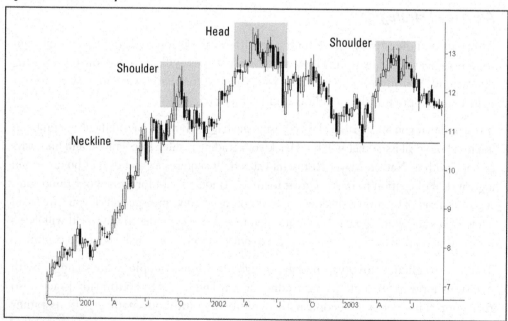

Source: SuperCharts version 4 by Omega Research © 1997.

Inverse head and shoulders

During a downtrend, inverse head and shoulder patterns are characterised by a central trough that is at a lower price than the first and last troughs. It looks like a head and shoulders pattern that has been flipped upside down (figure 6.26).

Location

This is a significant bottom reversal pattern. Resistance is formed at the neckline where the highs of this pattern align. When the share price closes above this level of resistance, particularly on heavy relative volume, the reversal pattern is confirmed. Trade in the direction of this break of resistance.

During a downtrend, inverse head and shoulder patterns are characterised by a central trough that is at a lower price than the first and last troughs.

This is a highly reliable pattern once the breakout has occurred. It is also quite probable that there will be a pullback to the level of the neckline after the breakout. Because the share price reaction to this pattern is so predictable, a breakout on low relative volume is not usually a sign of impending signal failure.

Figure 6.26: inverse head and shoulder

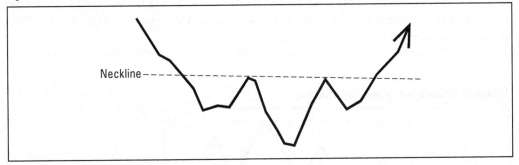

Psychology

The market has tried to continue the existing downtrend on three significant occasions but failed. The stale bears are washed out, and the bulls are free to fill the online screen with their 'buy' orders.

One way to think about macro patterns is to consider the principles behind the formation. The two central peaks of the inverse head and shoulders have a similar implication to a double top pattern. Once trading exceeds this double top, then it can be said that the top reversal pattern has failed. This is also at the point of confirmation for the inverse head and shoulders bottom reversal pattern. Quite nifty, don't you think?

Strategy

Trade these patterns in the same manner that you would trade a triple bottom pattern.

> ### *Advanced strategies*
>
> Waiting for the neckline to break on a white, bullish candle could trigger you to initiate a bought call option or warrant position, a written put option position, or you may choose to buy the share. If you do observe heavy volume, this will add confirmation to your signal. Some traders like to enter a partial position if there is low relative volume at the breakout and then add to their position at the pullback change of polarity. Set a stop for your long position below the neckline.

The measure rule

The measure rule can be used with both the head and shoulders and inverse head and shoulders patterns to provide you with a potential price target. This is of use to short-term traders especially. Take the tallest peak of the head and shoulders and calculate the height of this in relation to the neckline. When the neckline breaks, you can expect a fall of this amount or more. Use the same method to project a target for an inverse head and shoulders pattern (figures 6.27 and 6.28).

Figure 6.27: measure rule for head and shoulders

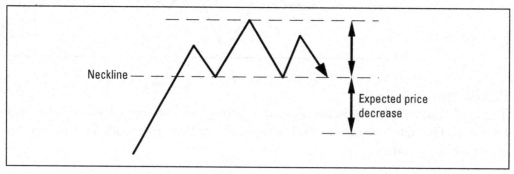

Figure 6.28: measure rule for inverse head and shoulders

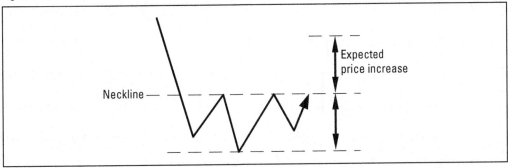

If these patterns experience signal failure, you could use the measure rule to project a likely trend continuation extension. This is true for all of the patterns that are subject to the measure rule. Just use the same method that you have used to calculate the expected price increase, for example, and this amount will translate to the expected price decrease if the signal fails.

The key to all pattern detection is to keep your approach simple. Over-complicating your approach will do nothing to enhance your bank balance. Kel Butcher, a disciplined trader whom I had the pleasure of personally training, once told me, 'Trading is like life — you can make it as complicated or as simple as you choose. In the end it all comes down to choices'.

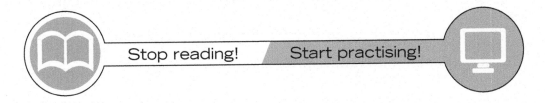

Here are three exercises that you can complete to test your skills.

Exercise 1

You should have enough information to identify the inverse head and shoulders in figure 6.29 (overleaf). Have a close look at the chart and pinpoint where you believe this macro pattern occurs. Record your thoughts in the space provided.

Figure 6.29: HDR weekly

Source: SuperCharts version 4 by Omega Research © 1997.

....

....

....

....

....

....

....

Have a look at figure 6.32—HDR weekly—on page 131 to see if you have correctly identified an inverse head and shoulders pattern from figure 6.29. Let's run through a couple more exercises before we move on to exploring macro continuation patterns.

Exercise 2

Have a look at the chart shown in figure 6.30. Circle any significant patterns you can identify. Jot down how you would trade this opportunity and the instruments that you would use to profit from your analysis. You could use the measure rule to assist with your profit projections. Wait until you have completed exercise 3 before checking your answers (see figure 6.33 on page 132).

Figure 6.30: WBC weekly

Source: SuperCharts version 4 by Omega Research © 1997.

....

....

....

....

....

....

Exercise 3

Circle any significant patterns you can see on the chart in figure 6.31 and discuss how you would trade this chart in order to profit from your analysis. Try combining your knowledge of pattern detection with some basic trendlines and support and resistance lines. If you notice any significant micro patterns, such as candlestick patterns, identify these on the chart also. This will help you gain an overall picture regarding the share price behaviour. Once you've completed exercises 2 and 3, turn to pages 132 and 133 to check your answers.

Figure 6.31: ALL weekly

Source: SuperCharts version 4 by Omega Research © 1997.

....

....

....

....

....

....

Answers

Exercise 1

Figure 6.32: HDR weekly

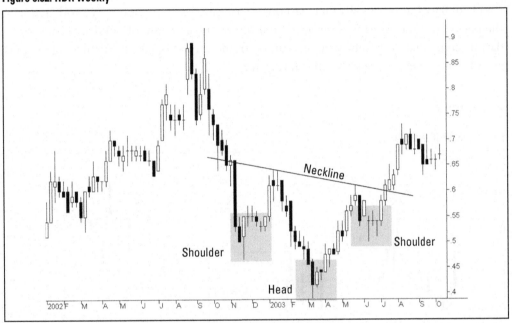

Source: SuperCharts version 4 by Omega Research © 1997.

Trader Tom Baldwin states, 'What separates the 1 per cent from the other 99 per cent is a lot of hard work. It's perseverance. You have to love to do it'. It may take you a while to conceptualise these macro patterns, but the effort will be worthwhile.

... I begin with an examination of a weekly chart, before progressing onto charts of shorter time increments ...

When looking at macro patterns, I first define whether the share is in a medium-term uptrend or downtrend. For this reason, I begin with an examination of a weekly chart, before progressing onto charts of shorter time increments such as daily and intra-day charts. The longer the time period of the chart, the more enduring the effect of the formation. For example, head and shoulder patterns on a weekly chart will have a more significant impact than if the same pattern is displayed on an intra-day chart. Now turn back to pages 129 and 130 and complete exercises 2 and 3.

It's important to actually use your skills to review charts, rather than just reading about the patterns. This practical experience will help you to improve your level of understanding.

I'm absolutely sure the majority of my pattern detection skills were honed while I watched shares automatically flick past on my computer screen, one after another, during the period of time that I was incapacitated. By seeing a couple of hundred charts every day, it seems that your subconscious can be trained to recognise particular formations, even before your conscious mind can register.

Exercise 2

Figure 6.33: WBC weekly

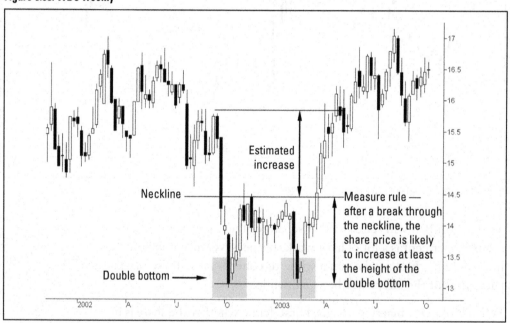

Source: SuperCharts version 4 by Omega Research © 1997.

If your chart doesn't look anything like mine, please do not be too concerned. It can take quite a lot of practise to develop confidence in this area. Remember to watch for signal failures as well as confirmations. This will provide you with two distinct opportunities for effective trading.

In exercise 2, the closing price above the neckline of the double bottom would encourage you to either buy the share, buy a call option or warrant, or write a put option.

Exercise 3

Figure 6.34 shows the power of a move when a signal fails. The double bottom failed with a spectacular bearish rush. Currently the share seems to be range trading. It probably wouldn't be wise to trade in a bullish direction until there was a heightened level of confirmation.

Figure 6.34: ALL weekly

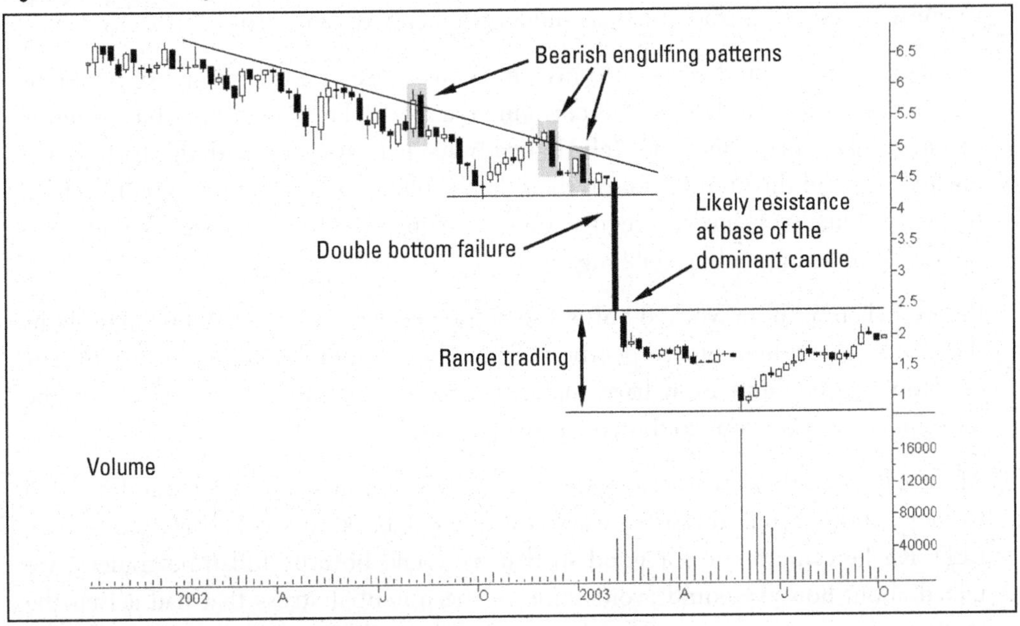

Source: SuperCharts version 4 by Omega Research © 1997.

Psychology secrets

Take pity on your spouse

Not long after I had my first baby, my husband (Chris Bedford) quit his job. This was awesome, except for the fact that now both of us were working from home and we constantly wanted to murder each other. I was trading, writing a book, and learning how to be a mum. Chris was still doing a bit of work as an industrial engineer, trading, and learning how to be a dad.

(continued)

Psychology secrets (cont'd)

He would stomp around the house yelling: 'BUY! SELL! WE NEED TO MAKE MORE PEAKS IN THE DAIRY WHIP!' — or something like that. Honestly, I don't really know because I just wasn't listening to the content. All I could hear was the volume. However, I can tell you that there's nothing more distracting than a man yelling to himself or nameless others on the end of a phone line while you're trying to unravel an options trade that has suddenly taken a wrong turn.

Inevitably, Chris would come into my office, just in the middle of one of my brain waves where I was on the brink of changing the world. I'd glare at him, but he never would get the hint to 'Shut the Hell Up or I'm likely to stab you with this fork!' Then one of us would threaten to poison the other's coffee, or storm off in a huff. In fact, it was a lot like working in a regular office, except that there was a baby there and the threat of an impending stabbing.

Before, when we both worked out of the house, we'd come home and whinge about the moronic people in our respective offices who were undoubtedly out to destroy us. Now, we couldn't even have that conversation because it was clear that the moronic co-workers out to destroy us were . . . us.

After many months of near-stabbings, we finally set some ground rules and decided to work through our territory wars. Chris went back to work part-time. Then, BEFORE he came home for good so that we could both be full-time traders, we talked about how we could avoid some of the potential stress that had arisen the first time.

Chris even told me once, 'You reckon it's tough being a trader — try being your husband!' Yikes. Something had to change — and I knew that something was me.

Whenever you're trying to learn a new skill, you're bound to be a bit on edge. Whether that skill is being a mother or becoming a trader. As you conquer the trading skills you need to make your dreams come true, make sure you remember the toll this can take on your spouse. Build in some time just for them. Tear yourself away from your computer screen. Try not to talk about trading every moment of every day. Go to the gym, or for a run and release your tension. Find other support mechanisms to help you blow off some steam.

I like to give my new traders an experienced 'Trading Buddy', to help them in those first few tender months of trading. Some of the members of my Mentor Program have told me that this is one of the best by-products of the course. If you haven't done my Mentor Program, I still suggest you find a friend who shares your obsession with the markets. It will be a great relief to your spouse, and it might even save your marriage.

Or...at least make sure you remove all sharp objects from the house, lest your spouse decide to take their revenge.

Summary

- Reversal patterns display reinforcement of either a support or resistance line.

- If support proves to be very strong, the future share price direction will be upwards.

- If resistance is continually reinforced, the breakout will be downwards.

- Volume expanding in line with the breakout increases the efficacy of the pattern.

By now, your confidence should be building as your brain sparks with technical analysis brilliance. We are nearly at the stage where, if we attached a bunch of electric cables to your head, we could light a small town at Christmas. Keep reading to develop your knowledge about macro continuation patterns.

7

Magic macro continuation patterns

Want to know if the pretty little trade you're profiting from is likely to continue bringing in money? Then, these little macro continuation patterns will give you your answer. You can't afford to miss out on reading about them ...

SO FAR WE HAVE COVERED some of the major macro patterns that suggest a trend reversal. You may find that you detect some patterns more easily than others, which is okay. Just aim to understand the principles behind each formation and you'll be well on your way to trading them successfully.

Why are continuations important?

This chapter is focused on revealing some macro patterns that imply trend *continuation*. This is equally as important as establishing when a trend is likely to reverse. Continuation patterns may give you another chance to enter a position. Alternatively, if you are already trading an instrument that presents a continuation pattern, it can bring you peace of mind.

Let's start out with one of the more colourfully named examples of a continuation pattern — the dead cat bounce.

Dead cat bounce

At the risk of offending feline fanatics everywhere, please understand that this definition merely clarifies a price action phenomenon.

So that cat lovers don't hold this against me personally, I will quote Chris Tate:

> **How would I define a dead cat bounce? Well, you take a dead cat and throw it at the ground … it will bounce … but the cat is still dead despite bouncing once.**

Crass, but descriptive …

The dead cat bounce looks like a bullish V-reversal pattern, but the subsequent share price action continues the existing downtrend. It is a bearish downtrend continuation pattern. Typically, the lack of heavy relative volume on the upswing will signal that the rally will be short-lived (see figure 7.1).

Figure 7.1: dead cat bounce

Location

This pattern looks as if the share decided to jump down an elevator shaft on a pogo stick. The first bounce is lots of fun, but the trip down the shaft is terrifying!

The first decline is often combined with a gap, or a solitary black bearish candle that scares the living daylights out of any remaining bulls. The subsequent incline is often on low volume, and lacklustre. The final decline is not usually as steep as the initial drop, but is still a nasty surprise for those deceived into believing that an uptrend was likely.

This pattern is a failed bottom V-reversal pattern. The dead cat bounce is sometimes known as a *sucker's rally*, particularly if it is not accompanied by heavy relative volume. Wait for an increased weight of evidence to suggest that the trend has altered before trading a V-reversal on low relative volume, as it may just be a dead cat bounce in disguise.

In general terms, the more dramatic the drop in the share price, the larger the bounce, and the more hideous the eventual decline. This is a nasty, openly vengeful pattern that you wouldn't want to meet in a dark alley.

There is no top reversal pattern equivalent to the dead cat bounce.

Psychology

Despite the view of some fundamental analysts, the market is not rational and does not act purely on economic information. After the significant market crash in 1987, US economist Robert Shiller sent out a questionnaire to a large number of institutional investors and private traders. His goal was to discover the emotions that fuelled the crash. He asked them, 'What reasons to buy or sell did you have during this period?' Almost every interviewee stated that he or she was selling because the market was beginning to drop. Economists would have expected that the rising inflation, financial news or political situation would have been the reason for the decline. In effect, the market crashed because a feedback loop that fed on itself was initiated.

Despite the view of some fundamental analysts, the market is not rational and does not act purely on economic information.

Sometimes the market can become temporarily excited because of a bullish news report. However, if the ripples of excitement do not spread with sufficient speed or conviction, the result is a continuation of the existing downtrend. A dead cat bounce shows the stale and exhausted bulls selling at the first sign of higher prices. Just as houses need a solid foundation to be a stable construction, shares need to have volume coinciding with a bullish movement in order to continue rising. Volume forms a solid foundation for future bullish price action.

Humans desperately need to think that they are 'right', and don't like to admit when they're wrong. They can only stand so much pain. If you've ever said to yourself, 'The next time that share price goes up, I'm going to sell', then you will understand exactly why a dead cat bounce forms in a share chart.

Some traders even use this type of pattern as a trigger to *average down* (buying more of a security that is not co-operating with the trader's initial view) by purchasing more stock on the bounce. These types of traders will soon become extinct, however, through their own exorbitant levels of ineptitude. By trading against the trend, you may lower the average price of your overall purchase, but you are then holding even more shares of a downtrending stock. Averaging down doesn't work.

If you are going to consistently trade bottom reversal patterns to trigger your entry, make sure that you have several pieces of evidence to suggest that a trend reversal is likely. In general terms, top reversal patterns require less confirmation than bottom reversals.

Prospect theory also helps to explain why a pattern like this can occur. This theory suggests that people have an irrational tendency to be more willing to gamble with profits than with losses. Driven by their own innate programming, ineffective traders tend to sell quickly when in profit but nurse their losses into the twilight years. Often, the traders who already own the share throughout the formation of the dead cat bounce will feel momentarily elated by the upswing. They may even tell people, 'See, I told you so... I knew that Dotgone.com would come good'. Yet they continue to hold on when the share drops back into the chasm.

There is one question that seems to plague newcomers to the market. If they commit their time to learning about these patterns, who is to say that the market won't suddenly display a completely new set of signals? Ed Seykota is one of the most profitable traders that the world has ever seen. He states: 'The markets are the same now as they were five or ten years ago because they keep changing—just like they did then'. Good traders maintain flexibility and adapt their techniques over time. Pattern recognition, exit methods and money management have always been the skills that distinguish brilliance from mediocrity in the markets.

Strategy

Setting a stop loss is an essential skill. The main premise behind this skill is to preserve your trading capital. Without adequate risk management a string of losses could prevent your ability to trade due to a lack of equity. Refer to chapter 10 for further information on stop losses.

> *Setting a stop loss is an essential skill. The main premise behind this skill is to preserve your trading capital.*

A dead cat bounce is hard to predict. For this reason, there are no effective methods for trading this pattern, other than preserving your trading equity so that you can trade another opportunity. Rather than seeking to trade a dead cat bounce, you should be aiming to avoid it entirely. Recognise the warning signs and then walk away in search of a more lucrative trade.

Warning for advanced traders

This pattern really drives the volatility of the instrument through the roof. There is actually an opportunity to get burned twice if you short sell at the base of this pattern (expecting lower prices), close out your short sale, and then go long after the initial reversal has become apparent. The first short sell will lose money because the share reversed its downtrend, and the long position will also be a net loser because the dead cat decided to stay dead and drop through the floor. It has happened to me in the past, so heed my warning—don't even try to trade these mongrels (not that I'm bitter and twisted about it).

Example

The daily chart of Southcorp in figure 7.2 gives an example of a dead cat bounce.

Figure 7.2: SRP daily

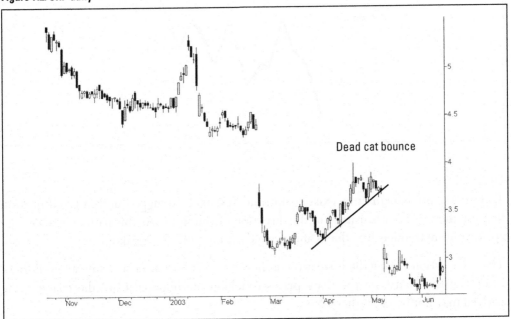

Source: SuperCharts version 4 by Omega Research © 1997.

Triangles

Triangles come in all shapes and sizes. These terrific tools can pre-empt a breakout. Once you start to recognise how they look, they are very easy to identify as they are forming.

Ascending triangles

The ascending triangle pattern shows a series of higher lows that creates a baseline which slopes upwards. A level of horizontal resistance forms the flat top of the triangle. This top is most often completely level but, if not, it can still be defined as an ascending triangle. The ascending trendline must display at least two higher low prices to be valid. The ultimate breakout may happen before the upward-sloping trendline and the horizontal line intersect at the triangle's apex (see figure 7.3, overleaf).

Figure 7.3: ascending triangle

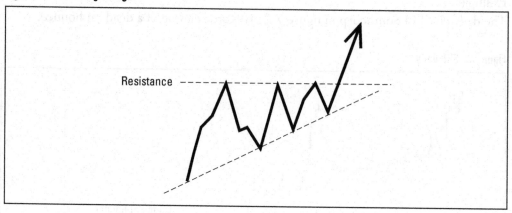

Location

This pattern often forms in an existing uptrend. It is likely to suggest uptrend continuation because the breakout is usually in the direction of the slope. As this pattern reaches the apex, volume frequently reduces and expands at the point of breakout.

The price action during the formation of the pattern is usually fairly compacted. If there is a lot of time between the share prices touching the boundaries of the triangle, the pattern may not be as predictable.

Signal failure is important to watch for. Trading below the level of the upward-sloping trendline is a bearish indication.

Psychology

A strong level of resistance is often formed by pockets of traders waiting for the share price to hit a certain value before selling. The horizontal line can coincide with a round dollar value for this reason. The uptrend line that forms the bottom boundary of the triangle shows that traders are interested in paying more and more for this share. Once the lid blows off, all hell breaks loose and the bulls charge.

Traders often cultivate *ego-defensive attitudes*. They look for evidence to confirm a decision that has already been made. The upward slope of the triangle suggests the decision to drive the share price upwards has already been made by the market participants. The breakout merely confirms this decision.

Strategies

The breakout doesn't often show signs of pullback so it's good to get involved as soon as you can. Because the medium-term trend is already upwards, you can act before the breakout has actually occurred with a fair degree of certainty. Towards the apex you'll actually notice quite a few small-bodied candlesticks that suggest indecision. Aggressive traders often enter on one of these small-bodied days, rather than waiting for the breakout. Often a very pointy apex does not form with a strongly uptrending share displaying an ascending triangle. The breakout is likely to occur in the final third of the triangle, so be prepared for a breakout that jumps before you are ready to catch it. Tricky little devils, aren't they?

The breakout is likely to occur in the final third of the triangle, so be prepared for a breakout that jumps before you are ready to catch it.

The measure rule

You can estimate the size of the expected price move using an ascending triangle pattern. The way to do this is to measure the height of the triangle at the start of the formation and then add this result to the horizontal line. This also provides you with a rationale for why tall triangles tend to produce fairly big kicks in price action. Short-term traders could sell their long positions when the share approaches this price target. Medium-term traders are more likely to endure the expected consolidation rather than close their positions at this price target level.

Advanced strategies

Call option and warrant buyers love this pattern, as do put option writers. Make sure you place your pattern-based stop just below the horizontal resistance line.

Descending triangles

This pattern shows a downward-sloping trendline that creates the upper boundary of the triangle. A level of support that is approximately horizontal forms the lower boundary of the triangle. A breakout will often occur prior to these two lines intersecting. It is especially common for the share to break out during the final third of the triangle formation. Breakouts are usually downward, in the same direction as the slope of the trendline. For this pattern to be valid, the trendline must be touched at least twice by the share price action (see figure 7.4).

Figure 7.4: descending triangle

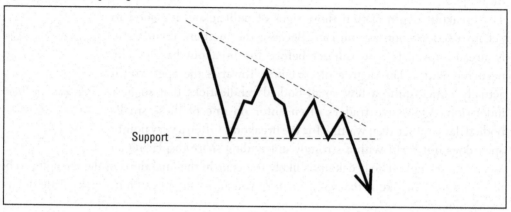

Location

These patterns are usually formed during an existing downtrend and act as downtrend continuation patterns. If a breakout occurs in an upward direction, it means that the signal has failed and is a bullish sign. For an example of a descending triangle, have a look at figure 2.18 on page 27.

Psychology

Every time the share price drops to a certain level, people start to buy shares because they are perceived as being 'cheap'. This is the equivalent of the doors opening at the Myer/Grace Bros stocktake sale as buyers scramble over each other to pick up a bargain. Once the price drops through this psychological level, the buyers realise their error and then push each other out of the way to sell. Fickle creatures! (Never underestimate the power of stupid people in large groups.)

Strategies

This is one of my favourite patterns to trigger a short sale, or a bought put. You can write calls with this as well, but often the move is quite significant, so you may as well use an approach which capitalises on this.

The measure rule

To estimate the expected fall in price action, measure the height of the pattern at the beginning of its formation. Take this result and subtract it from the horizontal line to give you a potential short-term price target. Of course, if the item is in downtrend already, this point will just provide you with a likely consolidation point before further falls are expected in the instrument. Short sellers could close their positions once the share approaches this price target, and await a re-entry signal to attack again if the trend continues.

Symmetrical triangles

The symmetrical triangle pattern is formed when the price action is enveloped by converging upward-sloping and downward-sloping trendlines. The breakout can be either upwards or downwards (see figure 7.5).

Figure 7.5: symmetrical triangles

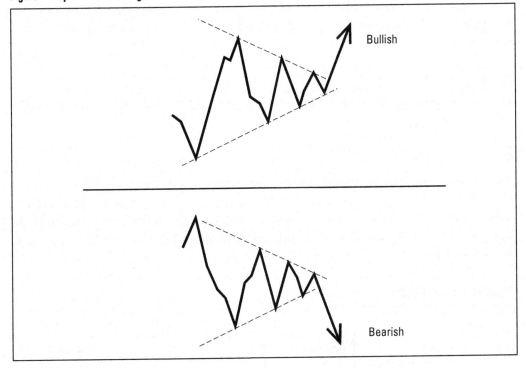

Location

If a symmetrical triangle has formed during a medium-term uptrend, it is likely that the breakout will be upwards. If this pattern is apparent in a medium-term downtrend, the breakout is likely to trigger your entry into a short sale. Unfortunately, there are no guarantees and the direction of the breakout cannot be known in advance. Confirmation is usually required before any action is taken.

The trendlines do not need to be the same length to qualify as a symmetrical triangle. Neither trendline is horizontal (otherwise you would most likely have identified an ascending or descending triangle). There should be at least two touches along the upper trendline and two along the lower trendline to establish a viable example of this pattern. Triangular patterns usually form over a period of more than three weeks. However, it is not unknown for a short, spunky little pattern to produce a tradeable breakout within just a few days.

Triangular patterns usually form over a period of more than three weeks.

Psychology

This pattern tips you off that something big is going to happen; however, you can't tell in which direction it is going to take the price action. Take your cue from the medium-term trend.

Strategies

Due to the nature of this pattern, I tend not to act until I actually receive confirmation of a breakout.

The measure rule

The measure rule can be applied to this type of pattern to assist you in determining the price target in either direction. Just have a look at the height of the formation by subtracting the lowest low from the highest high. For downside breaks, subtract the difference from the lowest low. For upside breaks, add the difference to the highest high. See figure 7.6.

Figure 7.6: the measure rule

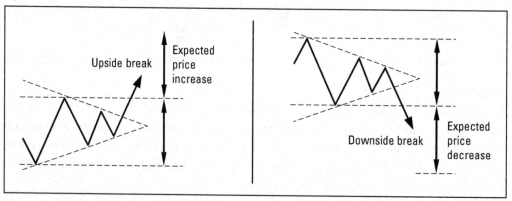

The use of triangles in your trading will often allow you to make an earlier entry than if you just waited for a break of a horizontal support or resistance line. The angle of the slope of the triangle and the clarity of a breakout can give you an edge with your entry technique.

Advanced strategies

If you are an astute option trader there is an absolute ripper of a strategy available. You could buy an *at-the-money straddle*. This involves buying put options and call options where you estimate the apex will eventuate. Once the breakout direction is established, the winning leg will be in profit and you can close out the losing leg. This clever little strategy lets you take advantage of the market's indecisiveness.

Example

Figure 7.7 gives you an example of a failed descending triangle and a symmetrical triangle. Both triangles represent valid trading opportunities. Because the uptrend is so strong, it is unlikely that the descending triangle would have produced anything other than a temporary pause.

Figure 7.7: MCP daily

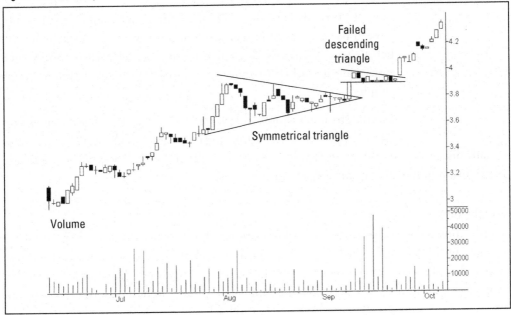

Source: SuperCharts version 4 by Omega Research © 1997.

147

Bullish channels

Channels fall into a few different categories. They all show the share price bouncing between parallel horizontal support and resistance lines, or between diagonal trendlines. A bullish channel is characterised by higher lows and higher highs. Often, top reversal candlestick patterns will be apparent along the upper line, and bottom candlestick reversal patterns occur along the lower line. (Candlestick patterns are discussed in appendix A.) The medium-term trend is upwards, so there is usually an increased weight of evidence to support that this trend will continue (see figure 7.8).

Figure 7.8: bullish channel

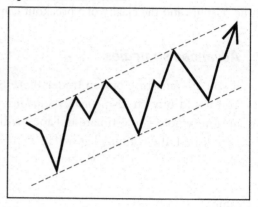

Location

Bullish channels represent an idealised uptrend. Low relative volume is often apparent on pullbacks. High relative volume on rallies inspires the bulls to greater heights.

Bullish channels almost always show share prices above a medium-term (approximately 30-period) moving average.

Not all uptrends have this type of channel appearance. Just because a trend has a series of higher lows does not mean that the highs will behave so consistently. So, when these types of patterns show such a great amount of consistency, it can make our lives as traders much simpler.

Bullish channels almost always show share prices above a medium-term (approximately 30-period) moving average. They will also usually display higher volume for white candles in comparison to black candles and have momentum indicators pointing skyward.

Psychology

To my knowledge there has been no adequate psychological explanation regarding the appearance of diagonal trendlines or trend channels. However, just because we can't find a logical explanation for our observations doesn't mean that these patterns are not valid. Any observation that you can make and duplicate has the potential to make you money.

During a trend, the market's perceptions about whether a share is 'cheap' or 'expensive' come into play. When the share price is trading at an all-time high, the share is perceived to be expensive. This often inspires selling pressure.

Any observation that you can make and duplicate has the potential to make you money.

When the stock drops in price, it is then considered cheap, and new buyers enter the market. Existing shareholders add to their portfolios. This buying pressure drives the price upwards and an entry into a share at this time will allow you to harness the power of this bullish wave.

The market players are comfortable paying higher and higher prices and the attitude is buoyant. They are convinced that the share price will continue its ascent and the red rag for the bulls is unfurled with a flourish.

Many traders suffer from overconfidence and a misunderstanding about *locus of control*. An *internal locus of control* is the tendency to take responsibility for all situations. An *external locus of control* is the tendency to believe that outside forces control everything. When markets go up and we are involved in a long position, we often think it's because we are smart. When markets drop, we tend to blame outside factors.

Because of the *certainty effect* traders prefer a small, but sure, gain now rather than a likely, larger gain in the future. This effect tends to encourage shareholders to sell when the market surges, producing a pullback to a support level. These shareholders think that they are incredibly clever and run around with a massively inflated ego. They practically dislocate their shoulders by patting themselves on the back so hard. They would prefer to 'feel good' rather than hold onto an uptrending share which has the ability to produce far greater profits in the future. Remember, keep your losses small and let your profits run.

Bearish channels

A bearish channel is characterised by lower highs and lower lows. The share price bounces between two downward-sloping trendlines that form the boundary of the share price action. Top reversal candlesticks along the upper line are confirmed vigorously. Bottom reversal candlestick patterns just don't seem to muster enough energy to really get the bulls charging with enthusiasm. The strength of the upward move is quickly eradicated by share price mini-avalanches (see figure 7.9, overleaf).

Location

Bearish channels epitomise the definition of a downtrend as they display a progression of lower highs and lower lows. Most indicators will be providing consistently bearish signals. This adds to the weight of evidence that the share is downtrending.

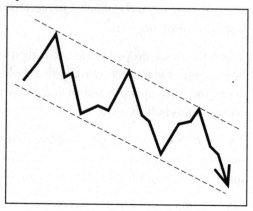

Figure 7.9: bearish channel

Psychology

Most market participants have been selling their holdings at the sign of any small rally. This suggests they are not optimistic about the prospects for this share. They do not expect higher prices in the near future and are keen to dump their shares on any passer-by who shows even a small amount of interest.

Why do some people, though, hold onto a share that looks like it's got Titanic delusions and is heading down at a rapid rate? One of the concepts behind people hanging onto a downtrending share is *endowment theory*, which suggests that people place an inordinate amount of value on items that they own. They also tend to focus on these items far more than logic would suggest is warranted. Traders convince themselves their holdings are of a higher value than the market would suggest, it's just that the market hasn't realised this yet. Self-delusion is a wonderful thing. It can make the trauma of being an adult so much more bearable, can't it?

Another reason people hang on, even when the evidence to exit is overwhelming, can be related to the theory of *cognitive dissonance*. Cognitive dissonance is the tendency to reject information that is contrary to the trading decision which has just been made, and to look for information to confirm that the decision was correct. Rather than facing the evidence that we have made a bad trading decision head on, we distort it, reject it, or turn on the football and reach for another beer. This is much more comfortable than confronting our inadequacies.

Regret theory is another psychological reason we still keep those dogs in our portfolios, even though we know we shouldn't. Humans try to avoid actions that confirm that we have made an error. Selling to crystallise a loss would mean that you would have to admit you were wrong. Have you ever heard someone try to justify holding a losing position by saying, 'You don't make a loss until you sell'? This is a prime example of regret theory.

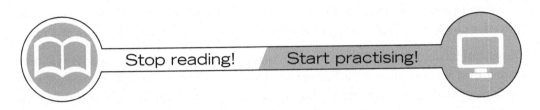

I want you to take some time to think about the courses of action you could follow to profit from these macro patterns. This will benefit you to a greater degree than if I just hand you the answer on a platter. While you're at it, open up your charting package. Slowly scroll through the top 200, one by one. Have a look at all of the charts and try to identify some patterns you're now familiar with. Especially aim to find an example of either a bullish or a bearish channel. Mark the chart with the appropriate lines to show support and resistance. The more you can practise and detect these patterns on your own charts, the more your skills will grow. Take some time to write down how you would trade these patterns:

....

....

....

....

....

....

....

Strategy

Many traders try in vain to enter a series of short-term trades using the turning points of the channel to signify their entry and exit. Known as *range trading,* this strategy may initially seem like a good idea. However, it is almost impossible to nail the exact turning point consistently, making this technique ineffective. The amount of brokerage that you will churn through will also tend to build up. A far better idea would be to trade these patterns by buying the share when you have identified a bullish channel, or short selling when you recognise a bearish channel. This lets you hook into the power part of the trend and profit from this sustained move over the medium term. This is a far more effective channel-trading strategy than seeking to range trade using options or warrants.

In general terms, share traders are best advised to trade when a definite trend is in action, rather than aiming to buy at the bottom of a channel and sell at the top. You may get away with range trading for a few trades, but sooner or later, the share is going to make a rude gesture in your direction and bound away, dragging your capital down the drain.

Share stages

My discussion of macro trend pattern analysis would not be complete unless I mentioned the concept of share stages. This is a terrific way to keep in mind the bigger picture of the trend, while using all of your accumulated knowledge of macro patterns and candlesticks.

The concept is that most shares go through several life stages, each of which is described in turn below. Although you cannot tell how long each stage will last, this overall concept will give you an idea of whether you should be long or short in any particular instrument. As an example of how these stages are likely to appear on a chart, have a look at figure 7.10.

Figure 7.10: SKE weekly

Source: SuperCharts version 4 by Omega Research © 1997.

Stage 1 — the base

After a period of downtrending, a share will often form a base. This range trading activity occurs predominantly between horizontal support and resistance lines. The share price is often located below the 30-week exponential moving average, and candlestick reversals can be noticed occurring along the support and resistance lines of a sideways channel. (Note that I use the 30-week exponential moving average as my standard indicator for this type of stage analysis.)

The longer the period of sideways consolidation, the more enduring and dramatic the breakout. You may notice a variety of macro bottom reversal patterns form in this stage. Typical patterns include the inverse head and shoulders pattern, double bottoms and triple bottoms. This phase is of most interest to call and put option writers. Some poor, deluded novices may try to trade share price ranges using bought options, warrants, short selling or equities. Trend trading is where the big bucks are.

Stage 2 — the uptrend

In stage 2 the share breaks above the resistance line established in stage 1, and usually displays a decisive gap, or a dominant white candle on higher relative volume levels. If volume does not accompany the breakout, this indicates that the move is unlikely to be maintained. Shares that break above the 30-week moving average also suggest that the rally is likely to continue. You may also notice a momentum indicator crossing up through an oversold line.

After an initial rally, shares will often pullback to the point of breakout on low relative volume levels. The line that acted as resistance in stage 1 may have undergone a change of polarity, and can now become a support level. If this level of support/resistance is penetrated from above, the rally may not be sustainable. True breakouts rarely collapse back into the share price range established within stage 1. If the prices bearishly penetrate the previous level of breakout, this will generally trigger my pattern-based stop loss, and I will exit the trade immediately.

In many cases, a candle reversal will be apparent at the base of this pullback (at the same level as the support/resistance level). Common candles at this point include piercing patterns and bullish engulfing patterns. This is a sign that the pullback is temporary, and these formations provide a second chance to enter a long trading position. The less a share pulls back, the stronger the bullish impulse. Unfortunately, if you wait for the pullback, you may miss an opportunity to enter a position.

The less a share pulls back, the stronger the bullish impulse ... if you wait for the pullback, you may miss an opportunity to enter a position.

Often, once the share has established an uptrend, several periods of consolidation will be evident. New breakout opportunities can be identified during these periods. White candles outnumber the black candles during this stage. The range of these bullish candles is often quite large in comparison to any black candles present.

Entry into the majority of my trades and *pyramiding* of existing trades generally occurs after the initial horse has bolted. (Pyramiding is where the trader adds more capital to an already profitable position.) However, many lucrative trades are conducted at this first point of breakout. By keeping several shares that are in stage 1 on a watch list, and being exceptionally attentive to any changes in share price and volume action, it is possible to enter the share either on the day of, or shortly after, the initial breakout.

The share is in uptrend during this phase and experiences a series of higher lows. Bullish channels are very common. Bottom reversal patterns during pullbacks are responded to with bullish enthusiasm. Top reversal formations have little impact on the bullish share price activity.

Be aware that the duration of this stage is not predictable. In terms of working out how long the bulls will stay in power, take your cues from the share's history. Some shares stay in this stage for several years, others just a few days, especially if the breakout was weak.

This phase is of most interest to share traders and investors, call option or warrant buyers, and put option writers.

Stage 3 — the top

The share forms a top, usually on heavy volume levels, and exceptionally positive media reports. Many traders have made a lot of money during stage 2, so the journalists tend to write glowing articles, extolling the virtues of this instrument. The buyers and sellers exchange many shares. The market is playing musical chairs, trying to establish a clear identity. When the music stops, we'll find out whether the bulls or the bears are the winners.

Top reversal macro patterns during this phase may include double and triple tops, as well as head and shoulders patterns.

Towards the end of this sideways-trending stage, the share price slips below the moving average. You may notice that momentum indicators collapse through their overbought lines. The bullish behaviour holding the price at this level is running out of energy, so watch for a solid break below a significant support line. This support line break is especially dire if it commences with a strong black candle. Increased volume does not always accompany a drop below support. If the relative volume levels do increase, however, this may trigger a dramatic bearish descent into lower prices.

Be vigilant if you observe a top reversal candlestick pattern signal during this time.

Be vigilant if you observe a top reversal candlestick pattern signal during this time. As you will remember, top reversals usually provide some level of resistance for future share price activity, and bottom reversals provide support. In stage 3, top reversals typically prove very difficult for the bulls to penetrate. In contrast, bottom reversals are easily defied by bearish activity, and typically do not result in significant rallies.

The ideal strategy during stage 3 is to write a call option. If you decide to write put options, then take prompt defensive actions to close out these positions if the share shows signs of progressing to stage 4. Also, consider buying a put option or warrant, or short selling towards the end of this phase.

Stage 4—the downtrend
During stage 4, the share trades below the moving average and experiences a series of lower highs and lower lows. Bearish channels and dead cat bounces are not uncommon. Black candles outnumber the white, and any level of support provided by a bottom reversal pattern is easily eradicated by bearish activity. The range of these black candles is often longer in relative terms than the black candles apparent in the previous stage. A share price increase will often rise up to a previous level of

support before continuing its downtrending activity. A top reversal pattern during this phase may provide an ideal opportunity to exit any long positions that you are still holding.

Ideal strategies during this phase include buying put options or warrants, writing call options and short selling shares. You should not be holding any shares in stage 4, unless you have a serious leaning towards self-sabotage.

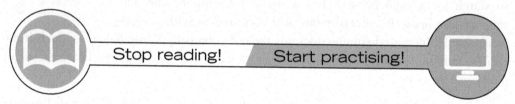

If you would like a simple way to remember all of the macro patterns described in this workbook, you can grab a copy of *The Secret of Pattern Detection Poster*. This is a full-colour, laminated wall chart (A2 size — 594 mm × 420 mm) available from www.tradingsecrets.com.au. You can order this poster, as well as *The Secret of Candlestick Charting Poster*, to help reinforce the principles of pattern detection.

It can take a little while to attune your eye to identifying stages. Have a look at the following examples. Take some time to identify the stage in which these shares are likely to be. Draw in significant support/resistance lines and trendlines to substantiate your arguments. Name any macro patterns that are apparent. Make some notes. You'll need to spend at least three to five minutes per chart, otherwise you're not analysing the charts in enough depth. Resist the urge to flick forward to discover the answers — there is no one correct answer in trading. A lot of it is to do with your own personal perceptions (see figures 7.11 to 7.15).

Figure 7.11: AAC daily

Source: SuperCharts version 4 by Omega Research © 1997.

....

....

....

....

....

....

....

....

....

Figure 7.12: AGL weekly

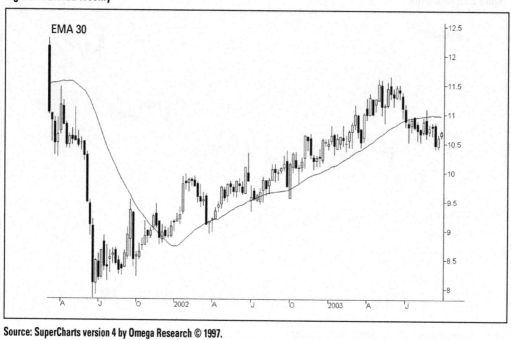

Source: SuperCharts version 4 by Omega Research © 1997.

Figure 7.13: AHD weekly

Source: SuperCharts version 4 by Omega Research © 1997.

....

....

....

....

....

....

....

....

....

Figure 7.14: AIX weekly

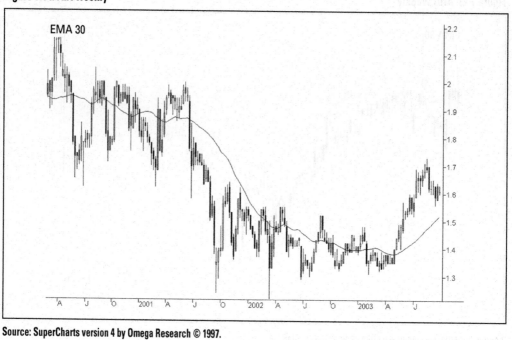

Source: SuperCharts version 4 by Omega Research © 1997.

....

....

....

....

....

....

....

....

....

Figure 7.15: ALS daily

Source: SuperCharts version 4 by Omega Research © 1997.

....

....

....

....

....

....

....

....

....

Answers

Figures 7.16 to 7.20 show some suggested answers:

Figure 7.16: AAC daily

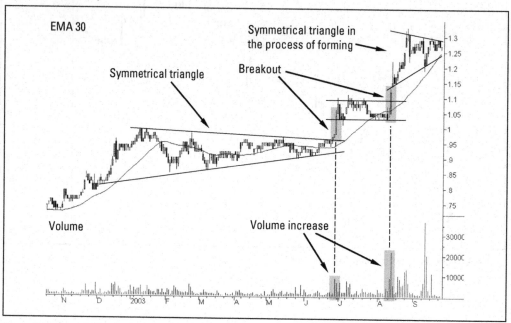

Source: SuperCharts version 4 by Omega Research © 1997.

AAC daily, the share depicted in figure 7.16, is likely to be in stage 2. There are several pieces of evidence that suggest this, such as a series of higher highs, higher lows, share prices above the moving average as well as a series of bullish breakouts. The final pattern in the process of forming is likely to be another symmetrical triangle.

AGL weekly in figure 7.17 may have dropped from stage 2 into stage 3. In stage 2, the predominant pattern was a huge bullish channel, characterised by higher lows and higher highs, above the weekly moving average. Current share price action has dropped below the channel and below the moving average, suggesting that the bulls' days are numbered.

Judging from the lower highs, lower lows, share prices below the EMA 30 and the bearish channel, we can say that AHD weekly, the share shown in figure 7.18, is currently in stage 4.

Figure 7.17: AGL weekly

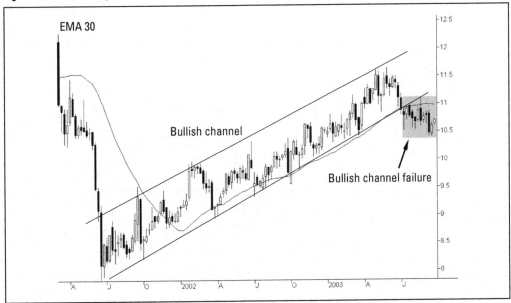

Source: SuperCharts version 4 by Omega Research © 1997.

Figure 7.18: AHD weekly

Source: SuperCharts version 4 by Omega Research © 1997.

Figure 7.19: AIX weekly

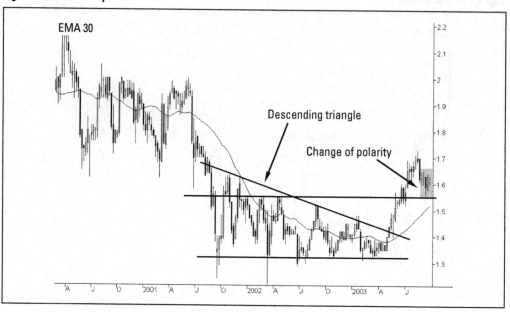

Source: SuperCharts version 4 by Omega Research © 1997.

Figure 7.20: ALS daily

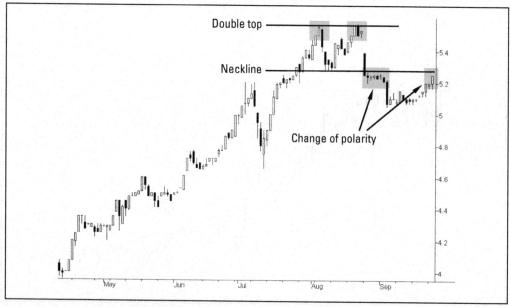

Source: SuperCharts version 4 by Omega Research © 1997.

AIX weekly in figure 7.19 (on page 164) has a basing formation in the shape of a failed descending triangle. There is a breakout upward and a change of polarity that suggests this is an early stage 2 pattern.

ALS daily in figure 7.20 (on page 164) has been in a sustained uptrend, but after the formation of a double top and share prices dropping through the neckline, it is possible that declines are likely in the future. It may be a little soon to tell, but this share could be in an early stage 4 formation.

Psychology secrets

At one stage ...

At one stage, Steve Jobs was working out of his Mum's garage.

At one stage, Martin Luther King was nervous about presenting in public.

At one stage, Benjamin Franklin was being called 'slow' by his third grade teacher.

At one stage, Charles Dickens left school early to work in a factory, after his dad was thrown into prison.

At one stage, Warren Buffett hadn't bought his first share.

Just because you started out in one place, doesn't mean you will end up in the same spot. What will the next chapter in your story hold?

Summary

- By fully understanding the importance of the line and volume families, you can identify a lot of the macro patterns just using these tools.

- After a continuation pattern, the breakout will usually be in line with the medium-term trend of that instrument.

- Remember to use the concept of share stages to help you determine the likely trend. Stage 1 shows consolidation, stage 2 is when the share is uptrending, stage 3 is a top plateau and stage 4 is a downtrend.

The macro patterns we have covered in the last two chapters are signals that I use again and again, and although I don't profit from every trade, they do give me an important edge. They indicate a broad set-up condition that tells me to watch closely for a trigger candle to enter a position. The next chapter will describe the exact triggers I use to enter a trade with confidence.

8

Candlesticks uncut

There's no doubt that candle charts can help you get rich and stay rich. They are single-handedly responsible for turning some sort of key in my brain that helped me to become profitable as a trader. Now it's time for them to work their magic on you too . . .

APPARENTLY, WHEN READING A NON-FICTION BOOK, only one-third of adults make it past the halfway mark. So, if you've made it to this part of the workbook, it is quite possible that you are in that disciplined minority. Congratulations! The remaining chapters will help round out your trading knowledge by giving you an insight into candlesticks, system development and trading psychology.

It is only since the early 1990s that candlestick charts have been discussed in Australian trading circles without the audience expecting a follow-up class on macramé and knitting. Luckily, candlesticks are now included in the majority of charting packages as a standard display of price action, alongside the more traditional bar charts and line charts.

As you've probably guessed, I am hopelessly biased. I adore candlestick charts. As far as I am concerned, candlesticks are as important to charting as oxygen is to breathing. Amusingly, in some trading circles I have become known as 'The Candlestick Queen'. I'm not sure if a tiara would match my usual trading attire — pyjamas are just not that formal.

Keep in mind that some instruments display specific candle-based characteristics — such as the FX market. Candles on FX charts typically have a greater number of long tails. However, the candle patterns still work on these charts. You just need to be a little bit flexible to trade them across every market.

By the end of this chapter, you will be able to detect a trigger that will empower you to engage a trade.

Set-ups

In the majority of cases, the macro patterns we have looked at so far form a *set-up* condition. A set-up is an environment of general conditions that suggest a share is either uptrending or downtrending.

If you have ever noticed a share that is trending but you have not actually been involved in that trade, you will know how incredibly frustrating this is. The ability to detect a trend is not enough—you must identify a clear signal that tells you when to act. If you are continually detecting strong trends, but you still have trouble entering a position, I can diagnose your problem from 100 metres. It will be either:

1   You have difficulty with procrastination.

OR

2   You have not identified a trigger to inspire you to act.

A set-up is an environment of general conditions that suggest a share is either uptrending or downtrending. The inability to recognise a trigger is much more common than you would think. At share trading seminars across the country, I can almost guarantee that more than half of the so-called traders present are actually only paper-trading. These poor, unfortunate souls watch the action from afar, living vicariously through their more aggressive trading brothers and sisters, salivating slightly whenever they tell you about the one that got away. Although I cannot turn a long-term procrastinator into 'Action Jackson', I can help people recognise when a share is giving them an unequivocal entry signal.

Triggers

The annoying thing about trends is that they're easy to recognise in retrospect but very difficult to spot when they begin. All you need to act on a trend that you think you have identified is a set-up (which includes macro patterns) and a *trigger* (a micro pattern). A trigger is the exact pattern, indicator or signal that will tell you when to buy or sell the instrument. For me, candlestick patterns act as the trigger. If I have everything else in place, a candle signals me into a trade as clearly as the guy with the ping-pong paddles waves a jet in to land safely.

If candlesticks do not initially strike a chord with you, give them (and yourself) a chance. For some people the wisdom of the candle is apparent immediately, but for others it may take time. Curtis Faith, an excellent trader, stated in an interview:

A trigger is the exact pattern, indicator or signal that will tell you when to buy or sell the instrument.

> **One of the greatest dangers that traders face is uncertainty about the approach they are taking, and whether or not it's going to continue working. I find, invariably, that just when people write something off is the exact wrong time to stop using it.**

Persist and you will grasp the lessons of the candlestick.

Let's have a look at some of the types of trades you can conduct using candlestick theory. I have broken this discussion into the following four areas:

1   the breakout trade

2   the retracement trade

3   gap trading

4   the dominant candle.

For this chapter of the workbook, I am expecting that you are familiar with basic candlestick patterns. If you are not yet comfortable with these formations, take the time to review appendix A on page 287 in preparation. I have included an index of each of these patterns on page 328. This will act as a quick reference guide when you need to find a pattern description in a hurry at a later date. For more in-depth information about these divine little creatures, have a look at my book *The Secret of Candlestick Charting*.

1 The breakout trade

One of the most common patterns that traders look for is the *breakout*.

Bullish breakouts are characterised by a continuation of an existing uptrend, initiated by a white candle, typically on heavy volume. They can be quite dramatic in nature.

Bearish breakouts usually act as a continuation pattern of an existing downtrend where a break past support is initiated by a black candle. If increased volume coincides with the breakdown of the share price, the downward movement is more likely to be sustained (see figure 8.1, overleaf).

Figure 8.1: the breakout trade

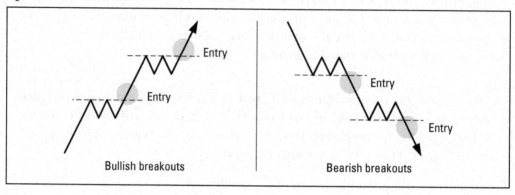

Bullish breakouts · Bearish breakouts

Location

Breakouts occur most frequently past a major level of support or resistance. The easiest breakouts to trade take place once the share has already displayed trending behaviour. The breakout follows a temporary pause within the existing trend. Periods of sideways consolidation give the share a chance to stop for a breather and take a puff on its asthma medication before running again.

Breakouts also confirm the appearance of many of the macro patterns we have already discussed. These include any of the triangular patterns, double tops and bottoms, as well as head and shoulders and inverse head and shoulders.

Identifying breakouts boosts your chances of making a profitable trade. If you only enter trades that have a high probability of trending in the expected direction, you are more likely to be successful. However, remember that: 'The simple truth is that there are no "sure things" in the market'. This is as true today as it was when Bernard Baruch first made the statement in the early part of last century.

A trigger you can use to open a long trade is a white candle above the level of resistance. A bearish trigger could be a black candle below the level of support.

A trigger you can use to open a long trade is a white candle above the level of resistance. A bearish trigger could be a black candle below the level of support. These signals tell you in no uncertain terms that it is time to get involved in a position. The set-ups are the 'cognitive' part of the trade and the trigger leads you to take the 'action'. So, as soon as your trigger is in place after the set-up, close your eyes (stop thinking) and take a leap of faith without hesitation.

Bullish breakouts

Here is a real-life example of a trade I made. As you can see, the share shown in figure 8.2 had just produced a breakout signal within an existing uptrend. Because this share's behaviour was in line with my trading plan, I chose to open a position. The confirming set-up factors included a series of higher lows, and more bullish candles than bearish candles. The bullish candles were also longer than the bearish candles. Increased volume at the point of breakout and share prices above the moving average also contributed to the weight of evidence, which triggered the buy.

Figure 8.2: AGX daily

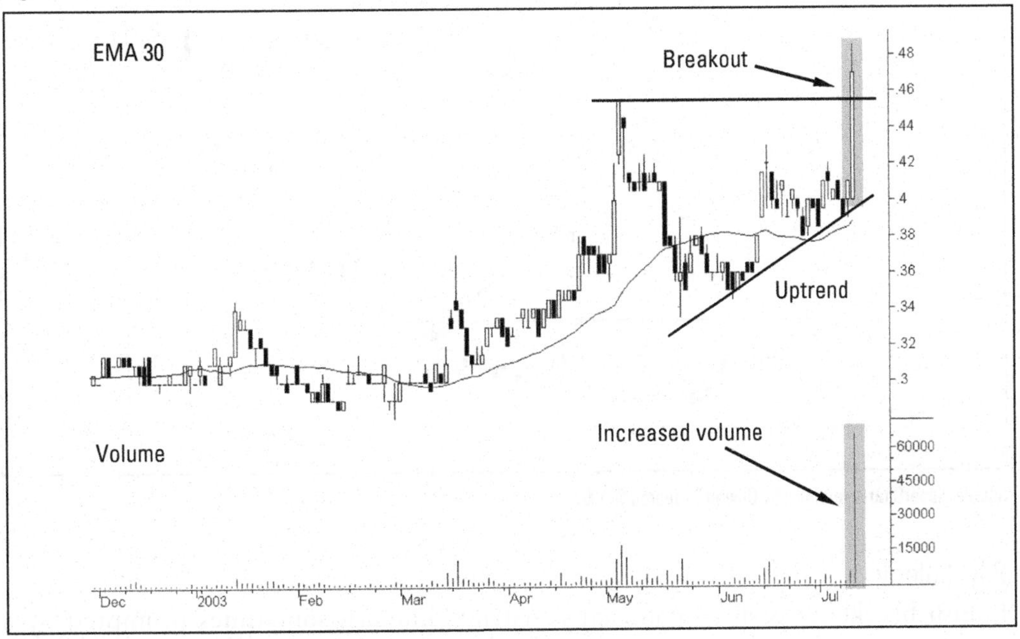

Source: SuperCharts version 4 by Omega Research © 1997.

These uptrend signals should be fairly familiar to you now after our discussion of macro pattern detection. A lot of the macro patterns suggest the share is warming up for something magnificent to occur. The breakout tells you when to act. Have a look at figure 8.3, overleaf, which shows how the share behaved after this bullish breakout. The strong uptrend resulted in a profitable trade.

For a bullish breakout you could either buy the share, buy a call option or warrant, or write a put option (if these option or warrant strategies are possible using that particular underlying share).You can check the candlestick chart at 3.30 pm before the market closes to see whether the breakout has occurred during the day, or wait until the market has closed and enter the trade the next day. Either way, you will be in the trade just after it has broken out from its range of trading, and if all goes well, you'll be in for one heck of a ride.

Figure 8.3: AGX Daily

Source: SuperCharts version 4 by Omega Research © 1997.

Psychology

Bullish breakouts past a significant resistance line are sometimes prompted by a positive company announcement, or as a minimum, a change in the market's perception of the value of this instrument. The number and enthusiasm of the buyers has overwhelmed the sellers, so the sellers continue raising their price. Hesitation at previous highs is overcome and momentum gains, producing heavy volume and increased excitement.

A lot of traders hold onto their shares and say to themselves, 'If the price ever gets to $3.00, I'll get out'. When they notice that the price has gone above this level, they sell. This often causes a temporary pullback to the previous level of resistance which results in a change of polarity. New buyers flood the market, after noticing the breakout. With the influx of new blood and funds, the share continues its bullish sprint.

Rounditis

Rounditis is an interesting affliction that takes a ferocious hold on even experienced traders in the market. Traders will generally buy and sell at levels they feel comfortable with. For example, it feels comfortable to buy a share at $5.00 and sell it at $6.00. The comfort of round dollar values, or even regular price increments, seems ingrained in our psyches.

Levels of support and resistance are often visible at psychologically significant values. It is uncanny to see how many times a reversal in share price will occur at $2.00, $2.20 or $2.50, for example.

Bearish breakouts

Bearish breakouts are characterised by fear as the market drops dramatically past support and the sellers flood the buyers. The shareholders may say to themselves, 'I know I've made a loss in this share, but as long as it stays above $2.00, I'll be fine'. Once the share drops below $2.00, they effectively 'freak out' and sell.

Bearish breakouts are characterised by fear as the market drops dramatically past support and the sellers flood the buyers.

Some deluded individuals see the drop in price and buy the share. Particularly stupid traders who own the share may even choose to buy more. Averaging down doesn't work. The result of the misguided traders' actions can drive the price back up to the previous level of support, which now becomes a resistance line. This is why change of polarity is a phenomenon, even in a downtrend. Ultimately, though, the sellers overwhelm the buyers and the downtrend becomes established.

In a falling trend, many traders put a lot of emphasis on the last top as providing the greatest level of resistance. However, in a strong downtrend, it is the last bottom that is often the most important. It has already acted as a level of support and is likely to change polarity to a level of resistance. In a rising trend, the last top is equally as important as this often forms the next level of support.

Signal failure

If the share pulls back into its previous range of trading, the breakout has failed. The use of a failed signal as a set-up condition requires a degree of psychological flexibility. If an expectation is not met most traders move onto the next stock unaware of the fact that the market has provided them with a powerful signal to act. It's important to look at failed signals as well as those that are confirmed.

If a breakout has failed, the share may take another run at it. If it does, before you act make sure you watch for enhanced levels of weight of evidence before believing that it will succeed in breaking out. It has bitten you once, so be wary before extending your hand again.

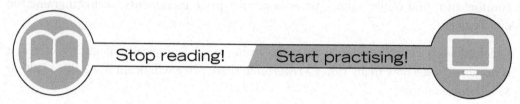

Have a look at the following charts (figures 8.4 to 8.7). Make some basic comments about share price direction. What has led you to consider that a trend is in place? Use methods such as trendlines and macro pattern analysis. Make sure that you use any of the other indicators provided on the chart. These observations will provide you with your set-up conditions. Once you have looked at the set-up, circle any breakouts that seem to be a potential entry point. These breakouts could act as your trigger so you could take a long or short position in this share. Most of the patterns I have shown have actually triggered my entry into a position, so this is as close to real life as you can get.

Suggested answers to this exercise are shown in figures 8.8 to 8.11.

Figure 8.4: ANN daily

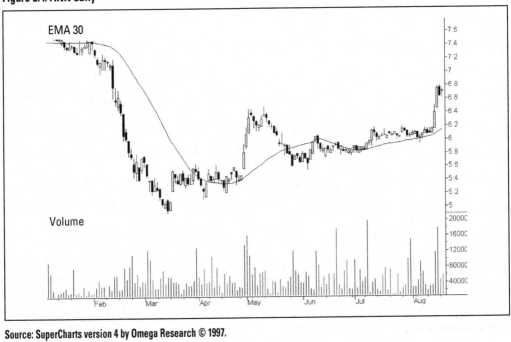

Source: SuperCharts version 4 by Omega Research © 1997.

....

....

....

....

....

....

....

....

....

Figure 8.5: VCR daily

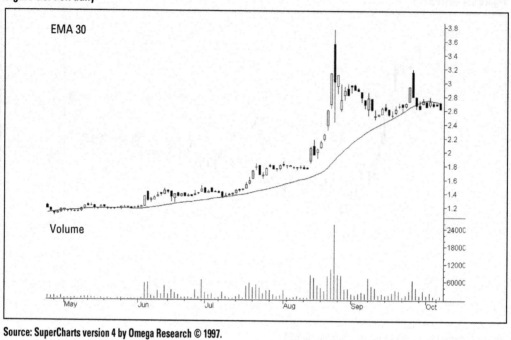

Source: SuperCharts version 4 by Omega Research © 1997.

....

....

....

....

....

....

....

....

....

....

Figure 8.6: SMS daily

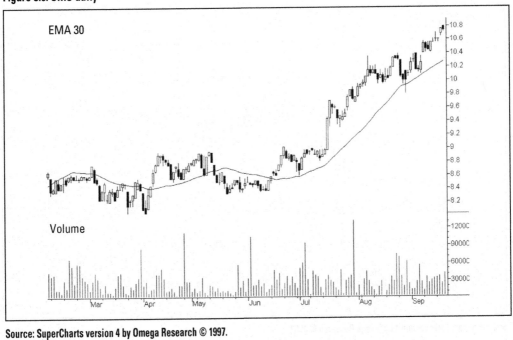

Source: SuperCharts version 4 by Omega Research © 1997.

....

....

....

....

....

....

....

....

....

Figure 8.7: SIG weekly

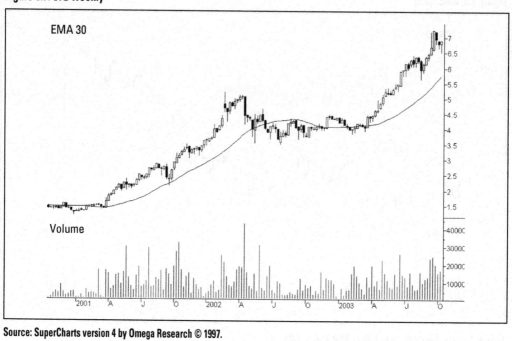

EMA 30

Volume

Source: SuperCharts version 4 by Omega Research © 1997.

....

....

....

....

....

....

....

....

....

Answers

Figure 8.8: ANN daily

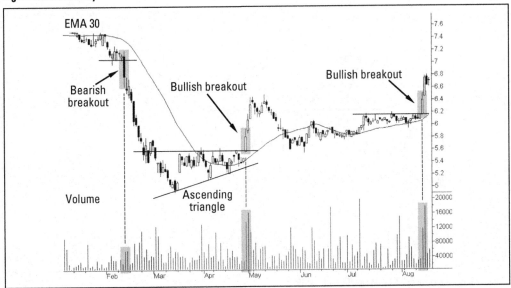

Source: SuperCharts version 4 by Omega Research © 1997.

Figure 8.9: VCR daily

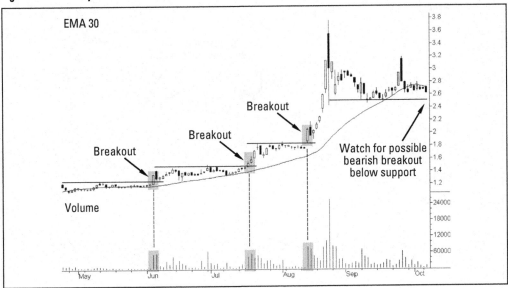

Source: SuperCharts version 4 by Omega Research © 1997.

Figure 8.10: SMS daily

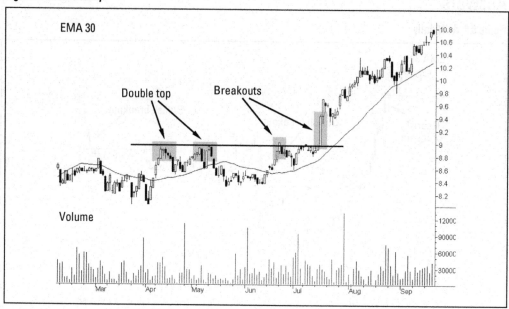

Source: SuperCharts version 4 by Omega Research © 1997.

Figure 8.11: SIG weekly

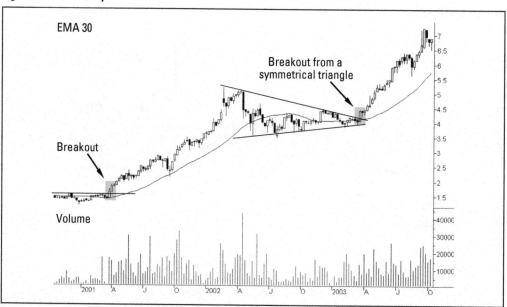

Source: SuperCharts version 4 by Omega Research © 1997.

2 The retracement trade

Another key method I use as an entry technique is the retracement trade. Retracements can either be in a bullish or a bearish direction. Let's have a closer look at this effective pattern in terms of its description, location and psychology.

Bullish retracements

When a share is in an existing uptrend and trading above its 30-week exponential moving average, a counter-trend reversal and rebound from a higher low can be used to trigger an entry into a long position. In other words, wait for a pullback to a lower price level, followed by a sign of recovery, before entering. This can be seen on a daily, weekly or intra-day chart (see figure 8.12).

You may have seen a ballet dancer crouch down before springing into the air in a graceful leap. Shares often behave in the same way. They will crouch down before thrusting upwards. If the weight of evidence suggests that an uptrend is likely to continue, you may as well enter the trade when the share shows signs of recovery from a small counter-trend reversal.

Figure 8.12: the bullish retracement trade

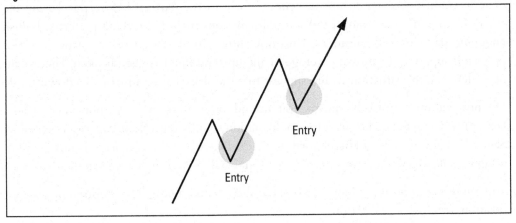

Location

The art of using this pattern as an entry signal is to ensure that the share has not begun a fully fledged downtrend. The pullback must be a temporary pause prior to the share uptrending again. The pullback can retrace to an existing trendline or a previous level of resistance. The instrument must form higher lows and higher highs in order to fulfil the definition of a continuing uptrend. Use a strong candlestick bottom reversal pattern to tell you when to enter a position. This will act as your trigger.

The instrument must form higher lows and higher highs in order to fulfil the definition of a continuing uptrend.

It's a gutsy move to act on a signal like this. You may feel like you are going out on a limb because the share has shown signs of a counter-trend movement, just when you are planning to enter. It takes courage to trade effectively. In *The Mind of a Trader* Alpesh B. Patel states: 'We are talking about the courage and self-confidence and ego, not just to go against the crowd, but to be wrong—a lot'.

Psychology

When the share falls in price during an uptrend, it is considered to be 'cheap' at this lower level and new buyers enter the market. Existing shareholders add to their current positions. This buying pressure drives the price upwards and an entry into a share at this time will allow you to harness the power of this bullish fervour.

Strategy

Entry into a long position can be made with a high degree of probability if there is a confirmed bottom candlestick reversal pattern. This is one strategy that requires definite confirmation to ensure the effectiveness of the pattern before purchasing the share. Commonly occurring candlestick formations include piercing patterns, bullish engulfing patterns and hammers. I do not enter a trade based on a bottom reversal pattern if support, the moving average or the uptrend line has been broken. The weight of evidence in this situation would suggest that the share has commenced a downtrend.

Do not act pre-emptively unless you intend on making a very short-term trade. Generally, you will need to wait for confirmation to fully trust your trigger. As stated by Shane Murphy and Doug Hirschhorn in *The Trading Athlete*: 'The market is not going to disappear. It will still be there tomorrow. Money will be waiting for you there. Patience'.

You can use bullish retracements to buy the share, enter a bought call option or warrant position, or write a put option.

You may find that you relate to one type of pattern more than another. If you prefer to trade breakouts rather than retracements, start with them, and when you are ready, add another pattern to your trading repertoire.

There is no guarantee that the method you have chosen as your favourite will continue to be effective ad infinitum. The best traders stay flexible in their approach, but are determined to progressively master more than just one entry technique.

Bullish retracements can trigger your entry into a long position. We will now have a look at bearish retracements and how they can help you enter a short position.

Bearish retracements

During an existing downtrend, temporary signs of bullish strength are quickly eradicated by bearish selling pressure (see figure 8.13). Small, bullish counter-trend reversals are brought to a halt, often by the arrival of a candlestick top reversal pattern. To trade these types of patterns with a higher level of certainty, it is advisable to focus on shares trading below their 30-week exponential moving average. Entry can be timed using daily or intra-day charts for short- to medium-term trades. Alternatively, longer term trades can be made using the weekly chart exclusively.

Top reversal candlestick patterns such as bearish engulfing patterns, dark cloud cover, spinning tops and doji can help you to time your entry into a short position.

Figure 8.13: the bearish retracement

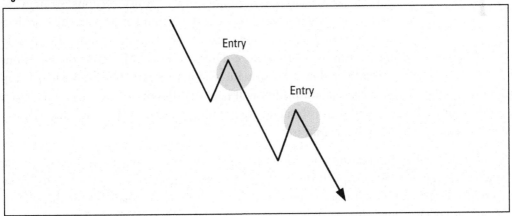

Location

Care must be taken to identify that this type of pattern is not the initiation of a new uptrend. Ideally, to confirm an ongoing downtrend, any show of share prices increasing in value should coincide with low relative volume levels. This suggests the enthusiasm of the bulls is only a temporary phenomenon. If heavy relative volume accompanies the bullish activity, it is possible that the share is about to form a V-reversal pattern and spike upwards.

If the share creates lower highs and lower lows, it can be assumed that the downtrend is continuing.

Psychology

During a downtrend, the egos of the current shareholders have taken a severe battering. They feel like failures because they have watched their portfolio value deplete steadily. This has made them vulnerable.

The toboggan ride down the mountain can be very quick and somewhat bumpy. At the first sign of bullish strength, the players sell their shares in order to bring their pain to a halt.

Strategy

When traders have ascertained that a downtrend is in action, they adopt strategies such as short selling, using a short CFD, writing call options, and buying put options or warrants. All of these are valid methods to capitalise on a downtrend.

... never negotiate whether to exit a position when a stop loss is hit.

Take a step back for a moment. The most obvious strategy to undertake when you observe a downtrend is to carefully analyse any current long positions. Look for the opportunity to actively move stop losses to a more defensive level. Monitor your positions carefully and never negotiate whether to exit a position when a stop loss is hit. Protect your capital and profits will naturally flow into your account. If you erode your capital, this will seriously affect your ability to continue trading. This will also take its emotional toll on your mindset.

Don't trade unless the market conditions are optimal. Sometimes it's best to sit on the sidelines and not enter new positions, biding your time, especially if you only know how to trade an uptrend. Good traders act like tigers, waiting in the shadows for the perfect set-up and conserving valuable energy and resources, before pouncing. Conditions must meet your trading plan requirements before you make your move.

I see many novice traders, full of enthusiasm, move into leveraged or volatile areas too early in their trading careers. This is often a catastrophic decision. The majority will destroy their hard-earned capital before they have a chance to learn the tricks of the trade. Take your time when you set out to develop your trading skills in a new market or with a new strategy. Sitting on the sidelines and waiting for an uptrend is a perfectly valid strategy.

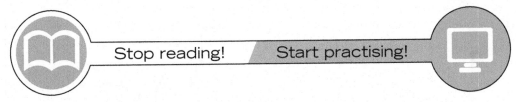

Stop reading! Start practising!

It is now time to practise your newly found analysis skills. I would like you to focus on identifying potential entry triggers by detecting breakout and retracement patterns.

Have a look at the charts shown in figures 8.14 to 8.17. Identify any potential entry points based on retracement patterns. You may want to use your knowledge of macro patterns as well as candlesticks to assist. If you can spot any previous viable breakouts, mark these on the chart too and make notes in the space provided. Assume that the volume and momentum indicator set-up is favourable for the entry you have in mind.

Even if you are not fully comfortable analysing shares at this stage, I urge you to do your best and have a shot at it. The easiest way to improve your trading results is to put your skills on the line and practise. The suggested solutions to these exercises are shown in figures 8.18 to 8.21.

Once you've finished these exercises, let's add to this knowledge by examining another type of pattern that can help us profit. Gaps can be used in conjunction with breakout trades and retracement techniques. The ability to use a gap to maximum advantage is essential for short-term trades, as well as trades that require specific timing to profit from a market move.

Figure 8.14: SGW weekly

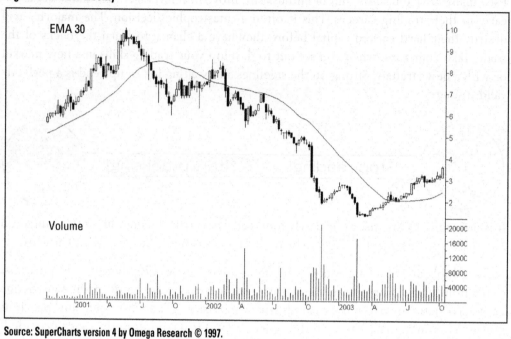

Source: SuperCharts version 4 by Omega Research © 1997.

....

....

....

....

....

....

....

....

....

....

Figure 8.15: SEV weekly

Source: SuperCharts version 4 by Omega Research © 1997.

Figure 8.16: PPX daily

EMA 30

Source: SuperCharts version 4 by Omega Research © 1997.

....

....

....

....

....

....

....

....

....

....

Figure 8.17: PMP daily

Source: SuperCharts version 4 by Omega Research © 1997.

....
....
....
....
....
....
....
....
....

Answers

Figure 8.18: SGW weekly

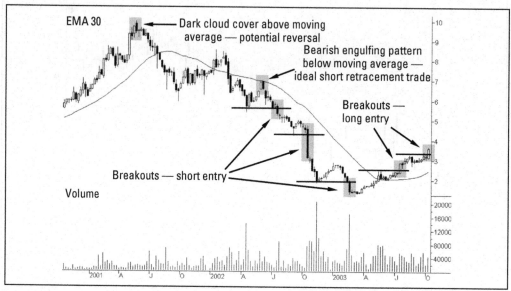

Source: SuperCharts version 4 by Omega Research © 1997.

Figure 8.19: SEV weekly

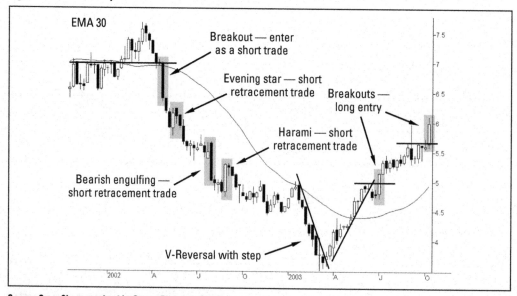

Source: SuperCharts version 4 by Omega Research © 1997.

Figure 8.20: PPX daily

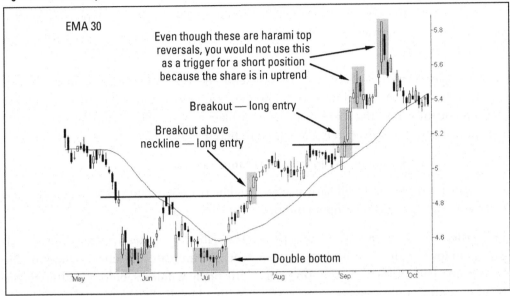

EMA 30

Even though these are harami top
reversals, you would not use this
as a trigger for a short position
because the share is in uptrend

Breakout — long entry

Breakout above
neckline — long entry

Double bottom

Source: SuperCharts version 4 by Omega Research © 1997.

Figure 8.21: PMP daily

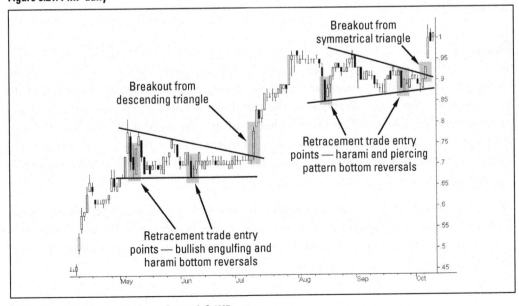

Breakout from
symmetrical triangle

Breakout from
descending triangle

Retracement trade entry
points — harami and piercing
pattern bottom reversals

Retracement trade entry
points — bullish engulfing and
harami bottom reversals

Source: SuperCharts version 4 by Omega Research © 1997.

3 Gap trading

A gap is essentially a hole in the share price action. There are several types of gaps that may be evident when viewing a chart. These are often described as sucker's gaps, false gaps and real gaps.

A *sucker's gap* is when a share goes ex-dividend and the corresponding share drop is visible in the chart. You will need to know the ex-dividend date in advance to observe the subsequent gap in the share price. Your broker may be able to supply ex-dividend date information, or at least tell you where to find it.

False gaps occur without an accompanying volume increase.

A *real gap* in a share chart will have an associated increase in volume. These types of gaps represent the most lucrative opportunities in which to trade.

In candlesticks terminology, real gaps are described as 'open windows'. Any real gap combined with a candlestick pattern tends to increase the effectiveness of the formation. For example, a shooting star with open windows before and after the trigger candle would suggest trend reversal with a higher degree of certainty than if no gaps were apparent.

Gaps are more often evident on daily and intra-day charts, in comparison to weekly charts.

Real gaps

In general, there are three types of real gap. A *breakaway gap* is a big gap on heavy volume at the start of a trend. A *continuation gap* (also known as a runaway gap) mostly leads to prices progressing in the direction of the trend. An *exhaustion gap* may indicate that a trend is running out of puff and that a change in the direction of the trend may occur. The first two real gaps are characterised by an increase in relative volume, whereas the latter is depicted by low relative volume. This is apparent in the AMP example shown in figure 8.22.

Many traders will trade in the direction of the real gap. For example, if a share is in an existing uptrend, and gaps upward on opening, it may be preferable to buy the share as soon as the gap has become evident. This can be an effective strategy if all of the other conditions suggest trend continuation.

Figure 8.22: AMP daily

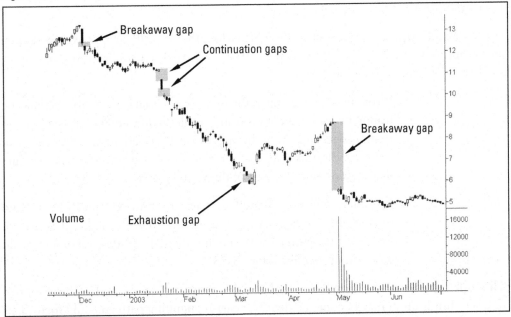

Source: SuperCharts version 4 by Omega Research © 1997.

A problem

There are several difficulties with buying a share as soon as the market opens. There is a saying that the 'amateurs open the market and the professionals close the market'. The amateurs have had all night to absorb the rumours and news about certain shares, and their anxious flurry of activity on the opening of the market reflects this. It is a well-known fact that in most markets around the world, the period of highest volatility for the day is the first hour of trading, and the Australian sharemarket is no exception. In the first hour of trading, there is a veritable scramble of punters trying to establish their positions. The more anxious the trader, the earlier he places an order with the broker. Once this early-morning scramble calms down, the market settles into a less volatile period during the middle of the day.

The final hour of the Australian sharemarket also experiences a definite increase in volatility as buyers and sellers review the price action that occurred during the day. They must quickly assess whether or not they can live with their trading decisions overnight, so they must be decisive and brave to buy or sell at the final hour. Again, emotions run high as traders buy and sell their shares in accordance with their view of the direction of the market for the following day.

For markets that never close, such as the FX market, there is still an approximated open and an approximated close. That's why the patterns we are discussing will work for every single market around the world.

If you insist on trading in the first hour of market activity, you may be trapped with the amateurs, and condemned to make a less informed trading decision. In addition, if you think about the formation of some candlestick patterns, the gap formed by early market trading may be closed by the end of the trading period.

Consider a bearish engulfing pattern, for example. The second session initially gaps away from the first bullish candle. If you were looking at the pattern at the beginning of the trading session, it could look something like figure 8.23.

This looks like the start of a bullish day, doesn't it? However, by the end of the session, a different implication may become evident. A bearish engulfing pattern could form. This means that the pattern would look like figure 8.24.

Figure 8.23: early phase of a bearish engulfing pattern

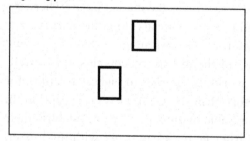

Figure 8.24: bearish engulfing pattern

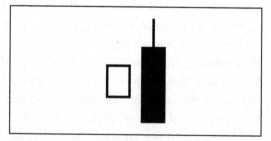

If you trade in the morning during amateur hour, you must be prepared for the possibility that some bullish signals will actually reverse by the end of the day. The same goes for bearish signals. Some gaps downward in the morning could eventually form bullish reversal patterns by the end of the session. One way to limit this possibility is to make sure you have other indicators giving you appropriate signs to act, in addition to the candlestick pattern. Candlesticks work best when you use them in conjunction with other indicators.

Strategies

As discussed, it would be wise to trade in the direction of the real gap, and to initiate your trade towards the end of the day. This will increase the probability that the gap will hold, and not close. Opening a trade at the beginning of the day would be appropriate if every other piece of weight of evidence suggested uptrend continuation.

Interestingly, gaps can act to confirm support or resistance levels. If a bullish gap is closed, you could use this to initiate a bearish strategy. Obviously this would make more sense if the overall trend was downward. If a bearish gap is closed, this could be a trigger for entering a long position. Gaps that remain open, in line with the medium-term trend, usually confirm the strength of the trend.

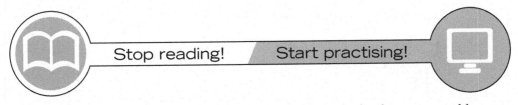

Stop reading! Start practising!

Have a look at the following charts (figures 8.25 to 8.28). Define how you would use any gaps you identify on the chart. Also, circle any breakout and retracement areas. (Assume that there is an appropriate volume and momentum set-up for your purposes.) Some suggested solutions are explored in figures 8.29 to 8.32.

Some shares are more likely to respond to gap trading techniques than others. Before you trade, look back over the history of the chart and briefly back-test to see which candlestick patterns a share is responsive towards. Look for *frequency* of pattern occurrence, the *immediate responsiveness* to individual patterns and the longer term *effectiveness* of these formations.

Some research suggests that particular patterns are more effective than others. I believe this varies according to the chart being viewed at the time. Additionally, the overall trending behaviour of the share must be taken into account to glean an accurate understanding of the likely effect of a particular candlestick pattern. Candlesticks, as well as the majority of technical analysis techniques, are subjective in their interpretation.

Figure 8.25: CTX daily

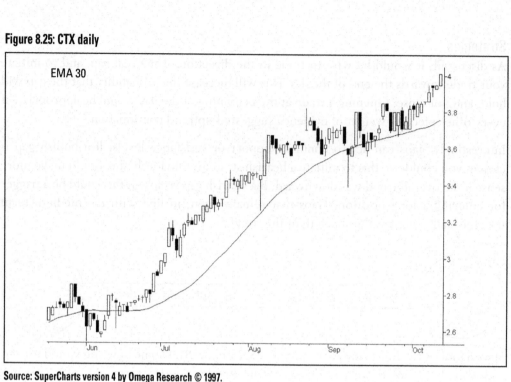

EMA 30

Source: SuperCharts version 4 by Omega Research © 1997.

Figure 8.26: ADA weekly

Source: SuperCharts version 4 by Omega Research © 1997.

....

....

....

....

....

....

....

....

....

....

Figure 8.27: ALT daily

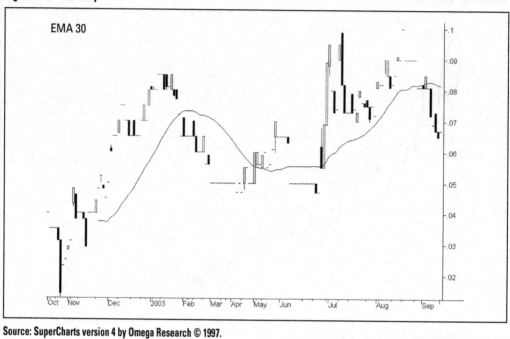

Source: SuperCharts version 4 by Omega Research © 1997.

....

....

....

....

....

....

....

....

....

....

Figure 8.28: PHY daily

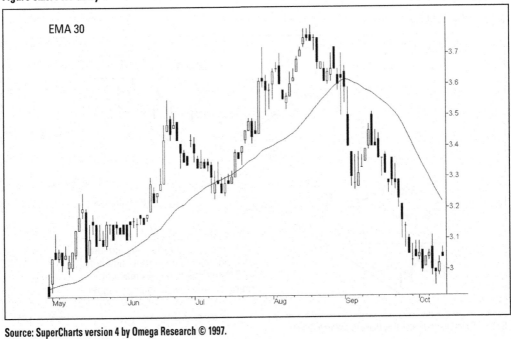

Source: SuperCharts version 4 by Omega Research © 1997.

....

....

....

....

....

....

....

....

....

Answers

Figure 8.29: CTX daily

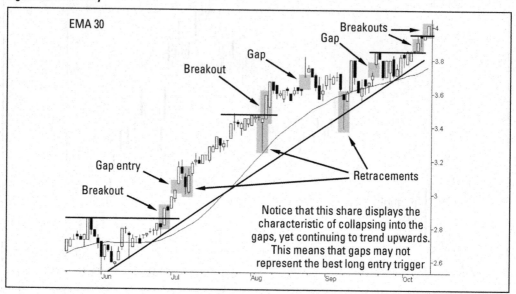

Source: SuperCharts version 4 by Omega Research © 1997.

Figure 8.30: ADA weekly

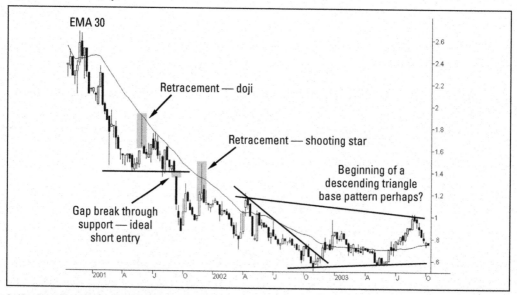

Source: SuperCharts version 4 by Omega Research © 1997.

Figure 8.31: ALT daily

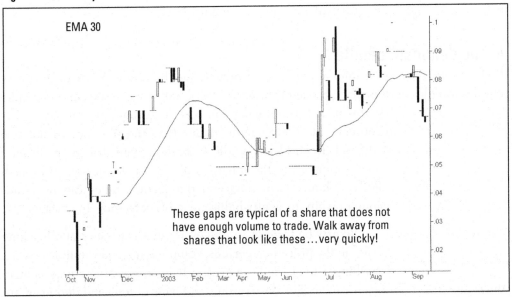

These gaps are typical of a share that does not have enough volume to trade. Walk away from shares that look like these... very quickly!

Source: SuperCharts version 4 by Omega Research © 1997.

Figure 8.32: PHY daily

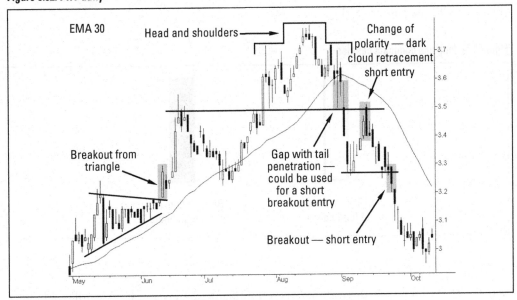

Source: SuperCharts version 4 by Omega Research © 1997.

Now we will look at dominant candlesticks and how you can use these single candle patterns to trigger your entry into short and long positions.

4 The dominant candle

Both *long* and *dominant* candles display a significantly longer body length than the majority of other candles on the chart. Some of these types of candles show tails on either side,

A dominant candle has a much greater impact than a long candle. It indicates a violent, unequivocal decision about the future market direction.

but this is of little bearing. The key to recognising this pattern is to observe the body length, rather than the presence or absence of the tail. I consider a candle to be dominant if it is significantly longer compared to the other candles *and* is accompanied by high relative volume. Both long and dominant candles can be either colour — white to signify bullishness, black to show bearishness.

A candle may be termed as long even if there are several other long candles in the preceding periods. Volume is not a key indicator when describing a long candle, whereas it is an essential component in the creation of a dominant candle. For this reason, the terms of long and dominant are not interchangeable. A dominant candle has a much greater impact than a long candle. It indicates a violent, unequivocal decision about the future market direction. The dominant candle clearly shows the victory of either the bulls (white candle) or the bears (black candle) (see figure 8.33).

Figure 8.33: long and dominant candles

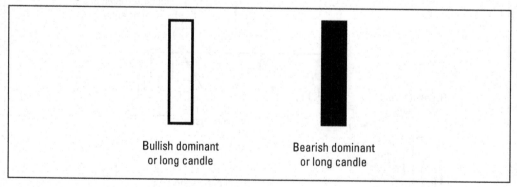

Bullish dominant
or long candle

Bearish dominant
or long candle

Psychology

Some analysts do not distinguish between dominant candles and long candles. I believe that the distinction between these two types of candles is essential. A dominant candle has a higher level of emotional significance than a long candle. When trading with a long candle, I require an increased weight of evidence before entering the trade. Long candles suggest the view of the direction is not held as vehemently by as many players in the market, otherwise the volume would have shown a definite increase relative to the preceding sessions. For this reason, the support and resistance that can be found within the body of a dominant candle is not as significant when looking at a long candle.

Support and resistance

Dominant candles actually show levels of support and resistance within the body of the candle. These diagrams show there are three essential areas in the body of the candle to consider — the base, the midpoint and the top. This is apparent regardless of the candle colour (see figure 8.34).

Figure 8.34: support and resistance

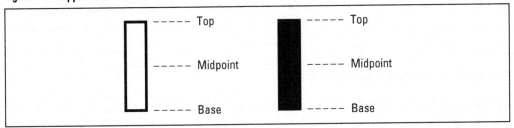

The top of the candle is defined as being the open of a bearish dominant candle or the close of a bullish dominant candle. The midpoint can be drawn at the 50 per cent level of the real body. If the candle has tails, the midpoint actually ignores these tails. The real body is the focus. The base of the candle is the opening price of a bullish dominant candle, or the closing price of a bearish dominant candle.

These three points are of particular relevance when looking to set a pattern-based stop loss for short-term trades. They also are essential when considering whether a candlestick pattern has been confirmed. Each of these levels display support and resistance characteristics. The following example should provide more of an insight into this concept.

Example

Have a look at the chart of Agenix daily in figure 8.35 (overleaf). The medium-term trend is up, and the short-term trend is up. There are two very long candles on this chart, relative to the lengths of the other candles shown. Because they display heavy relative volume, the two candles may be defined as dominant.

Figure 8.35: AGX daily

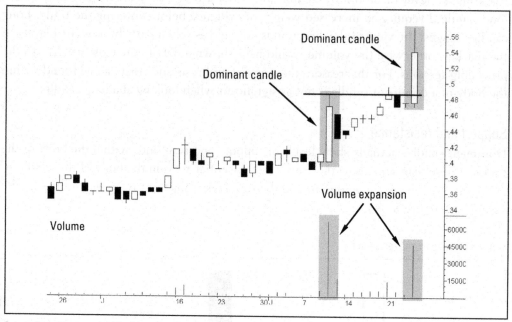

Source: SuperCharts version 4 by Omega Research © 1997.

If you refer to the *Candlestick basics* in appendix A, you may recognise that the two dominant candles in this example form the perimeter of the rising three method formation. It is quite common for dominant candles to represent a subsection of a larger candlestick pattern, or even confirm a macro formation such as a double top.

It was a bullish signal that the subsequent trading remained above the base of the initial dominant candle on this chart. From a very short-term perspective, it would have been even more bullish if all trading had been situated above the midpoint. Short-term traders could set their automatic stop loss just below the midpoint or under the base of this bullish dominant candle, so that a penetration of this price would result in an exit from their long position.

Notice that the high of the initial dominant candle formed a level of temporary resistance. This is a great example of the change of polarity principle. Short-term traders who are now trading the hard right edge of the chart could set their pattern-based stop loss just below the base, or the midpoint, of the new dominant candle.

Traders seeking an entry into this instrument could enter a bullish trade if the next day's price action closed above the midpoint of this new dominant candle. Any closing price above the base would be considered bullish, but a close above the midpoint would suggest a heightened level of confirmation. Short-term traders could choose to await a closing price above the top of the new dominant candle. Often, after such a dramatic push forward, a step backward in price action is likely.

Short-term traders could choose to await a closing price above the top of the new dominant candle.

Pattern combinations

Midpoint analysis is inherent in several candlestick formations. From your knowledge of candlesticks, you may recognise a dark cloud cover and a bearish engulfing pattern. Both are very effective top reversal candlestick patterns (see figure 8.36).

Figure 8.36: dark cloud cover and bearish engulfing pattern

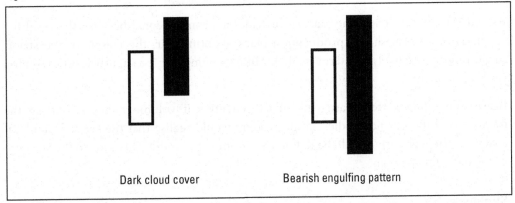

Dark cloud cover   Bearish engulfing pattern

Intuitively, it could be ascertained that the engulfing pattern is the stronger of the two patterns. To double-check this, you could perform candlestick addition (which is examined in appendix A) and compare the reduced candles. In this method, you take the open price of the first candle and the closing price of the second candle to form the real body of the resulting candle. Candlestick addition will provide you with an objective method of evaluating the strength of any multiple line candlestick patterns (see figure 8.37, overleaf).

Figure 8.37: candle addition

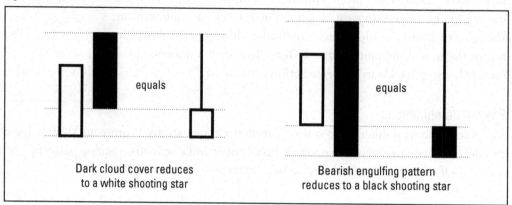

Dark cloud cover reduces
to a white shooting star

Bearish engulfing pattern
reduces to a black shooting star

As you can see, the engulfing pattern provides a stronger signal because the resulting candle is more bearish. By producing a black shooting star, the colour of the star is suggesting a more likely trend reversal. A white shooting star is a slightly less bearish top reversal pattern.

Bearish engulfing patterns are particularly effective if volume increases during the formation of the second candle. Astute readers would realise that the second candle, if analysed independently, would be defined as a dominant candle. This adds to the strength of the engulfing pattern.

Strategies

This concept of the dominant candle is of key importance in my trading strategy. It assists in the determination of support/resistance levels, helps to establish profit targets for volatile shares and short-term trades, and can even facilitate the identification of sustainable breakouts.

You may choose to tighten your stop loss after the appearance of a dominant candle in the expected trend direction. For short-term trading, moving your stop up to the base of the dominant candle would lock in your profits.

In instruments where the mid-term trend is established, dominant candles can provide an entry trigger, even if you have missed entering the share on the day the dominant candle formed. In the period after the dominant candle, entry signals could be established if the share displayed price action above the midpoint for bullish positions, or below the midpoint for bearish positions.

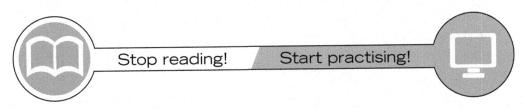

Here's a chance to test your knowledge of dominant candles and related concepts. Take the time to answer the following:

1 Imagine that you have identified a share that is downtrending strongly. Where would you like to see subsequent price action after a bearish engulfing pattern to encourage you to enter a short trade?

....

....

....

....

....

....

2 Why is volume important in the formation of bullish and bearish dominant candles?

....

....

....

....

....

3 Is heavy relative volume more important to confirm a bullish breakout or a bearish breakout?

....

....

....

....

....

....

4 If you miss the initial bullish breakout, rather than walking away from opportunity, you could seek alternative entry points. Describe as many other potential entry points that you can think of. If you come up with three potential entry points, that is 'average'; four is 'good'; and five and above is 'very clever'.

....

....

....

....

....

....

5   For a short trade, if you miss the initial bearish breakout you could seek alternative short entry triggers. Describe as many other potential short entry points that you can think of. If you come up with three potential entry points, that is 'average'; four is 'good'; and five and above is 'very clever'.

....

....

....

....

....

....

6   In the space below, summarise any of your discoveries regarding the types of triggers that you would like to use in your own trading.

....

....

....

....

....

....

Answers

1 Trading below the midpoint of the second candle of the bearish engulfing pattern would provide confirmation that an entry into a short position would be appropriate. For a heightened probability entry, trading below the base of this second candle would be even more bearish. A real gap following a bearish engulfing pattern would also suggest that the trend downwards is likely to continue.

2 Without heavy relative volume coinciding with the appearance of a dominant candle, it is actually just a long candle. Support and resistance is less applicable within the body of a long candle. Increased volume suggests that this view of share price direction is held by a large number of market participants.

3 Volume is more important with bullish breakouts. To experience an enduring uptrend, volume adds to the weight of evidence. Bearish breakouts can be strong with lower levels of volume because the emotion of fear is more pervasive than greed.

4 If you miss an entry into a bullish breakout, you could:

   — Open a position if the share price closes above the midpoint of the breakout candle.

   — Trade if the share price closes above the top of the breakout candle.

   — Seek a change of polarity back to the level of previous resistance which should now act as support.

   — Seek heavy volume on subsequent breakouts and low volume on pullbacks.

   — Await a bottom candlestick reversal pattern to trigger your entry.

   — Act on trading above a previous top reversal pattern, and use this as your entry signal.

   — Trade if there is price activity above a significant macro top reversal pattern. This would also be a bullish trigger.

   — Use a failed top reversal candlestick pattern, which is also a significant entry indicator.

   — Enter on a bullish technical indicator such as a golden cross of a moving average — if you don't find that candlesticks are your cup of tea.

— Read tea leaves and enter only when they give you the signal. This may be only slightly better than using horoscopes, but what would I know? I'm a Taurean and we are known to be stubborn and tactless.

5 If you miss a bearish breakout, and you would like to enter a short position, you could:

— Open a position if there is share price action below the midpoint of the bearish breakout candle.

— Trade if the price closes below the base of the bearish breakout candle.

— Seek a change of polarity back to the level of previous support, which should now act as resistance.

— Seek heavy volume on breaks downward and low volume on breaks upward.

— Await a top candlestick reversal pattern to trigger your entry.

— Use any bearish real gap as a trigger because it is likely to act as future resistance and drive strength into a downtrend.

— Enter on a failed bottom macro reversal pattern or a failed candlestick bottom reversal pattern.

6 Obviously, you may have come up with your own interpretations, but it is always wise to try and simplify your methods as much as possible. The more practice you get at identifying the set-ups and triggers, the better. I want to give you as many opportunities as I can to test out your skills before you trade all by yourself.

More exercises

In the charts shown in figures 8.38 to 8.41 identify any patterns you recognise. Using weight of evidence, describe whether you are more likely to enter a long or a short position. Circle any areas that could represent an entry position into a long or short trade. Use all of the analysis skills you have gleaned throughout this workbook. Give it your best shot! Figures 8.42 to 8.45 provide possible answers.

Figure 8.38: TLS daily

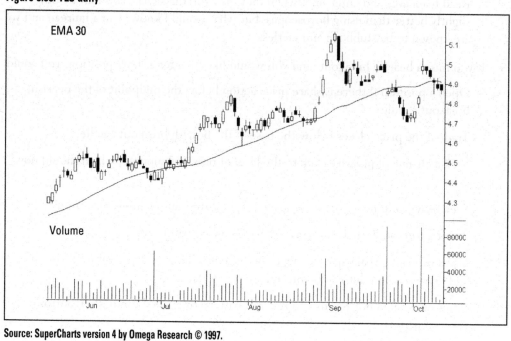

Source: SuperCharts version 4 by Omega Research © 1997.

....

....

....

....

....

....

....

....

....

....

Figure 8.39: UNI daily

Source: SuperCharts version 4 by Omega Research © 1997.

....

....

....

....

....

....

....

....

....

Figure 8.40: VSL weekly

Source: SuperCharts version 4 by Omega Research © 1997.

....

....

....

....

....

....

....

....

....

....

Figure 8.41: HSP daily

Source: SuperCharts version 4 by Omega Research © 1997.

....

....

....

....

....

....

....

....

....

Answers

Figure 8.42: TLS daily

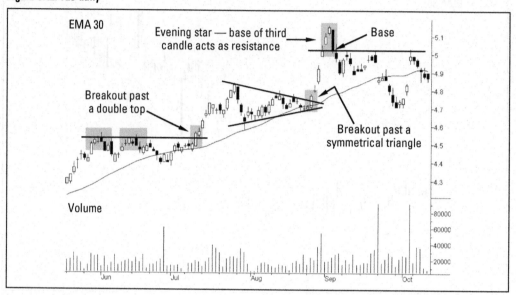

Source: SuperCharts version 4 by Omega Research © 1997.

Figure 8.43: UNI daily

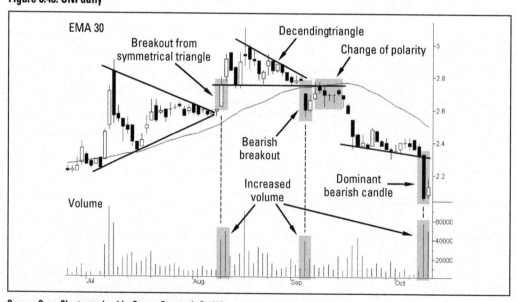

Source: SuperCharts version 4 by Omega Research © 1997.

Figure 8.44: VSL weekly

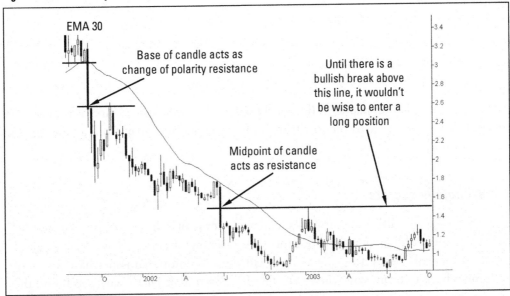

EMA 30

Base of candle acts as
change of polarity resistance

Until there is a
bullish break above
this line, it wouldn't
be wise to enter a
long position

Midpoint of candle
acts as resistance

Source: SuperCharts version 4 by Omega Research © 1997.

Figure 8.45: HSP daily

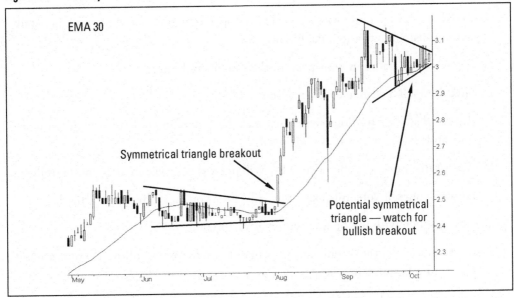

EMA 30

Symmetrical triangle breakout

Potential symmetrical
triangle — watch for
bullish breakout

Source: SuperCharts version 4 by Omega Research © 1997.

If you are struggling a little with these exercises, take heart. As stated by trader Bruce Kovner:

> **There are two things that are absolutely critical: You must have confidence, and you have to be willing to make mistakes regularly; there is nothing wrong with it.**

Make your mistakes on paper, in this workbook, before you apply your ideas in the real market. It will be easier to recover from a blow to your ego, than from a blow to your bank account.

Psychology secrets

Your level of wealth will rarely exceed your level of self-development. Without continually pushing yourself and improving your own mindset, your bank account will stubbornly refuse to grow as well. Unresolved emotional issues have a way of coming back to haunt you when you start life as a trader. That's why you'll find the best traders are obsessed with psychology. So, in the interests of improving your mindset and your bank balance, here are ...

Eighteen things to start doing as a trader

1 Avoid negative people. You are perfectly capable of generating negative self-talk without listening to them babble on.

2 Let go of the trades in your past, both winners and losers.

3 Give yourself a chance to learn a new skill.

4 Realise that your trading plan is the only thing standing between where you are now and chaos. Ignore it at your peril.

5 Accept that not everyone in your life will possess your vision, drive and intellect.

6 Forgive yourself your mistakes, but only after you've really learned the lesson.

7 Stay in touch with the people who matter to you.

8 Do something little to encourage yourself when you've followed your trading plan, but it resulted in a loss.

9 Take some time to simply think, rather than 'do'.

10   Do something little to encourage yourself when you've followed your trading plan, and it resulted in a profit.

11   Find some quiet and don't answer your phone, watch TV or answer your emails when you're trading.

12   Remember to take long deep breaths when you're feeling under pressure.

13   Stand up! You've been sitting down too long watching your computer screen.

14   Find a pet to stroke — or your spouse's hair, if you can't find a pet.

15   Remember that the little people in your life may not share your passion for charts.

16   Forgive people from your past and move on. If you don't, you're likely to end up sabotaging your trading results.

17   Seek out someone who knows more than you about a particular topic and immerse yourself in their world.

18   Give before you ask to receive.

Summary

- A set-up is a set of general conditions that suggest the share is either uptrending or downtrending.

- A trigger is the exact pattern, indicator or signal that tells you when to buy (or sell) a share, option or warrant.

- You will need to define your set-ups and triggers with mechanical precision so that you will have the courage and confidence to enter into positions.

- Uptrend triggers may include bullish dominant candles, gaps upward, bottom reversal candlesticks, bullish breakouts and trading above top reversal patterns to signal an entry into a long position.

- Downtrend triggers may include bearish dominant candles, gaps downward, top reversal candlesticks, bearish breakouts and trading below a bottom reversal pattern to signal an entry into a short position.

The next chapter will assist you in compiling all of your knowledge into an explosion of brilliance that will most likely be visible from the moon.

9

Putting it all together

You've been gathering the puzzle pieces. Now you're ready to strut your stuff and complete the picture. This chapter will be very revealing for you. It will give you confidence and allow you to realise just how far you've come already...

CHARTING IS SUCH A BROAD TOPIC. It's one thing to grasp the main concepts, but getting them to work together can be a challenge. This chapter is designed to test your knowledge by looking at several different charts and asking questions to help develop your skill.

Without fail, the traders who have been exposed to a wide variety of charts will be the ones who recognise these patterns in real time as they unfold. Successful traders look back into the past so that they can detect patterns in the future.

On www.turtletrader.com Paul Counsel states:

> Everything in this world involves risk but by far the greatest risk is staying in your comfort zone because this involves the risk of lost opportunities. The secret to risk lies in knowing how to minimise its impact on you. If you want to be a successful trader you must become passionate about the learning process. You must become totally focussed on trading well as opposed to making money. You must learn from someone who can show you how to trade successfully rather than rely on machines and promises of 'golden eggs'. You must become absolutely disciplined in the activity of trading.

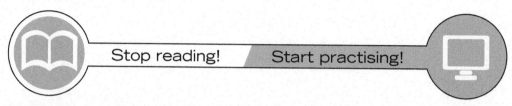

Take your time as you go through each of the six exercises and try to complete every one, even if you don't fully understand why I have placed that particular example in front of you. As Henry David Thoreau stated: 'Success usually comes to those who are too busy to be looking for it'. Go through the motions and those elusive charting secrets will gradually reveal themselves.

You may find that you need to flick back over your notes throughout this workbook or refer to the appendices. That's okay. There's no problem with using this book as a reference guide, even when you are trading with real money. You may choose to complete each of the six exercises sequentially before checking your answers at the back of the chapter. Alternatively, you can check the answers after you have completed each separate exercise in turn. Choose whichever method feels most comfortable for you.

Let's kick off...

Exercise 1

Analyse figures 9.1 to 9.3. Figure 9.1 shows a chart of GGL weekly and figure 9.2 shows a daily version of the same share. Figure 9.3 provides an expanded version of this daily chart, which should enable you to get really close to the share price action. Take into consideration and use evidence from all of the families that are relevant. If there are any usable candlestick patterns that you recognise on any of the charts, highlight these. What strategies could you use to profit from this share trend? What triggers would you look for to prompt you to enter a position?

Figure 9.1: GGL weekly

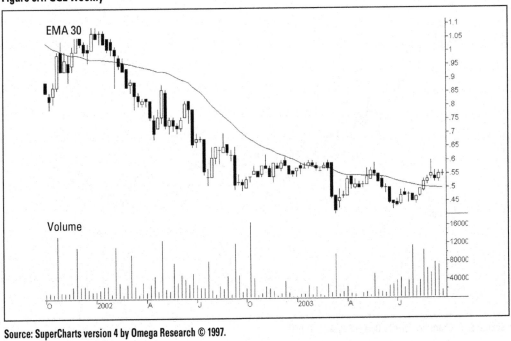

Source: SuperCharts version 4 by Omega Research © 1997.

Figure 9.2: GGL daily

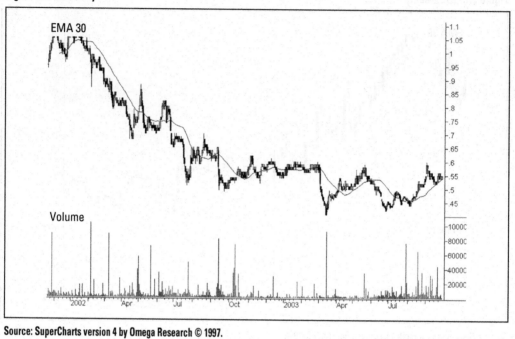

Source: SuperCharts version 4 by Omega Research © 1997.

....

....

....

....

....

....

....

....

....

....

Figure 9.3: GGL daily close-up

Source: SuperCharts version 4 by Omega Research © 1997.

....

....

....

....

....

....

....

....

....

Exercise 2

Analyse figures 9.4 to 9.7, which show different views of the same share—G.U.D Holdings. Use evidence from all of the families that are relevant. If there are any candlestick patterns that you recognise on any of the charts, highlight these. Are there any macro patterns on this chart that could have acted as an earlier trigger for entry? What strategies could you use to profit from this type of trend? What triggers would you look for to prompt you to enter a position? Is there anything to suggest that you shouldn't enter a trade?

Figure 9.4: GUD weekly

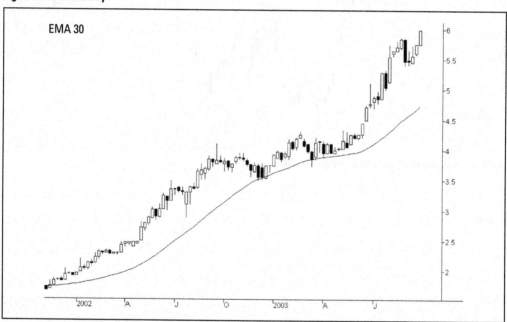

Source: SuperCharts version 4 by Omega Research © 1997.

....

....

....

....

....

Figure 9.5: GUD weekly

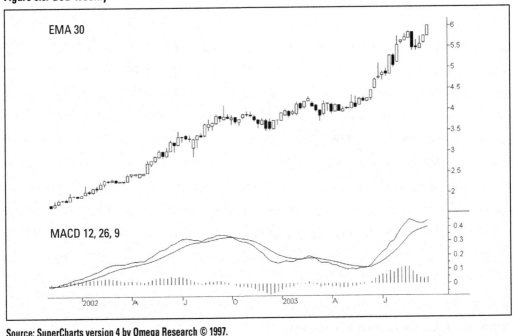

Source: SuperCharts version 4 by Omega Research © 1997.

. . . .

. . . .

. . . .

. . . .

. . . .

. . . .

. . . .

. . . .

. . . .

Figure 9.6: GUD daily

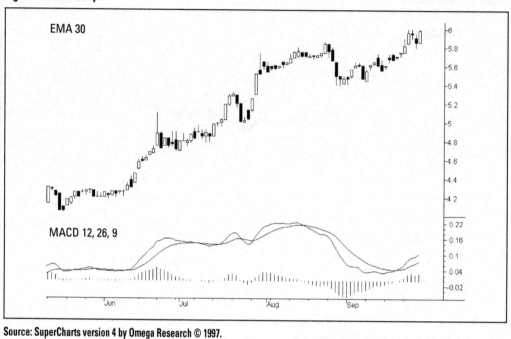

Source: SuperCharts version 4 by Omega Research © 1997.

....

....

....

....

....

....

....

....

....

....

Figure 9.7: GUD daily

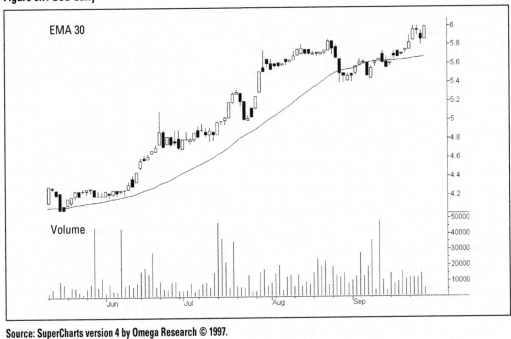

Source: SuperCharts version 4 by Omega Research © 1997.

....

....

....

....

....

....

....

....

....

Exercise 3

Have a think about all of the trend direction clues the various indicator families can give you. Organise them into a checklist to help you determine when a share is uptrending. Try compiling a personalised checklist here to assist you in ascertaining share price direction. (You may need to add a separate piece of paper, depending on how enthusiastic you are about this exercise.)

Line family ☐ ....
....

☐ ....
....

Volume family ☐ ....
....

☐ ....
....

Moving average
family ☐ ....
....

☐ ....
....

Momentum
family ☐ ....
....

☐ ....
....

Pattern family ☐ ....
....

☐ ....
....

Exercise 4

Repeat the thought process that you went through in the previous exercise, but apply it to a downtrending share. The goal is to have two very objective, indisputable lists that will help you become a trend direction hero. (Add your extra points to a separate piece of paper if you need to.)

Line family ☐ ....

....

☐ ....

....

Volume family ☐ ....

....

☐ ....

....

Moving average family ☐ ....

....

☐ ....

....

Momentum family ☐ ....

....

☐ ....

....

Pattern family ☐ ....

....

☐ ....

....

Exercise 5

Figures 9.8 to 9.10 show weekly and daily charts of Mincor Resources. Observe the trend, indicators and patterns, and summarise why you would be willing to go long in this share. Define your trigger, and record any reasons why you may choose not to get involved in this share. So now it's decision time: would you buy or would you walk away? Before you progress to exercise 6, commit to a course of action. Boldly write down your response.

Figure 9.8: MCR weekly

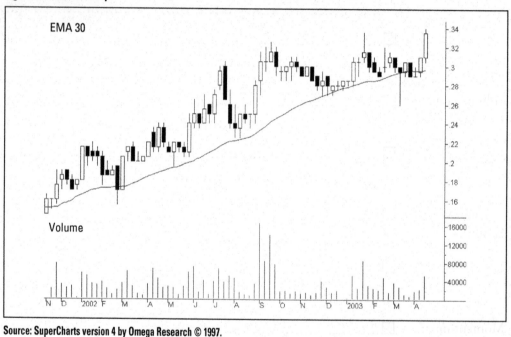

Source: SuperCharts version 4 by Omega Research © 1997.

....

....

....

....

....

....

Figure 9.9: MCR daily

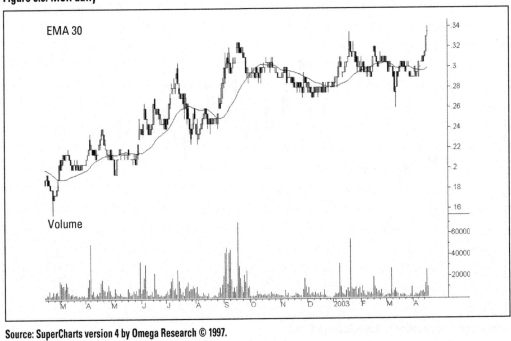

Source: SuperCharts version 4 by Omega Research © 1997.

....

....

....

....

....

....

....

....

....

....

Figure 9.10: MCR daily close-up

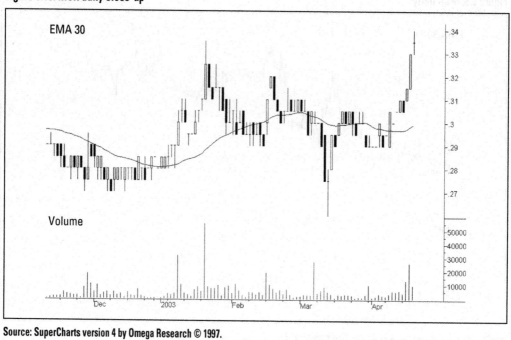

Source: SuperCharts version 4 by Omega Research © 1997.

....

....

....

....

....

....

....

....

....

....

Exercise 6

The charts in figures 9.11 to 9.14 show a share I would like you to analyse. Look at the weekly and daily charts and gain a perspective on the likely future share direction. Are you prepared to open a position? What strategies would you use to make money? Commit, one way or another. The time is 3.45 pm, and you have 15 minutes before the market closes for the day. Are you in or are you out?

Figure 9.11: CDO weekly

Source: SuperCharts version 4 by Omega Research © 1997.

....

....

....

....

....

....

Figure 9.12: CDO daily

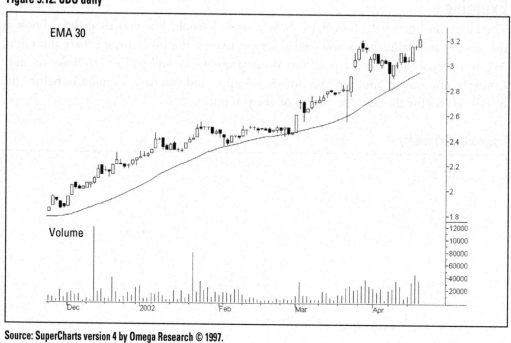

EMA 30

Volume

Source: SuperCharts version 4 by Omega Research © 1997.

....

....

....

....

....

....

....

....

....

....

Figure 9.13: CDO weekly

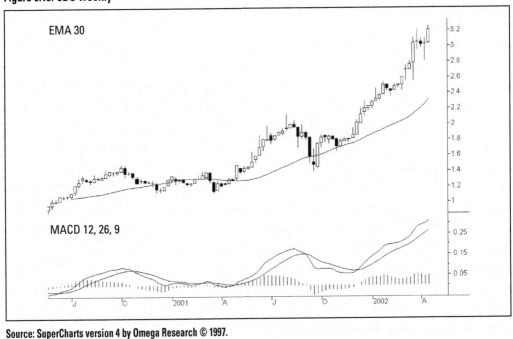

Source: SuperCharts version 4 by Omega Research © 1997.

....

....

....

....

....

....

....

....

....

Figure 9.14: CDO daily

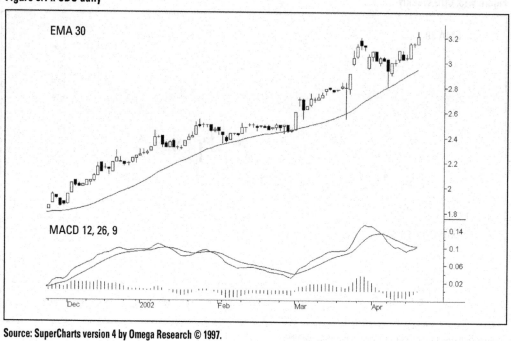

Source: SuperCharts version 4 by Omega Research © 1997.

Answers

Exercise 1

GGL on the weekly chart looks like it is forming a basing pattern, and is displaying stage 1 characteristics. Rather than showing you my chart analysis, I will leave this share for you to analyse and reach your own conclusions. As we've established, the market won't hand you all the answers on a platter. Most of the time you are left guessing. Here are my comments regarding how you could benefit from your analysis of this share forming a stage 1 pattern:

a) *signal confirmation*

If this share breaks above the resistance line at 60¢ on heavy relative volume, this would suggest an early stage 2 may be in progress. An ideal trigger to buy the share, buy a call option or warrant or write a put option would be a dominant white candle or a gap upwards. If you missed this chance, you could await a change of polarity indicated by a pullback to the line of previous resistance. An appropriate trigger in this situation would be to enter based on a bottom candlestick reversal pattern. You could either act on the pattern itself, or wait for confirmation that the pattern was effective. The longer the term of your trade, the more confirmation you can afford to wait for.

b) *signal failure*

If the stage 1 formation failed, you would see trading below the support line at approximately 42¢. This would suggest a short-selling strategy may be appropriate. Other strategies include writing call options or buying put options or warrants. In light of the share price, I would walk away from such an opportunity as I tend to only utilise downtrending strategies on shares that are more than $2.00 or so. It is important that they have a bit of room to move downwards so you can capitalise on the trend. This is a personal choice, though. If short-selling or derivative-based strategies (options and warrants) are appropriate, triggers could be a gap downwards, a dominant bearish candle, or a top reversal candle pattern at a change of polarity region if the share recovers slightly.

Exercise 2

Based on the weekly and the daily charts, G.U.D. Holdings looks like it is in a strong uptrend. I couldn't spot any significant macro patterns, but if you were able to recognise any, that is fine. One of the characteristics of a strong uptrend is that top reversal candlestick patterns tend not to hold a good share down for long. Have a look at the number of failed top reversal patterns during this uptrend. It is really quite significant (see figure 9.15).

Figure 9.15: GUD daily

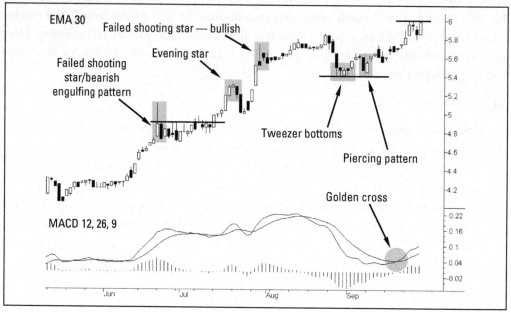

Source: SuperCharts version 4 by Omega Research © 1997.

There is a golden cross on the MACD oscillator on the weekly and daily charts, and the share prices are above their moving average. This is a good bullish sign. The share has just created a higher high, but the MACD histogram has traced to a shallower high. To see this clearly, look at figure 9.16. This sign of divergence seems to be the only sign of future share price weakness, but given the steady trend of this instrument, you may still choose to enter a long position. When you are trading in real life it is rare to find an absolutely perfect set-up and trigger. The breakout on the weekly chart is quite compelling, but some traders may wish to see a clean break above the $6.00 mark before buying to avoid the rounditis phenomenon (see page 173).

Appropriate strategies may include buying the share, buying a call option or warrant or writing a put option. Alternatively, if you are particularly aggravated with someone who you know owns the share, you could let it slip that you heard a nasty rumour that the company was going out of business. This is a cruel, yet effective way of seeking revenge in today's modern society (just joking, of course!).

Figure 9.16: GUD weekly

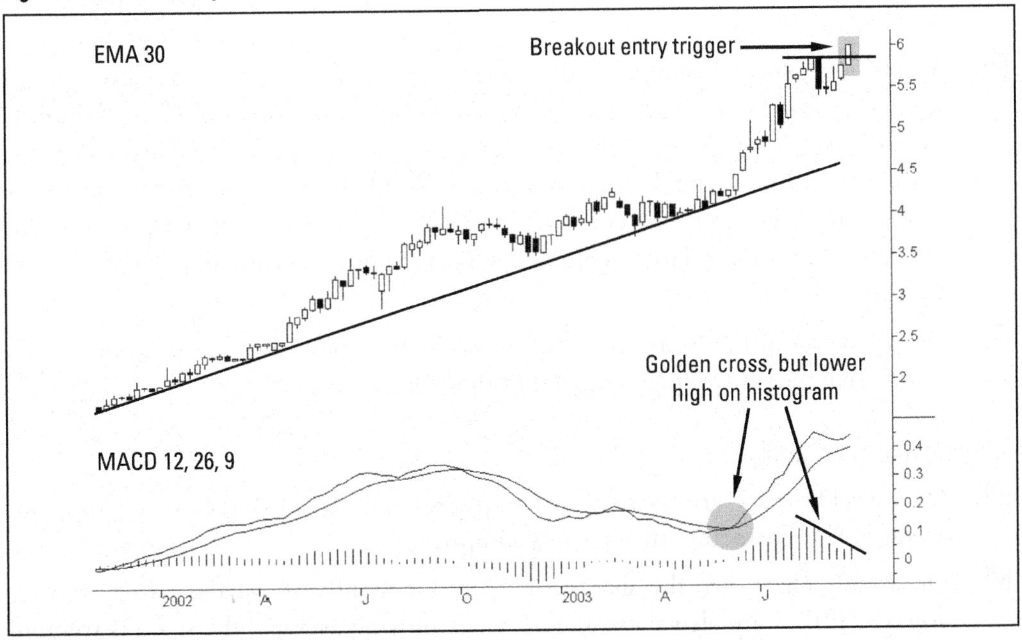
EMA 30
Breakout entry trigger
Golden cross, but lower high on histogram
MACD 12, 26, 9
6
5.5
5
4.5
4
3.5
3
2.5
2
0.4
0.3
0.2
0.1
0
2002
A
J
O
2003
A
J

Source: SuperCharts version 4 by Omega Research © 1997.

Exercise 3

Your uptrend checklist may have included different concepts, but have a look at my lists and see what you can use to build on your own ideas.

Line family

☑ Does the share display a series of progressively higher lows? If so, draw in a trendline below the share price action connecting two lows for a tentative uptrend line, or three lows for a confirmed uptrend line. Start with a weekly chart and then examine the daily chart.

☑ Is each level of resistance easily transcended, only to become a new level of support for future share price activity (change of polarity)?

Volume family

☑ Does volume expand on breakouts and contract on pullbacks? If so, this is a bullish sign. It means that traders are willing to pay higher and higher prices, yet when the share price decreases, they are reluctant to sell their shares.

☑ Is the volume higher when white candles are present than when black candles are present?

☑ Are volume spikes located predominantly above a short-term moving average applied to the volume chart in line with breakouts? (If you don't have the ability to run a moving average over the volume component of the chart, try drawing a horizontal line through roughly the middle of the volume. Then look to see where the spikes are located above and below the line. Spikes above the line indicate increased relative volume; spikes below indicate decreased relative volume levels.)

☑ Do pullbacks in the share price action show the volume spikes drop below the short-term moving average (applied to the volume chart)?

Moving average family

☑ On a weekly chart, are the share prices predominantly above the 30-week moving average? This characteristic indicates an uptrend.

☑ On a daily chart, are the share prices predominantly above the 30-day moving average? If they are also above the 30-week moving average, the share is trending up on a daily basis as well as on a weekly basis. If prices are above the 30-week moving average, yet below the 30-day moving average, the share is likely to be experiencing a counter-trend reversal. Probability suggests that the share will ultimately continue its uptrending behaviour in the near future.

Momentum family

☑ Is a medium-term oscillator (for example, RSI, STO, ROC, SIROC or MACD) rising on a weekly chart and a daily chart? This characteristic is common in a strongly uptrending share.

☑ If the chart of the price action shows a series of higher highs and higher lows, there should be no sign of divergence with the momentum indicator, preferably on either the daily or the weekly chart, to confirm an uptrend. Are there any visible signs of divergence? If divergence is present, this suggests the current prevailing trend is weakening and may be subject to a reversal. (If you need a refresher on the concept of divergence, take another look at chapter 5 or refer to Chris Tate's *The Art of Trading*.)

Pattern family

☑ Is the share breaking upwards from a base formation pattern (stage 1)?

☑ Is the stock displaying continuously higher highs and higher lows, located above the 30-week moving average (stage 2)?

☑ Are there more white than black candles?

☑ Are the white candles longer in length (that is, the range of the real body) than the black candles?

☑ Are there several candlestick tails pointing downward? This is a sign of buyer pressure. It indicates that the share price is likely to go upwards in the following periods.

☑ When there are candlestick tails pointing upwards (indicating seller pressure), does the share price stall briefly, only to propel to prices above these tails on heavy volume?

☑ On a weekly chart, when you stand back from the computer screen (ignoring the name of the chart) and squint at it, is the predominant direction upwards?

Exercise 4

The following points can act as a downtrend checklist.

Line family

☑ Does the share display a series of progressively lower highs? These highs can be connected with a line to show a downtrend. Start with a weekly chart and then examine the daily chart.

☑ Is each level of support easily broken, only to become a new level of resistance by future share price activity (that is, change of polarity)?

Volume family

☑ Compared to when white candles are present, is the volume higher when black candles are present?

☑ Does volume contract on movements upwards and expand on breakouts downwards? If volume decreases on upward moves, this characteristic suggests that the upthrust is running out of puff. If it increases on downward moves, the downtrend is likely to continue.

Moving average family

☑ On a weekly chart, are the share prices predominantly below the 30-week moving average?

☑ On a daily chart, are the share prices predominantly below the 30-day moving average? If they are above the 30-day moving average, but below the 30-week moving average, this represents a counter-trend reversal. If the trend is downwards on a weekly chart, the upward movement is likely to be temporary.

Momentum family

☑ Is a medium-term oscillator (for example, RSI, STO, ROC SIROC or MACD) falling on a weekly chart and a daily chart?

☑ If the share chart shows a series of lower highs, there should be no sign of divergence with a momentum indicator, preferably on both the daily and weekly charts, to confirm a downtrend. Are there any visible signs of divergence?

Pattern family

☑ Is the share breaking downwards from a top formation pattern (stage 3)?

☑ Is the share displaying progressively lower highs and lower lows, located below the 30-week moving average (stage 4)?

☑ Are there more black than white candles?

☑ Are the black candles longer in real body length than the white candles?

☑ Are there several candlestick tails pointing upward (seller pressure)?

☑ When there are candlestick tails pointing downward (indicating buyer pressure), does the share price stall briefly, only to fall below these tails on heavy volume?

☑ On a weekly chart, when you stand back from the computer screen (ignoring the name of the chart), is the predominant direction downwards?

Exercise 5

Have a look at how I have analysed Mincor Resources (MCR) in figures 9.17 to 9.19.

Figure 9.17: MCR weekly

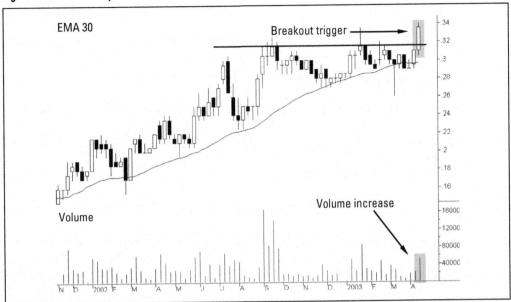

Source: SuperCharts version 4 by Omega Research © 1997.

Figure 9.18: MCR daily

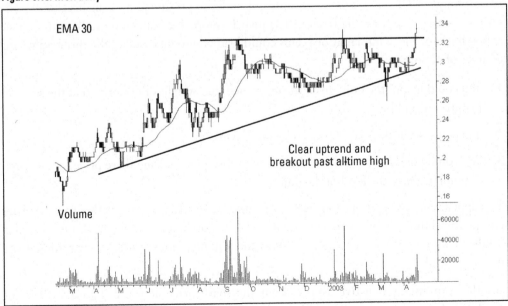

Source: SuperCharts version 4 by Omega Research © 1997.

Figure 9.19: MCR daily close-up

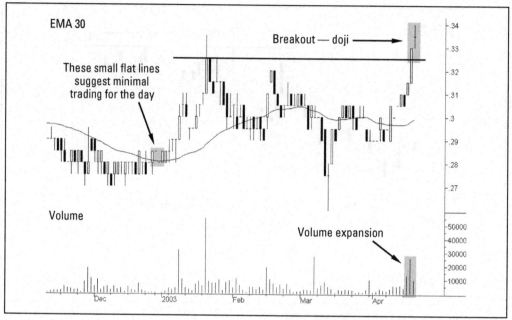

EMA 30

Breakout — doji

These small flat lines suggest minimal trading for the day

Volume

Volume expansion

Source: SuperCharts version 4 by Omega Research © 1997.

Even though MCR is clearly in an uptrend and has produced a clean breakout trade on the weekly chart, the daily chart has just developed a doji candlestick pattern (see appendix A for more information). This could lead you to take one of the three following courses of action:

1   You could ignore the doji, given the overwhelming weight of evidence that the share is in uptrend, and buy it.

2   You could see if the share retraced before buying it.

3   You could purchase the share if there was a subsequent closing share price, or any sign of trading, above the level of the doji.

The appearance of the doji does not mean that you walk away from this type of share completely, but it might mean a momentary hesitation before buying it. Remember that candlesticks are only short-term indicators and will help finesse your entry timing if you use them well.

Another potentially negative aspect about the share price action in figure 9.19 is the perilously low volume on several of the days.

There are three ways to handle this situation:

1 Walk away from the opportunity.

2 Put less capital towards this trade because of the liquidity risk.

3 Use the same amount of capital that you usually would, but be prepared to experience some difficulty and slippage when it comes time to sell.

The course of action you will follow is your choice.

If you had chosen to buy MCR, figure 9.20 below shows you the result of your trade.

Figure 9.20: MCR weekly

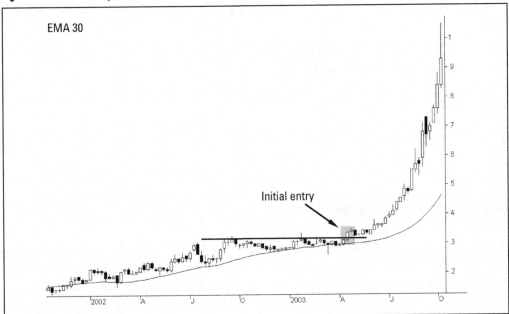

Source: SuperCharts version 4 by Omega Research © 1997.

It is possible to recognise trends early in the process and commit capital towards a trade. It's just a matter of attuning your eye to potential buy signals and backing your analysis. This trade is one of the more profitable ones I am holding at the time of writing. All you need is a couple of these types of trades per year and it can make an incredible difference to the performance of your portfolio. Other people are making money out of shares that look like this, so why not you?

Exercise 6

Have a look at the following charts (figures 9.21 to 9.24) to see how I have analysed this share.

Figure 9.21: CDO weekly

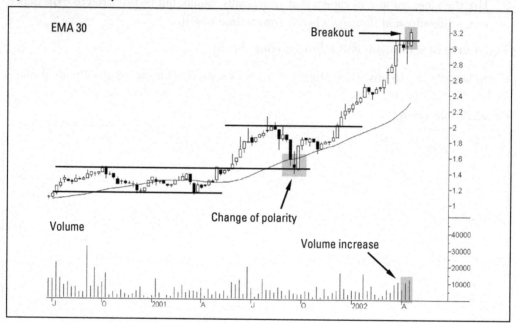

Source: SuperCharts version 4 by Omega Research © 1997.

I have to tell you that when I came across this opportunity, I thought I was onto a winner. The trend was clearly upwards on the weekly and daily charts. Higher lows and higher highs meant that the bulls were in control. There was no sign of divergence, and there was even a golden cross on the MACD oscillator. Lots of white candles were present and the volume on these bullish candles added a lot of strength to the apparent uptrend. Any black candle activity was easily overcome by bullish enthusiasm. What a little beauty, right?

Figure 9.22: CDO daily

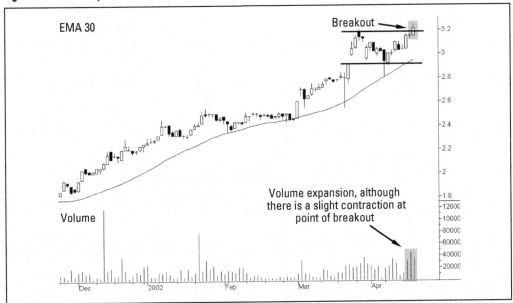

Source: SuperCharts version 4 by Omega Research © 1997.

Figure 9.23: CDO weekly

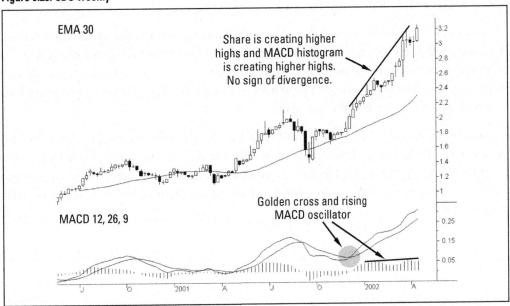

Source: SuperCharts version 4 by Omega Research © 1997.

Figure 9.24: CDO daily

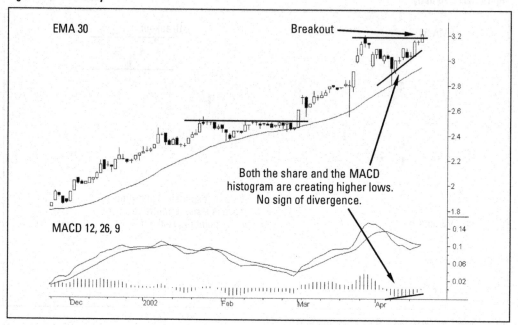

EMA 30   Breakout

Both the share and the MACD
histogram are creating higher lows.
No sign of divergence.

MACD 12, 26, 9

Source: SuperCharts version 4 by Omega Research © 1997.

Wrong! The result of all of my careful analysis is figure 9.25.

As you can see, the breakout was not sustained. Almost as soon as the signal was received, the share fell from the sky! So, what do you do? If you've planned an exit strategy in advance, then you will be fine. If not, you can hold on for the ride and hope the darned thing recovers. You may be in for a long wait — not every share rebounds. Some head for bedrock and are never heard from again.

This share eventually did regain its bullish form, but it took a while (see figure 9.26). You wouldn't have wanted to hold your breath! This is why the concept of a stop loss is so important. The next chapter will cover stop losses in much more detail so you can react defensively when the share that you have just bought ceases to co-operate with your initial view.

Figure 9.25: CDO daily

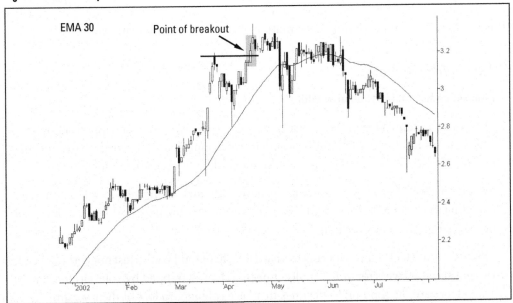

Source: SuperCharts version 4 by Omega Research © 1997.

Figure 9.26: CDO weekly

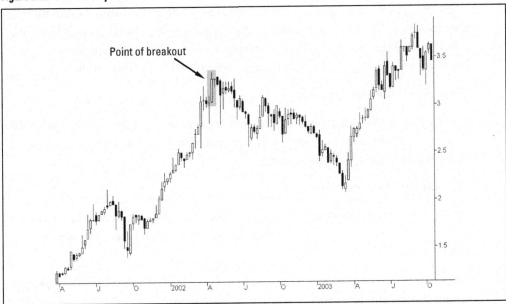

Source: SuperCharts version 4 by Omega Research © 1997.

Now that we are at the end of this chapter, you should be capable of emitting a bolt of mental energy that could stun next door's cat. If, however, you have not quite reached this lofty level, keep persisting. It's a matter of continually practising your skills.

Psychology Secrets

Mindset crimes robbing you of wealth

We live in a skeptical age. We've learned not to trust. We've been ripped off before. Our leaders have lied to us, new scandals are popping up on a daily basis and the companies we used to believe in are falling over like fir trees being logged.

We're on alert 24/7. No wonder we have difficulty rising above all of this and excelling as traders. We're scared we'll get our fingers burned, and we're wary as all heck. Scared money never wins.

However, if you feel you're working too hard for a living and you're just not getting ahead, I've got some answers for you. You don't need to feel so trapped by your circumstances again. Here are the top mindset crimes that I see robbing traders of their wealth.

1 We are stressed out of our minds

As previously discussed in chapter 4, we're plugged in to every electronic device, every blog, every newspaper . . . We're working long hours, tied to our mobile phones and are never alone long enough to gain some clarity in our lives. We jump around the place like cats following a laser pointer. Our attention spans have become shorter than a hyperactive teenager with an Xbox addiction.

Does any of this sound familiar?

You need to unplug, even just for a morning per week. I guarantee you that you'll gain more enthusiasm, and approach your problems with a different mindset if you just give yourself a chance to recover.

2 We want instant results

This is why farmers do so well as traders. They know that it takes a while to bring in the harvest, and if you skip one step of the preparation phase, the whole crop will be ruined.

It's not your fault that you expect trading to be easy. We're bombarded by people selling this dream. However, it really is only a dream.

3 We feel unworthy

We are terrified of making the wrong decision. Why? Because we don't want to show the world how we feel inside when we're lying in bed, alone, at night in the silence. We don't want our actions to reveal who we feel that we really are.

This one emotion drives us to save face.

I don't know about you, but frankly, I've got a bucketload of weaknesses. However, unless we train our subconscious to feel worthy, we'll never achieve what we really deserve in life. We'll be drained of the energy needed to seek out the answers to our problems, and find the people who can really help us excel.

By focusing on reading this book, you're taking a step in the right direction. You're showing that you have what it takes to excel as a trader.

So far in this workbook we have focused on defining trends and using triggers to enter into a position. Even though this is incredibly important to give you the confidence to trade, to profit from the sharemarket you will need a few other tools. System design and an understanding of psychology is essential. Keep reading to see how you can round out your trading education.

10
System development secrets

There's more to trading than just diagnosing the trend. It's time you looked at your entire trading system and filled in some of the blanks so you can trade like a machine.

PEOPLE ARE ATTRACTED TO THE MARKETS because they want to make money. They have high expectations about making this money using skills and techniques developed through other experiences. Just because you're a cardiac, orthopaedic, paediatric brain surgeon who works for NASA in your spare time doesn't mean you will instantly be a master trader.

Traders love the thought of being totally free from a boss, where their time is their own. It's an exhilarating, heady combination. This honeymoon period will last for as long as their accounts are not in *drawdown*. This may take a single trade or many trades, however, drawdown is inevitable. Drawdown occurs when your trading account value is less than the highest value that it reached (which is usually the opening balance when first starting out). Things generally get worse from this point on, as the novice trader wrestles with his emotions, the market, the broker and even his tools. This generally leads to an outcome which can account for all the trading mistakes and losses that follow — inconsistency.

All traders should aspire to consistency. Of course you must have a trading plan that sets out your financial goals and establishes why you are taking on the role of active investor. You should also have some personal development goals. With respect to trading, your personal development goal must be to become consistent. This is a requirement of many other pursuits, including all competitive sports.

Consistency is required when deciding the conditions under which you enter and exit trades, how much capital you commit to each trade, what markets you trade and how many open trades you monitor. Other considerations include how much time you will allocate to analysis, trade management and your trading paperwork, when you do these tasks and how they fit into your daily schedule. The list goes on.

The best weapon for beating indecision and achieving consistency is the development of a trading plan.

Achieving consistency is no mean feat. As trader John Hayden states: 'Indecisive traders will always produce inconsistent behaviour and, consequently, inconsistent profits'. The best weapon for beating indecision and achieving consistency is the development of a trading plan. Your trading plan will include answers to many questions, such as, 'What trading system will I use?'

Other aspects that need to be considered when writing your trading plan are covered more completely in other texts, including my book *Trading Secrets*.

In this chapter we will investigate trading system development.

Developing a trading system

When developing a trading system, or indeed, your overall trading plan, your aim is to be consistent. Consistent methods can be measured and repeated; inconsistency cannot.

A trading system typically includes three components: the entry/exit methodology, risk management and money management:

1   The *entry/exit methodology* deals with the techniques you will employ to enter/exit your trades.

2   *Risk management* deals with your risk profile. Your risk profile takes into consideration how much you are prepared to lose on a trade before you can no longer hold on, or how much of your portfolio you are prepared to lose before you stop trading altogether (that is, maximum portfolio drawdown). How much financial pain can you bear before you throw in the towel? The idea is to establish your trading approach so that you have very little chance of reaching such a point.

3   *Money management* deals with how much capital you invest in each trade as your portfolio value fluctuates. You must calculate how much of your capital to invest in each position. This is called *position size*.

We will discuss each of these components in turn.

Often traders aspire to being discretionary. These traders are successful when they use discretion consistently. Those who do not master consistency remain in the trading wilderness for years until, eventually, they give up because of a lack of trading funds or too many emotionally painful experiences. Rather than seek the freedom or confusion of trading on a whim, a good goal is to become a *mechanical trader* so you can trade like a machine. Mechanical traders apply a strict set of trading rules and never deviate from them. They do the same thing over and over again, just the way a machine would if it was capable of trading. Machines need to follow specific rules, and have no tolerance for ambiguity. Relying on a set of unambiguous rules will also keep your trading unemotional, which is essential to your wellbeing. Mechanical traders implement rules based on entry/exit signals, risk management and money management in all situations, without question. Every detail of the trade has been planned in advance.

1 Entry/exit methodology

This book is mainly focused on entry signals to use when trading shares, as well as leveraged instruments. You do not have enough information to start trading if this is all that you understand about putting money into the sharemarket. Even though it is essential to establish your own personal set-ups and triggers, you must also consider the other major aspects of a trading plan, or your success will be short-lived. Entry signals will only help you to engage trades with a high probability of success. They will not tell you how to exit or how much money to place into a trade.

Entry signals will only help you to engage trades with a high probability of success. They will not tell you how to exit or how much money to place into a trade.

If you would like some more assistance with these concepts, read my book *Trading Secrets*, which goes into each of these topics in-depth. My *Candlestick Charting Home Study Course* available through my website will provide even more trading insights and supplies you with specific exercises to complete.

Exit signals

In *24 Essential Lessons for Investment Success* William J. O'Neill stated:

> **Investors spend most of their time deciding what stock to buy. They spend little if any time thinking about when and under what circumstances their stock should be sold. This is a serious mistake.**

Before you place your order, you must decide on where you will exit. I advocate that you use a stop loss to capture your profits and avoid large losses.

The four main ways to set a stop loss are listed below:

1 *Pattern-based* stop-loss traders will exit trades if the share breaks downwards through a trendline, for example, or a significant line of support. Throughout this workbook I have given you many examples of appropriate places to position a pattern-based stop loss.

2 *Technical indicators* can be used as a stop. For example, a dead cross of two moving averages may trigger an exit.

3 *Per cent drawdown* or retracement methods suggest that if the instrument drops in value by a set percentage (for example, 7 per cent) then an exit should be made.

4 *Volatility-based* stops rely on significant changes in volatility past a pre-defined level to trigger an exit.

To exit a position in the sharemarket, you can choose to implement one of these types of stops or even a hybrid of any of these methods. Derivatives traders can use all of these types of stops and more. If you are unfamiliar with any of these techniques, it is essential that you research them to find out the most appropriate stop loss for your own requirements.

Successful technical traders have a defined set of rules to enter a position, to exit from the market promptly at the first sign of a downtrend, or to preserve their capital after the share or derivative has retraced in value. Some traders even set auto-stop losses so that when the share price reaches a certain level, the computer software exits their positions automatically. If you are struggling with the discipline required to take an exit when your stop has been hit, this is probably a good alternative.

It actually doesn't really matter what techniques you use for entering and exiting positions in the market, provided that over a large sample of trades using the selected techniques, you end up with more cash in your trading account than your starting capital! The more cash added and the longer the cash accumulates in your account, the better the method.

What matters is that the total winnings add up to more than the total losses net of trading costs.

While trading through the large sample of trades, it also does not matter how many winning trades you had compared to the number of losing trades. What matters is that the total winnings add up to more than the total losses net of trading costs. It also matters that the techniques for entry and exit which you deployed in the market are able to be repeated in the future so you can continue to use those techniques to generate more profits.

Deciding when you will take profits means that you have gone a long way towards ensuring your success as a trader. You could apply a trailing stop loss, or apply profit targets. The decision is up to you.

The question is: how can you determine whether an entry and exit combination over a large sample of trades will result in a net profit *before* you start trading it? For some ideas regarding how to effectively back-test your trading system, have a look at appendix B.

It's also important not to let your trading results dictate how you feel about a potential transaction. A good trade will be made by following your trading plan to the letter, regardless of a profit or loss result. It is a sign of a disciplined trader. If you are having trouble developing your own system, I suggest that you copy the ideas of other traders or authors you relate to. After you have tried out their concepts, you can make alterations to suit your situation. Duplicate before you innovate.

A good trade will be made by following your trading plan to the letter, regardless of a profit or loss result. It is a sign of a disciplined trader.

2 Risk management

Risk management is about limiting the size of loss trades. It also has to do with limiting the amount of drawdown that could result from a portfolio of open positions in the market and from recently closed trades.

Your risk management rules and processes should be closely aligned with the entry/exit methodology you design. Obviously, there will be less risk if you take medium- to long-term, non-leveraged positions rather than short-term, leveraged positions. Rules need to be customised accordingly.

Your risk management rules should not only match your entry/exit methodology, they should also match your risk profile. Are you a risk taker or are you more risk averse? A good methodology should allow risk to be customised to reflect a trader's risk appetite, which will change over time.

The sorts of indicators that can be used to assess risk include overall market direction, sector direction, liquidity, traded volume, market volatility, stock volatility, stock direction and market capitalisation. Using these tools you can construct unambiguous rules that assess risk as high, medium or low, or even according to a scale of one to ten.

Risk management rules should also determine how much risk you can take with your overall portfolio funds. This involves determining how much drawdown you can expect in certain market conditions in the future. Compiling portfolios of historical trades will give you an excellent idea of what drawdowns are likely.

3 Money management

Once risk is assessed it can be managed by adjusting the amount of capital you commit to each trade and/or to the market.

Your trade size should be determined by how much risk you are prepared to take. Your portfolio value and other factors will also come into the position sizing calculation, such as the amount of leverage you are trading with and the risk assessment for each individual trade.

As a rule, when your portfolio value increases, so do your position sizes. If your portfolio value decreases into drawdown, your position sizes should also decrease. Also, the higher the risk assessment, the smaller your position size should be.

The objective of money management is to define how much capital you should commit to each trade to consistently generate portfolio profits.

Write your trading plan for someone else

Want some help writing your trading plan? Well, it seems that solving a problem is easier when it belongs to someone else. So perhaps you could pretend that you're writing a plan for a special trader in your life, rather than for yourself.

A study published in the *Personality and Social Psychology Bulletin* suggests you are more likely to succeed if you believe a complex problem belongs to someone else.

Psychologists asked 137 students to picture themselves stuck in a tower or to picture a stranger stuck in a tower, with the only means of escape being a rope that doesn't go all the way to the ground.

Sixty-six per cent found the solution in the 'help someone else' group, compared with 48 per cent who pictured themselves in the tower.

What would you do to get yourself or someone else out of the tower? Bonus good karma points if you get it right. (Turn to the end of this chapter to read the answer.)

Psychology secrets

Five hurdles between you and trading success

To grow, you must first feel safe. If you're in a bad personal situation, take heart. You can climb out of hell one inch at a time. First of all though, surround yourself with people who make you feel safe. People who think support doesn't count simply haven't progressed very far in life.

Sure you have to be willing to stand on your own two feet, but every successful person I've ever known has had at least one person who has cheered them on in the past.

If you don't have someone who supports your vision for the future, draw on my belief in you. Rarely have I ever met a person who didn't have the seeds of trading ability within them. All it takes is someone to recognise this, draw it out of you, and to cheer for your successes. If you don't have a cheerleader in your life, let that role fall to me.

Here are five hurdles standing between you and trading success:

1 Quitting too soon

 You can't win if you don't finish anything.

2 Who you listen to

 If you don't start listening to people who have already achieved what you want in life, you'll be stuck in exactly the same place as you are currently. You are a sum total of the books you read, the people you hang out with and the educational sources you follow. Change your inputs and you'll change your outcome.

3 Procrastination

 Either you have a lack of clarity about where you're headed and what it takes to succeed, or ... you know but you're just delaying getting going. Both are mindset crimes. Both flaws will mean you won't progress.

(continued)

Psychology secrets (cont'd)

4   Believing you don't deserve success

Feeling unworthy is how the majority of sharemarket losers feel. Alter this, or suffer the consequences. You deserve success. You deserve the best in life. Now, get your actions to follow and you'll hardly recognise the results that this brings into your life. Work out what you need to unlearn to achieve the results you desire.

5   A trading system that doesn't work, isn't complete or doesn't function over a wide range of market conditions. This, my friend, is a huge one. Sure, you can get your mindset as bright as a sparkling diamond in the sun, but if you don't have the strategies to back you up—you'll never be a sharemarket superstar.

Sure, most people quit too early, feel like a failure and grapple with their own mindset. Ever wondered whether the reason for this is simply because they're just not applying themselves to a trading system that works? Ever felt that that creeping doubt you're feeling about trading well is justified because you actually don't have a system that kicks butt when it comes to results?

If you're like me, for the first few years of trading, I felt like I was stumbling around in the dark, clutching at straws, getting ready for a windfall that just never quite came. Frustrating, isn't it?

Know this: the basic principles in trading of entry, exit and position sizing do the heavy lifting in the sharemarket—always and forever.

Conquer these principles and you too will be able to trade any market around the world. If you'd like my ongoing support as you learn, make sure you register for my free monthly newsletter at www.tradinggame.com.au. I'll give you a feast of hints and tips every single month so that you can be a sharemarket winner, this year and every year. Plus, I'll give you my trading plan template which distils the essential areas you must consider as you write your plan.

Summary

System design can be personally rewarding, but don't kid yourself that it is a simple task. By reading this book, you have proved that you are in the small minority that even attempt trading-systems design at all. The great majority of traders start trading the markets based on nothing more than a newsletter or a broker's advice. I wonder what the exit methodology of the newsletter might be? And what are the money management rules that should be integrated with the broker's stock tips?

If the concept of controlling your risk makes sense to you, hopefully you will realise how futile it is engaging the market based on newsletter, magazine, broker, chat forum or other tips. In order to achieve the consistency required to make money in the market over the long term, you must have a robust entry / exit methodology integrated with risk management and money management.

If you are feeling overwhelmed by the task of doing all this yourself, then at least take comfort in the fact that you now know what to look for in a methodology that is available for purchase. You may consider this if you haven't the time to design and back-test your own approach to trading the sharemarket. Gary Stone from www.sharewealthsystems.com.au has designed several successful methodologies for the Australian markets. I would like to thank Gary for his assistance in writing this chapter, as well his ongoing support of my trading concepts over the past several years.

The answer

The answer to the 'stuck in a tower' question on page 260 is that you would have needed to split the rope lengthwise, and tie all of the pieces together.

The next chapter will help you to consolidate your knowledge of different trading vehicles such as options and short selling.

11

The short and the long of it

Markets have a habit of reversing trend and fouling up your plans of attaining a neat and easy profit. To last in this game, you need to make money when the market is going down as well as up. Keep reading as all will be revealed...

PROFESSIONALS MAKE MONEY REGARDLESS of the market direction. This chapter will discuss strategies to help you apply your knowledge of share price direction. It will also help you to benefit from strategies involving leverage.

How to make money out of a downtrend

Most people know how to make money in a bull market, but few know how to profit from a bear market. Let's have a look at four methods you can use to profit from a downtrending market.

1 Act on your stops

Aldous Huxley stated, 'Facts do not cease to exist because they are ignored'. If you recognise that a bear market is in place, your first step should be to review your existing portfolio. Take a close look at where you have set your stop losses, and make sure that these levels are consistent with your trading plan. If your stop is hit, exit immediately. Do not 'hope' that your shares will recover. Traders tend to hold onto shares that are trending down, yet prematurely sell shares that are trending up. This trait ensures that you will stay among the mediocre masses and never fight your way to the top of the class.

2 Write call options

This chapter of the workbook is designed to give you a brief understanding of options, rather than a full explanation of how to trade them. Once you've worked out how to trade shares, you may feel ready to apply leverage and take a walk on the wild side. Before you dive in, read my book *The Secret of Writing Options*. These will give you everything you need to know to get started trading these tasty little morsels.

The options market allows you to either buy options (also known as option taking) or write options. There are two types of options—call options and put options. Table 11.1 summarises which strategy is appropriate to profit based on the sharemarket direction.

Table 11.1: options and market direction

	Uptrending share	Downtrending share	Sideways trending share
Call options	Buy	Write	Write
Put options	Write	Buy	Write

In this chapter we will look at each of these strategies. This will put the odds in your favour of choosing the correct tactic based on your analysis of the share price direction.

Generally, this information can also be applied to the warrants market as a warrant is essentially a long-dated option. One of the key differences between these two instruments is that you cannot *write* a warrant. Writing means that you are selling to initiate a transaction. Both warrants and options are known as derivatives.

Writing a call option assumes that you have a sideways or downtrending view on the future share price action prior to the expiry date of the option. There are two types of call options—a covered call and a naked call. A *covered call* is where you own the underlying stock. If you have written a call with an option strike price greater than your share purchase price and you are exercised (that is, you are told to sell your shares), you will realise a capital gain on the share. This is in addition to the premium (for example, 40¢ a share) that you received for writing the call. This is the safest way to begin in the options market. Be aware that you should only write options against shares that you are willing to sell, or you will need to take defensive actions to remove yourself from risk before you are exercised. By consistently writing calls over shares that you own, you will receive a cash flow similar to receiving a dividend cheque in the mail every month.

Be aware that you should only write options against shares that you are willing to sell ...

To profit from a sideways-moving or downtrending share, you could write a *naked call*. This means that you have written a call option without actually owning the underlying share. As long as the share price stays below the strike price of the option, you will get to keep the full premium you were paid by the option taker. If the share price goes above the option strike price, you are likely to be exercised, and told to deliver shares to sell to the option taker. As you don't own these shares, you will be required to buy them at market value, and then deliver them to the option taker. This strategy is best reserved for professional traders, or traders who fully understand the risks involved.

Bought options depreciate in value, right up until a defined expiry date. This is called *time decay*. Once you have sold an option to another trader (that is, written an option), if all other things remain equal, the option will expire worthless. You will have the premium money in your bank account and the buyer of the option will be holding a worthless asset. In fact, up to 80 per cent of people lose money when *buying* options. However, if you understand the dynamics of buying options, even though your hit rate is often low, the amount of money you can make from the few trades that do pan out can be astronomical.

Exposure

When I first started writing naked options on National Australia Bank (NAB), I reached a startling conclusion. I was initially presented with a choice. Firstly, I could choose to write five close-to-the-money option contracts where I would seemingly take on more risk as the share price could easily break through my strike price. Alternatively, I could write 28 option contracts that were miles out-of-the-money, yet receive the same amount of money overall...For a brief moment I thought I was a genius! Can you see the problem with writing more contracts but receiving the same amount of money in total?

If you can't see the problem with this, then stop writing options immediately! There is one concept that you must learn about before you progress—EXPOSURE.

By writing many more cheap option contracts, it seems like your trade has a higher probability of success. However, what happens if a huge announcement is made, and the share price goes ballistic? Your exposure sets you up to be completely blown out of the water! Rather than being liable for 5000 NAB, I would have become responsible for 28 000 NAB if the trade had backfired. Yikes! (At that stage, one options contract covered 1000 shares. Now though, one contract covers 100 shares.)

Sometimes at the outset of a trading career, the risks can seem as though they do not apply to us—we are strong and brave and bulletproof. The market had better remember this and not cross us. Unfortunately, the trading world doesn't work that way and, often, the market will provide a proverbial kick to our soft underbelly to ensure that we don't repeat our past errors of being too sure of ourselves.

3 Buy put options or warrants

Writing options involves collecting a small fixed premium, yet incurring a theoretically unlimited loss. Buying options or warrants has a lower probability of success, yet due to the leveraged nature of this strategy, the rewards from the 20 per cent of trades that do work may outweigh the losses from the 80 per cent of losing trades.

In the options market, as the share price drops, the price of put options increases, often very dramatically. That is why you can make significant profits by buying options on downtrending shares. If you buy a short-dated option, then time decay will erode your profit. For this reason, it is preferable to buy an option that expires in at least three or more months, and exit before the final month.

Novice option buyers are particularly attracted to 'cheap' options which, ironically, have very little probability of appreciating in value. This assists in explaining why a vast majority of option buyers end up net losers in the market. In terms of risk/reward and probability, buyers of low-priced options make a trade with a low probability of success, where the rewards are high and the risk is minimal.

Why are they cheap?

Traders often buy options that have nominal time to expiry, which means that their bought asset is depreciating like a time bomb. The majority of options expire worthless and are only ever traded once. People don't like to be 'wrong'. They would rather sweep their bad trade under the carpet, along with any remaining value they could claim by closing out their position, than confess that the trade didn't work. There is no room for this type of ego in trading.

They would rather sweep their bad trade under the carpet, along with any remaining value they could claim by closing out their position, than confess that the trade didn't work.

Often, naïve traders underestimate the strength of a move required to impact the price of the option. These unfortunate souls truly believe that even though BHP may have only increased by 10¢ throughout the course of the month, it could potentially jump up $10 within three days (because that is when their option expires). Magically, BHP should recognise the skill of the trader with the deal in play and co-operate!

Brokers often promote cheap options to buy that are a long way out-of-the-money, which severely impacts upon the likelihood of success. If a broker is receiving commission based on the number of contracts you are buying, rather than your overall exposure—the desire for their children to experience the benefits of a private education just may stand in their way of giving you effective advice. Don't rely on your broker to guide you in this area. Stand on your own two feet and take responsibility for your future by learning more about options, and how to identify trades with a higher probability of success.

Brokers may inspire you to buy cheap options with a small amount of time before expiry because they are much more likely to fulfil their own personal goals. By turning over these types of trades quickly and efficiently, they can convert your trading capital to brokerage with lightning speed.

Buying at- or in-the-money options with three or more months to expiry will often seem like a more expensive trade, but it is more likely to eventuate in a profit.

Don't kid yourself that the market will reward your lack of understanding about value. If you're a cheap option addict, you'd be better off going in the next Super Draw with all of the other Saturday-night hopefuls. When you next see that amazing bargain option at 2¢, ask yourself why it is that price. Maybe there is a reason you haven't discovered. Perhaps you are about to buy an option that is actually worth that small amount, not an option that has been mistakenly underpriced by market dynamics.

4 Short sell

Short selling is another way we can profit in a downtrending market. Usually when we buy a share, we are hoping to buy it at $5.00, for example, and sell it at $10.00 at a later date. Short selling performs this same process, but in reverse. In effect, you borrow shares that you do not own, sell them with the expectation that the share price will drop, then buy them back at a later date. Your profit or loss is the difference between your sell price, and your buy price—so if the share price drops, you make a profit. If the price increases, you will incur a loss. It is actually quite a simple concept, yet less than 1 per cent of stock transactions in Australia are executed utilising this method. In rough terms, only the Top 200 shares in the ASX can be short-sold.

In the majority of cases, a leverage of 5:1 applies as brokerage firms usually require you to lodge 20 per cent of the value of the initial share price in a cash management account. Be aware that you will be *margin called* and required to place more money into this account if the share price trends upwards (against your initial view). Remember that these strategies must be used with shares that have sufficient liquidity, or you will have trouble extracting yourself from the position if the market suddenly turns bullish. This is absolutely critical, as there is nothing worse than being trapped in a trade due to lack of volume.

The other way to short sell is to use CFDs (contracts for difference). You can make money using CFDs whether there is an uptrend or a downtrend, and because it is a leveraged trade, you'll get a lot of bang for your buck. It's worth investigating because a lot of traders have decided to swing over into the CFD market rather than the options market. It's a simpler trade in comparison to an options trade and I'm sure you'll really enjoy them as an instrument. They are basically a virtual share, so they're easier to understand than other more complicated instruments. You can see my broker recommendations to trade them on my website — www.tradingsecrets.com.au.

Options or short selling?

Now that we've discussed the basics behind each strategy, let's have a look at some of the factors you should consider before you decide whether to trade options or short sell.

Length of your view

A significant benefit with short selling is that, unlike the options and warrants market, there is no time decay issue. Options and warrants decrease in value as they approach their expiration date.

> *A significant benefit with short selling is that, unlike the options and warrants market, there is no time decay issue.*

Time decay works in favour of the option writer, but against the option buyer. This is essential to understand when assessing whether to short sell, or to use an option to make money out of a downtrend.

Some brokers purport to only allow short-sold positions to be active for a limited time period — for example three days — before they will close your position. This is not an ideal situation, and I would query this condition with your broker.

Strength of the move

Another consideration is the expected strength of the move. If a strong move downwards is expected, writing a call does not often represent significant profit potential. It will result in a small fixed profit, regardless of the strength of the ensuing move in the expected direction. The logical choices would be to buy a put option or to short sell.

The majority of option buyers are unsophisticated in the markets and see leverage as a way to 'get rich quick'. Unfortunately, trading options well relies on a greater level of skill than that possessed by the average share trader. Most traders only look at direction, but options require consideration of several components, such as:

- direction
- type of option
- time decay implications
- volatility analysis
- liquidity issues.

Usually only the top 15 or so shares by market capitalisation have sufficient volume for options to be traded effectively. If I had the ideal options set-up and there was enough liquidity, I would buy a put option as opposed to short selling the share. The leveraged returns are exponentially superior, and the trade is often concluded in a shorter timeframe.

However, if the option trade I am considering does not provide an ideal combination of all of the factors listed above, I walk away from using options as a strategy for that particular instrument. There is no point in entering into an option trade unless the set-up is ideal.

There is no point in entering into an option trade unless the set-up is ideal.

If an option trade is not appropriate, and you still believe that the likely future direction of the share is downwards, consider short selling the share. Aim to understand and perfect the process of shorting with your first few trades, rather than trying to make excessive amounts of money. As stated by Mark Boucher, trader and author of *The Hedge Fund Edge,* 'Don't concentrate on winning; concentrate on the process that creates winning'.

Dividend considerations

When you are learning to short sell, don't short anything where the underlying share is due to pay a dividend. You may end up being responsible for the amount of this dividend and, perhaps, any associated franking credits.

Option prices have the dividend price plus the franking credits factored into the premium. Dividends have implications for in-the-money written calls as there is vested interest on the part of the buyer to exercise these positions, call the shares away from you and pocket the dividend. Prior to writing calls, as well as prior to entering a short-sold position, always check the ex-dividend schedule — or face the consequences. With CFDs, you'll find that any dividends are cash-adjusted to your account, so keep your eye on when those dividends are due for this type of trade as well.

Pyramiding

If you are an experienced short seller, you could take advantage of the leverage offered via a short sale and pyramid aggressively. Pyramiding adds capital to a winning position and is a very effective strategy when implemented with care.

Learning to pyramid effectively is an essential skill. As stated by Bill Lipschutz in a Market Wizards interview:

> **It's not enough to simply have the insight to see something apart from the rest of the crowd, you also need to have the courage to act on it and to stay with it.**

Shares tend to increase in value slowly, but are subject to quick and dramatic price falls. For this reason, you may find that you will pyramid into your short sold positions more quickly than your long share positions. It may also mean that your average hold time will decrease significantly for your short-sold positions compared to your bought share positions. For those beginning with short selling as a strategy, I suggest that you initially avoid pyramiding. Wait until you've managed to take off your 'L plates' before progressing to more complex strategies. Consistent profitability is important to achieve, prior to innovation.

Shares tend to increase in value slowly, but are subject to quick and dramatic price falls.

Few traders operate a pyramiding strategy in relation to option positions. Because of the effect of time decay, and the whipsaw nature of the options market, pyramiding becomes a less likely proposition. For this reason, options operate best in a quickly trending, clearly defined market, when your entry and exit timing is impeccable.

With any strategy comparison, it is important that you give yourself time to learn about the benefits and drawbacks. As stated by J. Peter Steidlmayer, Chicago Board of Trade floor trader:

> **Remember that you can learn a lot about trading from your mistakes. When you make a mistake — and you will — don't dwell on the negative. Take your lesson and keep going.**

Some definitions

Let's define some important concepts.

Going long means that you are buying to initiate a transaction. If you are *long* the share, this means you are buying the share in the hope that the future will reveal higher prices and allow you to capture a profit. If you are *short* the share, this means you are selling to initiate a transaction. Short sellers sell shares and profit from buying back their position when the share has dropped in value.

Short sellers sell shares and profit from buying back their position when the share has dropped in value.

The situation is slightly more complex when you add options to the equation. You can be long the share, but short the option. This means that you want the share to go up, but you are selling to initiate a written put option position. If you are short the share but long the option, you want the share price to drop and you are buying to initiate an option position. The appropriate type of option to buy if you are expecting the share price to plummet is a put option. The terms long and short mean that you are buying or selling to initiate a transaction—they don't refer to the share price direction.

It gets a bit confusing, doesn't it?! As with all bits of jargon, the more you are exposed to them, the more their use will become second nature to you. Now that you are a little more familiar with how to trade a bear market, let's discuss the ways you can capitalise on a share displaying upward-trending behaviour.

How to make money out of an uptrend

Most traders are intuitively more comfortable with making money from a share that is trending upwards. Let's have a look at the four strategies you can use to make money from a bull market.

1 Close out your written call, bought put and short-sold positions

If the trend is not unravelling as you were expecting, get out!

2 Buy the share or CFD

If a share is trending upwards, one of the main ways you can capitalise is to buy the share, or the equivalent CFD. The majority of technical analysts tend to be 'trend-followers'. They wait for a trend to display a particular direction prior to taking action. For trend-followers, there are a few simple rules. The first is, if a share is trending up, buy it. The second rule is, if it is going down, sell it. There are some traders who continually try to trade against the prevailing trend. People who trade against the trend will ultimately run out of money and self-destruct.

3 Buy call options or warrants

If the call option buyer's view is correct, and the share increases in value, he can either sell the option at a profit or choose to exercise the option. The buyer has the right to purchase the writer's shares at the strike price (which will represent a lower than current market value). Most players in the options market do not exercise their rights. If their position has co-operated, they sell their options, which have increased in value, to experience a capital gain. An overwhelming majority of options are only ever traded once and then left to expire worthless.

4 Write put options

A put option writer is of the opinion that a share will be trading in a sideways band, or is bullish. The writer is under an obligation to buy the shares from a put option taker at the strike price (if the taker exercises his rights). You could write a put option if you were happy to buy the share at a certain value below the current market price. You could also write a put if you were of the view that the share you are interested in trading would not penetrate a certain price within a certain time period. Most written positions are opened three to six weeks before expiry.

The perfect combination that would encourage me to write a put option, rather than employ an alternative strategy, would be where the option had a limited time to expire in a highly liquid share and option series. Ideally the volatility set-up would suggest the option is overpriced, and that the option is likely to decrease in value. It would also be wise to consider the expected strength of the move. If a strong move upwards is expected, writing a put does not often represent significant profit potential. It will result in a small fixed profit, regardless of the strength of the ensuing move in the expected direction. Buying a call, or the share itself, would capitalise more on a strong move upwards.

Even though these strategy examples provide some ideas about how to make money by backing your view with leverage, the trading world is not so simple in real life. Unfortunately, we are not given a crystal ball as soon as we decide to become a trader.

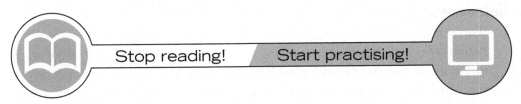

Stop reading! | Start practising!

Trading with leverage is quite a complex area. Fill out the following quiz to check your understanding of the strategies we have discussed so far in this chapter.

Quiz

1 Define short selling.

....

....

2 Describe a signal that would be likely to trigger your entry into a written call position.

....

....

3 How do you plan to exit your short-sale position?

....

....

4 If you observed that BHP is trending upwards strongly, what strategies could you engage to profit?

....

....

Once you've filled out your answers to this quiz, have a look at my suggested answers.

Quiz answers

1   Short selling is similar to buying a share, only the buying/selling order is reversed. Instead of buying a stock and then selling it, you sell the stock first and then buy it back at a later time. Your profit or loss is the difference between your sell price, and your buy price — so if the share price drops, you make a profit. If the price increases, you will incur a loss.

2   This is a personal decision, but any bearish chart pattern, preferably within an existing downtrend, could trigger your entry into a written call position. If you have written a covered call, your stop loss should trigger an exit from your physical position if the share downtrends significantly.

3   Exits can be made on the same basis as the signal required to exit a long position, only in reverse. For example, you could use a volatility stop loss, a pattern-based stop or a bullish technical indicator. Some people use a per cent retracement method.

4   There are several strategies to engage if you observe that a share is uptrending. You should firstly close out any written call, bought put or short-sold position. Acting on a set-up and trigger, you could buy a share, write a put, or buy a call option or warrant.

If you didn't score too well on the quiz, don't be too hard on yourself. You probably just haven't been exposed to these types of concepts before. It can take a while to feel comfortable with leveraged instruments.

If you did score well on the quick quiz, you have my permission to lapse into a temporary euphoric coma before continuing. Congratulations!

A final word

I would not encourage you to jump into a leveraged area if you are not a proficient share trader. Wait until you can control the pony before you hop onto the racehorse. There is no harm in building up your skills before you try out every strategy under the sun. The emotional consequences of trading with leverage can be dire if you are not ready for this arena.

Take the charting techniques you have learned from this book and combine them with an effective exit strategy, a risk management plan and sound money management. Give yourself time to become skilled and consistently profitable with trading shares. Once you have achieved this you can consider using leverage as a part of your overall trading plan.

Psychology secrets

Working without a net

We, as a society, have had our wings clipped. We've become reliant, instead of headstrong, opinionated and free. We've become dependent on hand-outs, instead of hand-ups.

This is true regardless of the political party in power. In your heart, you know I speak the truth.

We are told that the government has our best interests at heart and will protect us. But who truly believes this? I put it to you that this is propaganda. Propaganda to keep the dominant political party in power.

In our society, we have the comfort of knowing that if we fail, the government will step in and we will not starve. However, the effect of this so-called support is far more insidious in nature. We are offered the eroding facade of cradle-to-grave support, regardless of how able-bodied we are, or how intellectually gifted we may be.

However, the fallout from this societal shift has been obscured. Because we've become reliant, we've become complacent. We sit on a couch instead of struggle, fail and then succeed. Our senses are numbed because we no longer have to scramble to survive or excel. We accept mediocrity and do not rally against it.

A world in which you have the freedom to fail is also a world that offers you untold riches when success is achieved. This is the world of traders and I make no apology for it.

I am asking your help to spread the word. Self-reliance, rather than reliance on flawed government systems, is the only way to excel. It is only then that Australians will be what they were born to be: brave, strong and independent.

Summary

- If the share trends against your initial expectations, your first step should be to close out any threatened open positions.

- If you have identified a share that is trending up, you could profit from either buying the share, writing a put option, or buying a call option or warrant. Most people are more comfortable with these types of bull market strategies than the bear market strategies.

- To profit from a bearish downtrending share you could short sell, write a call option, or buy a put option or warrant.

Keep reading to explore some ways to help you develop emotional detachment and improve your trading results.

12

More psychology secrets

Sophisticated traders value their own psychology just as much they do their trading system. Underestimate the importance of your emotions and you'll shoot yourself in the foot.

ONE THING THAT HAS BECOME CLEAR during the Mentor Program that I run with Chris Tate is that people are struggling to put the GFC behind them. It's like some of the mentorees are stuck in the past.

Even though there is every reason to be optimistic about the future and the level of income you can achieve, it's hard to focus on the positive when you keep looking at your mistakes. (And if you haven't started trading yet, you can't tell me that you haven't been influenced by doom and gloom reports about the markets, or rumours about pensioners needing to go back to work to make ends meet.)

I want to address these fears in this chapter and give you a new perspective on how to view this.

If you've found your self-talk is suffering after taking a battering on the markets, I want to remind you that you are not your mistakes.

I love this quote from Stephen Covey: 'Live out of your imagination, not your history'. Look forward, not in your rear view mirror—or you're sure to crash.

Your mistakes are completely separate from who you are as a person. Take pride that you're moving one step closer towards your goals. Don't cripple your future growth by being cruel to yourself because you made a screw up.

Sure, doing the same dumb thing again and again is plain stupid. However, keep in mind that making a number of mistakes once, or even a few times, is part of being a human and part of becoming an exceptional trader.

The fear time bomb

Fear is a crippling emotion. It's a time bomb ready to explode and send your trading results into oblivion. Traders don't just experience fear about the markets, or their own skill levels. They often fear what other people think of them — especially those they live with. This is insidious because it's prefaced by the words, 'I love you ... but ...'

Fear of being judged, disapproved of, criticised or gossiped about has been known to stop grown men in their tracks. People often build themselves prisons, where the bars are their own emotional reactions to other people's disapproval.

Successful people have inoculated themselves against criticism. Their immunity has only grown because they've faced so much of it in their past. True wealth is granted to those who attain power by soldiering on regardless. You see, when you have both money and power — you'll gain independence.

If it's your dream to be a trader, realise that you'll be up against some resistance. Sometimes from those who love you, sometimes from yourself. No great trader ever rose to the top of their equity curve without it. Expect it, and even welcome it as you recognise that you're doing what it takes to get ahead.

If you're the one with the vision for the family, don't you ever give up on your dream.

Be prepared for it and when it comes in the guise of care for your wellbeing, get ready to stick up for what you believe in. If you're the one with the vision for the family, don't you ever give up on your dream. It's people like you who walked on the moon, sailed across the world to discover a new country and founded companies that changed the world. Avoiding toxic people is an essential part of the puzzle as well.

Whingers unite ... and then leave us the hell alone

Have you got someone who is negative and drags you down in your life? The type of person who can create doubt and a little black place in your mind that didn't exist before you started a conversation with them?

Sure, you could argue that because of that person's life, he or she has a reason to carry on and moan. After all, they're really not making enough money/didn't marry the right person/are in the wrong job or cast a hideous reflection in the mirror. You could argue that the people with positive attitudes have less to bitch about because things are going well for them.

Yes, I do see the point in your argument, but it's logically flawed.

The moaners actually focus on the things that are going wrong in their lives. Their situation is likely to be equal, or even better than the bloke with a perpetual smile on his face, or the lady with a good attitude as she goes for chemotherapy.

You've got to be successful in your own mind before success comes your way. Once your thinking changes, so does your reality.

Once your thinking changes, so does your reality.

Actively search out others of the same mould as you. Don't allow yourself to be infected by the venomous words of the serial-whinger. Make a hasty exit if you see one coming towards you ... by running away, arms flailing, hair flying.

Three success squashers

I want you to work on these three success 'squashers' today so you'll be one step closer to achieving your goals.

1   Not being accountable.

    If you don't take responsibility for your own goals and dreams, you just won't make it as a trader.

    Got something you really want to achieve? Tell someone you trust. Get them to check up on you. Get specific. When you become answerable to a mate, you're more likely to slam dunk your goal, rather than just pushing it aside for another month.

2   Over-complicating things.

    Stop over-thinking, over-analysing and over-complicating your objective. Break it down into baby steps, write it down and do step 1 today. If you're always 'about to change your life', then this is your problem. I guarantee it.

    I also guarantee that you'll never freaking well get the results you crave until you complete step 1. You owe it to the people who rely on you. Far out—you owe it to yourself.

Do you really think you have all the time in the world to achieve what you truly desire? Bollocks to that.

None of us know how much time we've got left, so take that first step today. Urgency counts. Winners rush. They don't dawdle.

3   Relying on others for a pat on the back.

Expect more from yourself and less from others. Provide your own rewards. The need for approval is exhausting and unnecessary. Relieve others from their duty on this one. Give yourself the accolades you've been craving.

Time to kick you out of the nest

Michael Johnson has stated:

> We do the strangest things to scuttle our success. Whether it's because we're afraid of leaving our nest, or afraid of failing, we can freeze when it comes time to open our wings ... be bold.

Since writing the first edition of this book I have grown to appreciate trading more than ever. At that time, it was just a few months since I had given birth to my son, Ryan, and I was totally besotted. (I've since had a daughter as well.) As I typed the first edition of this book, Ryan played at my feet, desperately trying to learn how to crawl.

Many women who had babies around the same time returned to full-time employment almost immediately. Some were happy about that prospect, but some were not.

The stark reality is that we are exactly where we are in life as a result of our past decisions. I am more grateful than ever that I decided to master some of the challenges that the sharemarket laid before me. I can now choose how much time I spend outside the home, away from the ones I love. Some people do not have this choice.

I believe there is more opportunity today than ever before in history — and this is especially true in the world of trading. There are more tools available and instruments to trade with more quality education than there has ever been.

A glimpse into your future

Imagine a time in your future, in just a few years. Imagine completing a trade so perfectly, so well executed, so flawlessly that you know in your gut that you are worthy of the title — Trader.

There you are, in front of your computer, leaning forward slightly, watching the market action, every part of you alive, the picture of complete concentration.

You look at the chart and your set-up is ideal. Now, if you can just wait for the trigger to occur ... there it is. You wait, tiger-like, stalking your prey. And then, bam — there's the trigger you've been waiting for.

You move in for the kill, hit enter, set your stop, lean back in your chair and then with a deep sigh, cross your arms behind your head. This is what you've been working for, educating yourself for, hoping for. A trading life where you act with no hesitation, and with complete confidence — protected by your trading system's method of setting stop losses and precision position sizing. You have traded like a machine and every cell in your body recognises this as fact.

You feel worthy and even more determined to seek out even greater levels of success. This is your aim. To be totally self-assured as a trader, knowing you can rely on support of your peers, and to continue to grow, to develop and to polish your skills.

In five years' time, your life could look very different from the way that it does today. What decisions are you currently making that will affect the shape of your life in the years to come? If you really focus on developing and practising your trading skills, what will this mean to you in the future? What are you prepared to do today so you can achieve your goals?

Just as I could not help my children crawl and walk before they were ready, I cannot help you to answer these important questions. Before my little ones could walk, they had to fall over many times. You will probably have to fail a few times on your way to trading profitably, although I hope the lessons you have completed in this book will cushion your fall. If you persist, and commit yourself to your education, success may be closer than you think.

But, isn't it easy for you now, Louise?

Personally, there are days when I hesitate to pull the trigger. The trades are few and far between, and I feel frustrated. The kids are making too much of a racket for me to think, my 'to-do' list seems like it's a mile long and I'm starting to get a sore throat. I doubt myself and wonder why in the heck I ever decided to become a full-time trader.

However, sometimes I sit at my computer, and trades jump out at me like I'm watching a 3D movie. Everything seems so bright and clear, as if I'm seeing a sunlit coral reef through 30 feet of sparkling azure water.

Those days are like magic. I pull the trigger, I'm in the zone, and everything else in my life fades into the background. I am one with the markets.

I can't tell you exactly where those days come from, but I can tell you that these occasions don't come from a particularly logical place. It's my guess that usually, my feelings about a particular trading day spring less from my actual circumstances, and more from a deeper subconscious level. That's why you have to focus on more than just learning the charting techniques. It's your job now to immerse yourself in mindset tricks to help drive you onwards to success.

Hundreds of brand new members join my Trading Game community every month by registering for my free newsletter on www.tradinggame.com.au. Some are flushed out before they even slow down to take a good look around. I know why. Trading looks like work. It requires a certain level of persistence just to even dip their toe in the water and some shiver and run away before they give themselves a chance to 'get it'.

This is exactly why the wealth of the population is pyramid shaped, with only a few people rising to the upper echelons. Personally, I've never entertained any dreams about creating the first community where everyone can make it to the top of the tree.

I work with the small minority of people who are persistent and do what they say they are setting out to do. I have very little interest in the rest. This is the exact same approach that money takes, by the way.

Makes you think, doesn't it?

We've come a long way together throughout this book. The secrets of the chart have been unveiled and I've begun to get you curious about the fulfilling life of a trader. Because you've completed the exercises I've set for you, you should now be able to detect a trend from 100 paces. You ought to understand set-ups and triggers and be ready to put together a strategy to help guide your entry conditions. With a bit of work, you will be able to establish your stop-loss procedures and your risk and money management methodologies to round out your trading system. Combined with your goals and contingency planning, your trading plan will be taking shape.

You now have much more knowledge than I ever did when I started to trade. Have courage. You have my support. However, to reach the top, you'll have to persist, grow and become the person worthy of making the money you feel you deserve.

I want to be your lighthouse in the fog and encourage you to take one more step. I want to celebrate your successes, and point out where you can learn from your errors.

I feel very grateful that our paths have crossed in life. I appreciate each and every person who tells me about their accomplishments and that in some small way I've helped them achieve their goals. You are my soul food.

Take my encouragement and create your own destiny.

Go out there and make me proud!

Appendix A
Candlestick basics

Information in this appendix is taken from my book *The Secret of Candlestick Charting*.

Candlestick patterns fall into two broad groups, continuation patterns and reversal patterns. Continuation patterns suggest that the share will continue over the short term in a particular direction. Reversal patterns imply that a share is likely to change direction completely or simply flatten into a sideways trend (figure A.1, overleaf).

Reversal patterns will be the focus for the following discussion.

Some common candlestick patterns

The shooting star
This pattern displays an upper tail length that is at least two times the length of the real body (figure A.2, overleaf). When a gap (or a hole in the share price action) is present between the previous candle and the shooting star, the significance of this formation is intensified. This principle is relevant for all candlestick patterns. The shooting star, as with all top reversal candlestick formations, has greater significance if it is black. Shooting stars appear at the top of a trend and signify that the bears are likely to move in with strength and that a downtrend could occur.

Figure A.1: reversal patterns

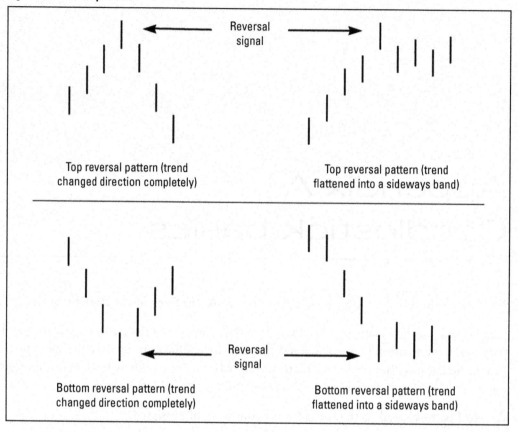

Figure A.2: the shooting star

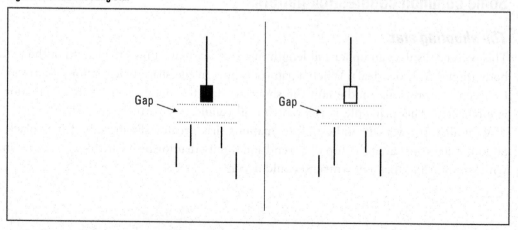

In these figures, the small bars positioned before and after the candlestick formation represent the direction of the preceding and following prices on the chart. They have no other special significance.

The doji

The doji displays an extremely small real body (figure A.3). The open and close are at the same price (or nearly at the same price) for that period. A doji shows that the market has temporarily come to an agreement that this particular price represents a fair value in the minds of the traders. The share will typically reverse its direction the day after a doji appears in the chart of an uptrending or downtrending stock.

Figure A.3: the doji

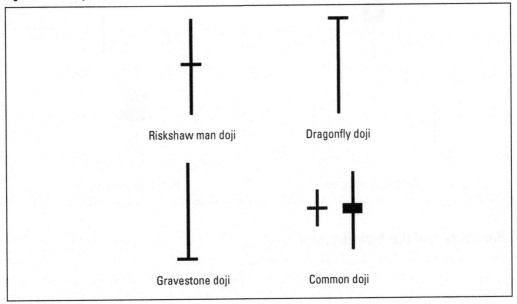

Riskshaw man doji   Dragonfly doji

Gravestone doji   Common doji

The spinning top

Spinning tops are similar to doji, in that they both display a small real body (figure A.4). The real body in a spinning top formation depicts a greater range from the open to the close in comparison to a doji pattern. The tail length is largely unimportant and the candle can be either white or black. This pattern represents a tug of war between bulls and bears and is accentuated by the presence of a gap before and after its formation.

Figure A.4: the spinning top

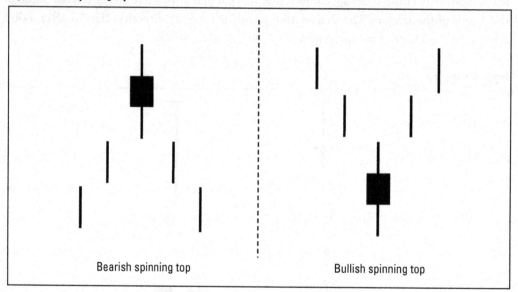

Bearish spinning top   Bullish spinning top

Hammers and the hanging man

These patterns display a long tail above or below their real bodies (figure A.5). There is likely to be no tail, or a very short tail on the other side of their real body. The tail length is required to be two times the length of the real body to fulfil the exact definition of this candle. Gaps increase the significance of the pattern. Look for these patterns at the top or bottom of trends to signify that a reversal is likely.

Figure A.5: hammers and the hanging man

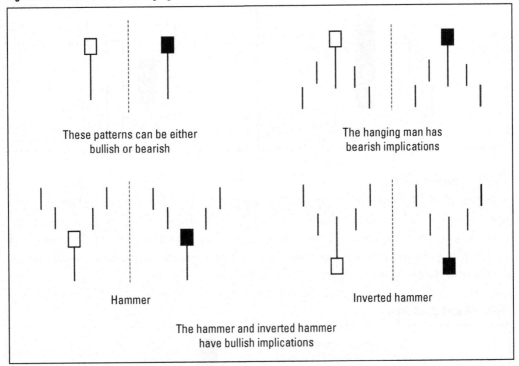

These patterns can be either
bullish or bearish

The hanging man has
bearish implications

Hammer

Inverted hammer

The hammer and inverted hammer
have bullish implications

The bearish engulfing pattern

This two-candle combination is an extremely effective pattern that often dramatically signifies the end of an uptrend (figure A.6, overleaf). After the appearance of this pattern, prices typically plunge downwards steeply. The second real body of this pattern totally engulfs the first real body and is a bearish sign as the price has closed lower than it opened for that period. The colour of the candles must be white for the first candle and black for the second candle.

The bullish engulfing pattern

This candle pattern often signifies the end of a downtrend (figure A.7, overleaf). After the pattern has been formed, prices often surge upwards. The colour of the candles must be black for the first candle and white for the second candle.

Figure A.6: bearish engulfing pattern **Figure A.7: bullish engulfing pattern**

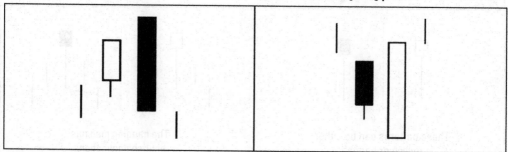

Dark cloud cover

This two-candle formation is a top reversal pattern (figure A.8). The second black candle must penetrate 50 per cent or more into the body of the white candle. The dark cloud cover pattern is not quite as significant as the bearish engulfing pattern. In candlestick philosophy, patterns that are more significant display greater penetration levels of one candle into the body of another.

Figure A.8: dark cloud cover

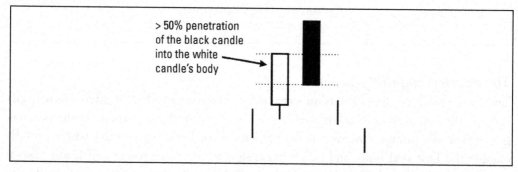

The piercing pattern

This two-candle bottom reversal pattern is the inverse of a dark cloud cover (figure A.9). The 50 per cent, or more, penetration level of the second candle into the body of the first is essential to fulfil the definition of this pattern.

The evening star

This bearish three-candle top reversal pattern shows a long white real body (1), a small star of either colour (2), then a black real body (3) (figure A.10). The evening star pattern is especially significant if there are gaps between each candle.

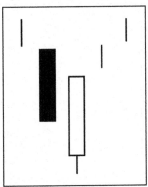

Figure A.9: the piercing pattern

Figure A.10: the evening star

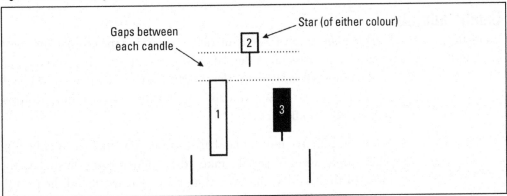

The morning star

This bullish three-candle bottom reversal pattern shows a long black real body (1), a small star of either colour (2), then a white real body (3) (figure A.11, overleaf).

Figure A.11: the morning star

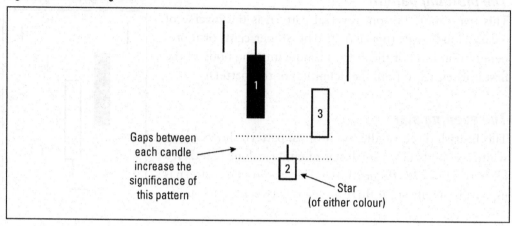

Gaps between each candle increase the significance of this pattern →

Star (of either colour)

Candle addition

Using the process of *candle addition* can assist in further ascertaining the ultimate meaning of a candlestick pattern. This process takes the data from several periods and reduces it to the one session. Perhaps the simplest way to learn about this skill is to think about how five daily candlesticks can combine to form one weekly candlestick.

Candle addition takes the data from several periods and reduces it to the one session.

For example, five individual daily candles may form a weekly doji. This single weekly candle takes the open for the first day, the close of the last day, the overall high for that week and the overall low for that week. Using this data, a single candle can be drawn, rather than five separate candles.

For multiple line candlestick patterns it is useful to use the process of candle addition to determine whether the meaning of the formation is unambiguously bullish or bearish. Let's have a look at the process of candle addition with the bearish engulfing pattern as a practical example (figure A.12). When we take the open of candle (1) and the close of candle (2), the real body of candle (3) is formed. The highest high of candle (1) *or* (2) forms the high for candle (3). The lowest low of candle (1) *or* (2) forms the low for candle (3).

Figure A.12: candle addition

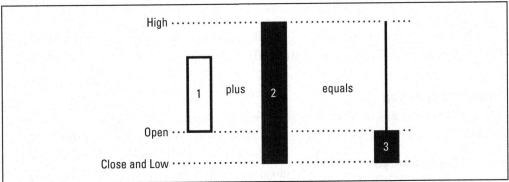

The bearish engulfing pattern reduces to a formation with a clear bearish direction bias — a black shooting star. This demonstrates that this type of pattern is unambiguously bearish. Remember to look at the lead-up to the candlestick pattern, the pattern itself and whether it has been confirmed to evaluate the efficacy of the formation.

If you feel inspired, you can go back through the other multiple line reversal patterns and use the process of candle addition to give you an understanding regarding which patterns are more powerful.

Continuation patterns

Continuation patterns suggest that the share will continue over the short term in a specific direction. Often they will imply a temporary hesitation before the share continues its vigorous trending behaviour. It is a positive sign if an instrument pauses, prior to commencing its uptrend, especially after a major push upwards. This pause will often be displayed as a band of consolidation of trading activity and will, in all probability, form a base of support through which future trading activity is unlikely to penetrate.

The use of a reversal pattern is generally related to entry and exit procedures. They can indicate it is time to take profits on a position, or tell you to get involved with a share because it is ripe and ready to be plucked. Continuation patterns are more likely to give you the confidence to stay with your winning trade. They may also present you with a belated entry trigger, just in case you missed the original signal.

Let's have a look at some of the more common continuation patterns available, and use the process of candle addition to evaluate their strength.

Upside tasuki gap

The upside tasuki gap occurs when an uptrend is in process. The initial white candle is followed by an upward gap to the next white candle. The third session shows a black candle that closes into the gap, but does not fully close the gap. If the gap was fully closed by this black candle, it would have to close at or below the closing price of the first white candle. The final black candle must open within the body of the second session, to strictly adhere to the traditional definition (figure A.13).

Figure A.13: upside tasuki gap

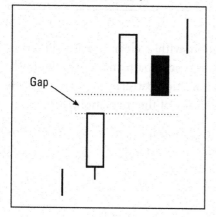

Candle addition

The upside tasuki gap reduces to a long line with the white body at the base. A white body is considered to be bullish, suggesting an uptrend continuation. However, the upper shadow suggests potential rejection of higher prices, which indicates a *lack* of strong bullish support. This is important to note, as you will need to identify stronger confirmation in comparison to a pattern with a more bullish reduction (figure A.14).

Figure A.14: candle addition, upside tasuki gap

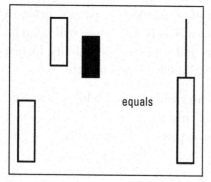

The share must already be in uptrend prior to the appearance of the trigger candle. The upside tasuki gap is likely to continue this upward trend. Adequate confirmation should involve the next session's trading activity maintaining above the gap created between the first and the final candle.

If this gap is closed, it is unlikely that the uptrend will be sustained in the short term at least.

Downside tasuki gap

This bearish counterpart to the upside tasuki gap shows the first black day gapping strongly down at the opening of the next session. The second candle is also black. The third line is white and opens within the body of the second candle. It fails to close the gap formed between the first and second candles (figure A.15). In effect, this gap acts as resistance.

Figure A.15: downside tasuki gap

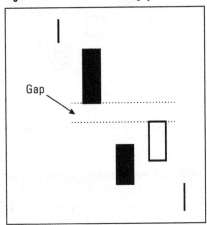

Candle addition

This pattern reduces to a long black line with a black real body located at the top. The black body is bearish, but the long lower shadow signifies rejection of lower prices. You should seek a more stringent form of confirmation prior to acting on the basis of this resulting candlestick (figure A.16).

The downside gap tasuki should be located within a downtrend. To signify a reversal, the candle following this pattern should close the gap. If this does not occur, the gap is likely to provide a band of resistance for future trading activity. For this reason, this pattern is likely to extend the existing trend, rather than reverse it.

Figure A.16: candle addition, downside tasuki gap

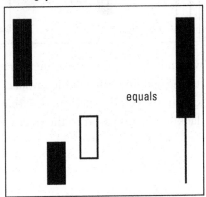

Rising three method

This is a continuation pattern that consists of five separate candles. The first candle is a white long day, and the following three candles are small bodied and usually confined to the trading range of the initial candle. These three central candles can be either black or white. It is the placement of these candles that implies a weak bearish downtrend, not their colour.

Figure A.17: rising three method

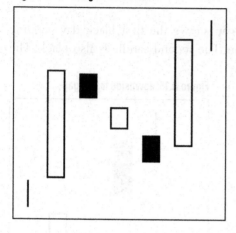

The final candle is also a long white candle that often opens at, or above, the opening price of the initial candle. It closes above the closing price of the initial candle, indicating a bullish perspective (figure A.17).

Candle addition

The rising three method reduces to a long white candle. This bullish reduction shows the power of the rising three method, and indicates that a less stringent form of confirmation is necessary. Any subsequent candle with a trading range above the midpoint of the final white candle would be confirmation of a bullish continuation (figure A.18).

Figure A.18: candle addition, rising three method

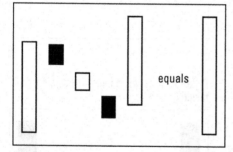

equals

A common definition of an uptrend is for an instrument to consistently experience higher lows and higher highs. This pattern complies with this definition because the final candle displays a more bullish close than the initial candle.

The rising three method offers a high probability of bullish trend continuation. You will notice that it takes three bearish sessions for the share price to drop to a value close to the opening price of the initial candle. In addition, this bearish effort to drive the price down was totally eradicated within the one final bullish session. The bearish sessions are lacklustre compared to the decisive direction of the bullish white candles.

Falling three method

This bearish continuation pattern shows the first black long candle preceding three small-bodied candles. These three candles are mostly contained within the real body range of the initial candle and can be either black or white. It is the placement of these candles that implies a weak bullish uptrend, not their colour.

The final candle has a long black real body that closes below the body of the initial candle. This close at a lower price level ensures that the pattern has made a lower low, therefore it is undeniably bearish (figure A.19).

Candle addition

The falling three method reduces to one long black candle, which fully supports the bearish continuation (figure A.20).

The share must be in downtrend when the falling three method forms. It will often penetrate a previous level of support.

Figure A.19: falling three method

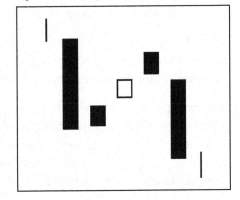

Figure A.20: candle addition, falling three method

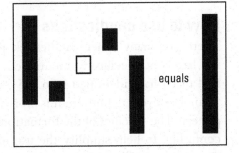

Final thoughts on continuation patterns

You will find *many* other examples of continuation patterns in other candlestick texts. For years I have sought to find clear consistently occurring examples in Australian charts. Unfortunately, I have not been able to utilise the continuation patterns in the same way that I have profitably traded with reversals.

Allow the continuation patterns we have discussed to confirm your knowledge about the psychology guiding the creation of the candle, rather than dismiss them altogether. The lessons they can teach us are valuable, even if the frequency of their appearance in Australian charts is not as significant.

The three point back-testing plan

Whilst reviewing the chart history of the instrument, I have found that it is of assistance to note the three main aspects:

Look for the *frequency* of pattern occurrence, the *immediate responsiveness* to individual patterns and the longer term *effectiveness* of these formations. Effectiveness refers to whether or not this pattern had an enduring effect.

For example, if there are many doji on a chart that did *not* appear to influence the share price action, then the appearance of a new doji is likely to be ineffective. The appearance of an infrequent, but powerful doji should catch your eye. Perhaps, after the appearance of a doji, a gap of 2 per cent was historically common. It is likely that a gap of this magnitude may occur again if another doji appears.

With practise, you will be able to evaluate the strength of particular multiple line patterns without resorting to the process of candlestick addition.

How to use candlesticks

There are many other candlestick patterns that appear in Australian charts. Even if I have not specifically mentioned a particular pattern in this appendix, you may find that I have identified it in the exercises you are about to complete. Rather than memorise every definition, it is more important to internalise the meaning behind each pattern. The specifics of the formation of candlestick patterns may initially seem a little confusing. To help simplify the use of the candlestick, try focusing on the following aspects of a candle:

- **Candle colour:** Look at the chart, and see whether there are more white candles or more black candles. If there are more white candles, it is likely that the predominant emotion in the market is bullish. If there are more black candles, the bears are more likely to be in control of the bulls.

- **Candle length:** Observe the length of the candles. Look at the real body length, as well as the length of the tails. If there are longer white candles, compared to black, then the bulls are in control. If the black candles are longer than the white, the bears are winning the battle. Roughly equal numbers of black and white candles imply that the share is likely to be travelling in a sideways band, and neither the bulls nor the bears are dominating.

- **Tail location:** If there are lots of tails pointing upwards, this indicates selling pressure and the share is likely to fall in value. If there are many tails pointing downwards, then the buyers are moving into the market and the share is likely to increase in value.

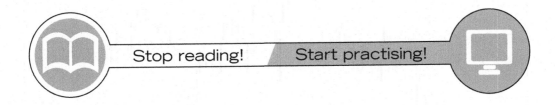

Have a look at the following charts (figures A.21 to A.24) and circle any relevant candlestick patterns you can see. In the space provided write as many notes as you need to help you reveal their secrets. My suggested answers to these exercises are illustrated in figures A.25 to A.28.

Figure A.21: ANZ weekly

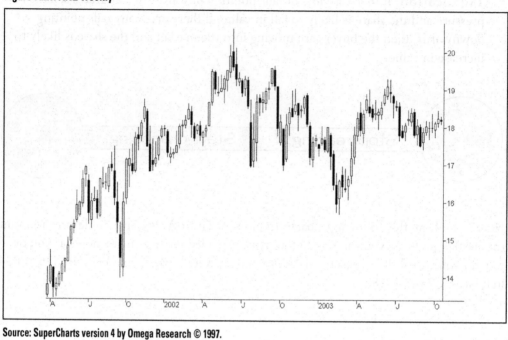

Source: SuperCharts version 4 by Omega Research © 1997.

....

....

....

....

....

....

....

....

....

Figure A.22: BIL weekly

Source: SuperCharts version 4 by Omega Research © 1997.

....

....

....

....

....

....

....

....

....

....

Figure A.23: TLS daily

Source: SuperCharts version 4 by Omega Research © 1997.

Figure A.24: WBC daily

Source: SuperCharts version 4 by Omega Research © 1997.

Answers

Figure A.25: ANZ weekly

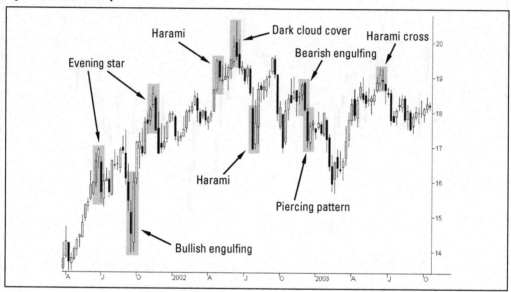

Source: SuperCharts version 4 by Omega Research © 1997.

Figure A.26: BIL weekly

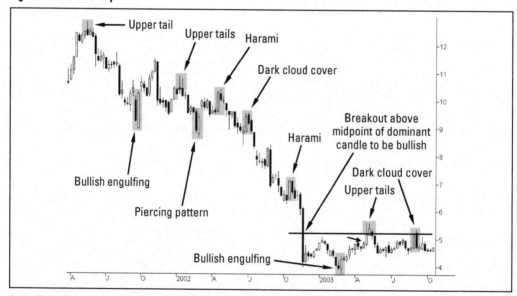

Source: SuperCharts version 4 by Omega Research © 1997.

Figure A.27: TLS daily

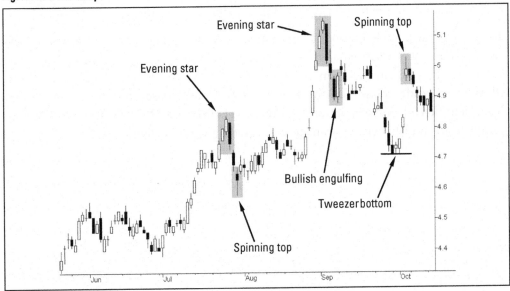

Source: SuperCharts version 4 by Omega Research © 1997.

Figure A.28: WBC daily

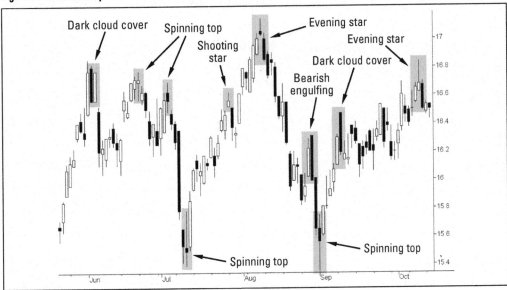

Source: SuperCharts version 4 by Omega Research © 1997.

Think about the share price direction and the ingenious way that candlesticks reveal the mass psychology of the market. Clever little darlings, aren't they?

To extend your knowledge about candlestick patterns, I suggest you read my book *The Secret of Candlestick Charting* and complete my DVD program of the same title. Once you're ready, you can then progress onto my *Candlestick Charting Home Study Course*. (If you've already completed the Home Study Course, you almost certainly would have identified a few extra patterns on the charts in figures A.21 to A.24). All of these products are available via my website www.tradingsecrets.com.au.

Appendix B
Back-testing

In this appendix, we will examine the research required to effectively back-test a trading system. Conducting in-depth research using technical analysis techniques can be quite a complex task. You should set some objectives and consider the following:

1   Establish your term for trading: intra-day; short term — one day to three weeks; medium term — two to 40 weeks; long term — nine or more months.

2   Direction of trade: long or short, or both.

3   Market to trade: equities, equity derivatives, index futures or derivatives, foreign exchange, commodity futures or bonds. Essentially you need to decide whether you wish to trade leveraged or non-leveraged markets. When you are starting, it is best to trade non-leveraged areas and slower-moving markets until you are ready to take off your training wheels.

4   Instruments to trade: all equities, only volatile equities, large cap equities, equity exchange-traded options (ETOs), equity warrants, instalment warrants, selection of commodity futures.

5   Exchanges to trade: local or overseas, multiple exchanges.

6   Average move that you wish to capture: the more leveraged the market you trade, the smaller the market move that you need to capture, and the shorter the hold period need be. Longer term systems need to capture larger market moves.

7   Minimum winning rate: the larger the market move you are trying to capture, the lower the winning rate required.

8   Minimum profit ratio (that is, the ratio of average profit trade size to average loss trade size): the longer the term you wish to hold trades, the higher this will need to be.

9   Frequency of trading: the more frequently you trade, the more time you will require for your whole trading business and the smaller the market move that you will need to capture.

Now that you have set some objectives for your trading system you can start thinking of entry and exit concepts that may suit your chosen objectives.

By now you may be getting the idea that there are limitless permutations of concepts you can research. This can be a never-ending exercise unless you remain focused on meeting the objectives that you have set and your expectations for your final system are not too high. It can be daunting, but just remember that every trader had to start somewhere, and there are many people less intelligent than you who are successfully trading somewhere in the world.

Research

Research is an objective, structured process. It aims to determine entry and exit rules based on historical data. This will provide the trader with an edge.

The research of entry and exit concepts excludes brokerage costs and slippage. You will need to account for these costs at a later stage.

The trader of a researched trading system does not try to find profitable trades or try to avoid loss trades. The focus is not necessarily on analysis; it is on following regular processes that result in engaging the market according to the rules of the trading system.

Successful discretionary traders are also the product of research. Their research is a more subtle process that has been completed over many years of experience in the markets. They follow intuitive rules on a consistent basis.

Measuring your entry/exit methodology

The objective of doing this research is to define a set of unambiguous entry and exit signals that:

- have a positive expectancy

- are able to be repeated in the future

- are practical for you to use to engage the market.

A positive expectancy should be measured over a large enough sample of historical trades. Obviously, the larger the sample of trades that are researched, the more robust the expectancy will be over the long haul. My book *Trading Secrets* shows you how to measure your expectancy.

Developing confidence in your entry/exit methodology is an essential step. If you trust your methodology, and you have internalised the concepts, you are much more likely to follow it during periods of trading pressure.

Paper trading

Rather than risking 'real' money in the markets, a lot of traders begin by paper trading. They write down every detail of their trade in a trading diary, including their position sizing, stop loss and profit-taking procedures. They imagine that they're really going to take the trade and record their entry price and monitor the stock as time goes on. This has the effect of the trader gaining some valuable experience using the trading signals and processes provided by the trading system without the risk that goes along with investing.

Unfortunately, there are a couple of problems with this idea. In *The Tao of Trading*, Robert Koppel says:

> You can't kid yourself in trading. You have to deal with who you really are, and take responsibility for all your shortcomings, which the markets have a way of revealing rather starkly. You have to confront all your fears and tame them. You have to check your ego at the door. You learn from each experience. What I have learned is this: Patience and diligence are rewarded. Profits will eventually accrue if you do the right thing and stick with it.

Paper trading sometimes allows people to bluff themselves that they are actually more skilled than reality suggests.

It is wise to try at least a few trades on paper at first, especially if you are testing a new trading system. This is especially true if you are beginning to trade a new instrument that you haven't traded before, such as options and short selling. This will give you a chance to understand how these instruments work before risking your capital. However, no matter how clever we are at paper trading, there is nothing like putting your own money into the market and experiencing the ultimate emotional roller-coaster. Our emotions have a very real impact on our ability as traders.

Gaining confidence in your system

In *The Best: Conversations with Top Traders*, Marder and Dupee comment:

> One of the most important things in trading the markets is finding that critical balance between a good level of confidence in your trading and a real sense of perpetual humility.

Some people find by trading small packages, or even just buying or selling one or two shares at a time can help them develop confidence in their system. Contracts for difference (CFDs) can help you do this while paying minimal brokerage. You can take a position in a share without having to put up the full underlying contract value. Instead, you put up a deposit or margin as initial collateral. The minimum margin requirement can be just 10 per cent of the contract value. With CFDs you are trading a contract that represents the share. This has many benefits.

Although you are only charged minimal brokerage, other fees may be charged such as a holding fee for keeping the trade open overnight. However, this cost is usually negligible in comparison to the full service fees charged by some brokers. The benefit of paying minimal brokerage is, of course, immediately apparent. One of the side benefits is that you can test out your theories in real life, without being penalised for gaining this knowledge. This is one way to accumulate trading experience when using a new system or just regaining some confidence. Another benefit is that a CFD position on a stock index remains open until you decide to close it. There are no automatic expiries or roll-overs, so many traders consider them to be a simpler transaction compared to an options trade.

CFDs have literally caused a trading revolution. Traders have flocked to this new tool to gain access to leverage, and have the ability to go long and short on a variety of tools such as the ASX Top 100 shares. Other possibilities include CFDs on stock market indices, foreign exchange and metals. For ideas on which CFD provider to utilise, refer to my website www.tradingsecrets.com.au.

Another way to develop confidence in your system is to enter the annual ASX trading competition. Information about this competition is available through www.asx.com.au. The competition forces you to be answerable for your trading decisions because you must register your trades with a third party. This has worked well for many traders.

When developing a robust trading plan, you will need to consider the issues we have just discussed. If you would like to follow a trading plan template, have a look in my book *Trading Secrets* or on my website.

Even though it seems that there is a lot of work in effectively back-testing a trading system, try not to get caught in an analysis-paralysis trap. Commit money to the market and you will receive the most honest feedback available. Don't be daunted by the amount of detail trading can sometimes involve. Endeavour to gain confidence in your system and jump in. The market rewards the brave and vigilant.

Further reading and education

Introductory

Bedford, Louise, *The Secret of Candlestick Charting*, Wrightbooks, 1999

Bedford, Louise, *The Secret of Candlestick Charting Poster*, via www.tradingsecrets.com.au

Bedford, Louise, *The Secret of Candlestick Charting Video Program*, available on DVD via www.tradingsecrets.com.au

Bedford, Louise, *The Secret of Pattern Detection Poster*, via www.tradingsecrets.com.au

Bedford, Louise, *Trading Secrets: Killer trading strategies to beat the markets and finally achieve the success you deserve*, 3rd edition, Wrightbooks, 2012

Bedford, Louise; Tate, Chris; & Dr Stanton, Harry, *Psychology Secrets — Peak Performance for Traders Double CD*, via www.tradingsecrets.com.au

Darvas, Nicolas, *How I Made $2,000,000 in the Stockmarket*, Lyle Stuart Inc., 1986

Tate, Chris, *The Art of Trading*, Wrightbooks, 2001

Weinstein, Stan, *Secrets for Profiting in Bull and Bear Markets*, Irwin Professional Publishing, 1988

Intermediate/advanced

Bedford, Louise, *Candlestick Charting Home Study Course*, via www.tradingsecrets.com.au

Bedford, Louise, *The Secret of Writing Options*, Wrightbooks, Reprint 2000

Bedford, Louise; Tate, Chris; & Dr Stanton, Harry, *Psychology Secrets — Peak Performance for Traders Double CD*, via www.tradingsecrets.com.au

Bulkowski, Thomas N., *Encyclopedia of Chart Patterns*, John Wiley & Sons, 2000

Seligman, Martin E.P., *Learned Optimism*, Random House Australia, 1992

Tate, Chris, *The Art of Options Trading*, 2nd Edition, Wrightbooks, 2001

Tharp, Van K., *Trade Your Way to Financial Freedom*, McGraw Hill, 199

Glossary

aggressability   The tendency to make up words that vaguely suggest a heightened level of aggression, but then to react aggressively when tackled on the origin of the word ... so watch your step!

ask   See *bid*.

at-market or at-the-market   An order to buy or sell an option or a share at the prevailing market price.

at-the-money   When the exercise price of the option is close to, or equal to, the current market price.

average down   Buying more of a security that is not co-operating with your initial view. For example, buying more of a downtrending share. You are trading against the trend. Only ever buy more of uptrending shares.

average true range   The average of the true ranges over the past x periods (where x is specified by the user). See also *true range*.

average up   To buy more of a share that is co-operating with your initial view.

back-test   A method of testing an indicator's performance by applying it to historical data.

bar chart   The standard form of chart utilised in Western technical analysis. A single bar consists of an open price, a high, a low and a close price for a particular session.

bear/bearish   A trader with a negative expectation of the market or share. Some texts use this phrase to signify a sideways-trending market as well as a downtrending market. For the sake of simplicity, this text will use 'bearish' to represent a downtrending market or share.

bid   The price at which buyers have registered their interest in a share. A real-time screen will show the buyers that are queuing to buy the share as bids, and the sellers queuing to sell their shares as asks.

black box system   A trading system where all buy and sell signals are generated, yet the calculation or rationale for these signals is not disclosed.

black candle   A bearish session showing the close lower than the opening price.

breakaway gap   See *gaps*.

breakout trade   An entry into a long position in an instrument in an existing uptrend after a significant level of resistance has been bullishly transcended.

bull/bullish   A trader with a positive expectation that prices will rise in the market or for a particular share.

call option   A call option gives the buyer the right, but not the obligation, to buy a given security at a particular price up to and including the day of expiry.

candle body size   The size of the real body can provide a clue as to the level of conviction of either the bulls or the bears. The presence of a long candle in relation to the most recent candles of previous sessions holds special significance.

candle range   The range from the high to the low, or the peak of the upper shadow to the base of the lower shadow, is a general indicator of the level of volatility for that period.

candlesticks   A 17th-century Japanese technique that contains the same information as a Western bar chart, but in a different graphic representation. Candlestick patterns of one, two, three or more candles (bars) provide an excellent timing/confirmation tool when used in conjunction with other indicators.

capital   The amount of equity or money that you have set aside with which to begin trading.

capitalisation   See *market capitalisation*.

confirmation   The activity of the share price action after the appearance of a *trigger* pattern. Some patterns require greater levels of confirmation than others.

consolidation   See *sideways trend*.

continuation gap   See *gaps*.

continuation pattern   After the appearance of this pattern, a share is likely to continue in the direction of the predominant, established trend. These patterns imply a pause or consolidation within the prevailing trend.

contracts   Options are sold by the contract. One option contract usually controls 1000 shares. For example, five BHP options contracts would control 5000 BHP shares.

correction   A movement in prices against the general trend, which typically occurs with little or no warning. For instance, the market periodically loses value as many of the underlying securities drop in price by several per cent. This typically occurs with little or no warning.

counter-trend reversals   A brief pause before the share continues its vigorous trending activity.

defensive actions   A last resort when the share goes against the view you had when initially writing the option. Defensive actions are a way of removing yourself from risk and minimising your potential loss if the trade goes against you.

delta   The sensitivity of option price to changes in share price.

derivatives   A derivative is a financial instrument that has another asset as its underlying base; for example, options and/or warrants.

dividend   A part of a company's net profit that is paid periodically to shareholders as a cash reward for investing in the company's shares.

double top   This pattern is where price action on a chart displays that the price has rallied twice in quick succession and stopped at or near the same high. This pattern forms two prominent peaks in the share price action and often signifies that a downtrend is imminent.

downtick   Any downward movement in price action. This downward movement can even be by the smallest available price increment available on the price scale; for example, 1¢.

downtrend   Prices are making consistently lower highs and lower lows.

downtrend line   A straight line is drawn in at downward right-slanting angle connecting the peaks of the share price action. Once the prices show evidence of rising above this line in a sustainable manner, it is likely that the downtrend has been broken. Ideally, this should be accompanied by an increase in volume.

drawdown   The term for when your trading account value is less than the highest value that it reached (which is usually the opening balance when first starting out).

equities   Another word for shares.

exchange-traded options   The options traded over shares in Australia are called 'exchange-traded options' or 'American options'. This type of option allows the optionholder to exercise the option at any time during the life of the contract.

ex-dividend   The day after the shareholders have taken the dividend. This typically results in a share price drop.

exercise   To exercise your rights as an option *buyer* means that the option has reached or is close to its strike price and you may exercise your *right* to buy or sell the shares covered by the option. You can do this at or before expiration. It is likely, however, that you will exercise your rights only after the share price has transcended the strike price of the option, or if there is a vested interest to exercise due to the effect of an ex-dividend scenario.

exhaustion gap   See *gaps*.

expectancy   This is a mathematical calculation that will provide a measure to show that for every dollar that you have invested in the market, how many dollars you will extract. Expectancy = (probability of winning × average win) − (probability of losing × average loss).

expiration date   The final date of the option contract. The duration of each option contract will often be 12 months or more in advance. As a writer, you can choose to write contracts on options with six months to expiry, or one month to expiry. The choice is up to you.

exponential moving average (EMA)   The exponential moving average places more emphasis (on an exponential basis) on the most recent sessions and forms a moving average line. A moving average takes the closes of several periods and plots a point. When several of these points are connected, a moving average line is formed. Moving averages are most effective as trend-following tools. They smooth out the price action but incorporate a time lag. A moving average in a sideways-moving market is less effective.

exposure   As a writer, this is the total possible amount of money that you would be liable for, if the options were to be exercised.

formation   See *pattern*.

fundamentals   Fundamental analysis assists in detecting which shares have a probability of increasing or decreasing in value, based on the company balance sheet and profit/loss details. Economic supply and demand information is analysed rather than the market activity of price and volume action on a share chart.

futures   An agreement which is legally binding to buy and sell specific quantities of specified commodities or financial instruments at a particular date in the future.

gaps   Gaps show that the price activity of the preceding period is completely above or below the next candlestick or bar apparent on the chart. Spaces or holes are left on the share chart when viewing candlestick charts or bar charts and these are called gaps. In Western analysis there are three main types of real gaps; continuation, exhaustion and breakaway. A continuation gap suggests that the prevailing trend direction is likely to continue. An exhaustion gap occurs after a trend that signals the trend direction is likely to end. These can often be observed prior to a reversal trigger candlestick pattern. A breakaway gap usually signals the beginning of a new trend and often confirms the new trend direction after a reversal trigger candle pattern. There are also false gaps—gaps that occur on low volume. Suckers' gaps are gaps that occur because of an ex-dividend situation.

illiquid   Instruments with low levels of trading are considered illiquid and are best avoided. By trading in illiquid options/shares, if the trade goes against you, exiting from your open positions will be considerably more difficult.

in-the-money   A call option that has the current share price above the strike price, or a put option that has the current share price below the strike price.

leverage   The degree to which an investor relies on borrowed money. Short selling and derivatives are leveraged tools, as you are not required to commit the full dollar amount of the underlying instrument to open a position.

line chart   A type of chart which connects the closing prices for each period to provide a continuous line that depicts share price action.

liquid   Shares or options with a significant number of buyers and sellers already participating in actively trading this instrument.

long candle   A candle showing a larger real body range than previous sessions on the chart.

long, or going long   This implies a bullish view of the market and describes when a trader purchases an instrument to initiate a transaction. When buying shares, traders have a long view of the market.

managed fund   A pool of money where investors relinquish power regarding buy and sell decisions to a fund manager, or a so-called professional trader.

margin   The amount of money retained in trust by the Options Clearing House or your broker, while you have an open written options position, a futures contract or a short-sold position. This insures your broker or the clearing house against a loss on your open positions.

margin loan   A sum of money that is available for you to borrow in order to purchase a select group of stocks; for example, top 100. Although specific firms' allocations will vary, you may be able to borrow up to 70 per cent of the value of the shares that you would like to purchase.

margin called   When the share price trends against your initial expectation, your broker will require an increased amount of money to be deposited, often within 24 hours, in order to maintain the original leveraged position margin ratio.

market capitalisation   The number of shares that have been issued in total, multiplied by the share price.

momentum   The velocity of a price trend. This type of indicator shows whether prices are declining at a faster or slower pace. Examples of momentum indicators are RSI, MACD, ROC and SIROC.

moving average   See *exponential moving average*.

moving average convergence divergence (MACD)   A momentum oscillator. It can also be displayed as a histogram, and displays likely overbought and oversold regions.

naked calls   Writing calls where you do not own the underlying security.

open interest   The number of outstanding option contracts at a particular strike price. This is a comparable concept to volume.

open-market risk   When you combine all of your active positions, calculate the exposure from the current share price to the stop price that you have stipulated, you will calculate your open-market risk.

out-of-the-money   The term for when the share price is below the strike price of the call option, or when the share price is above the strike price of a put option. Writing out-of-the-money call and put options is the most conservative and safe method of writing options.

overbought   This term and the following term are usually used in relation to momentum indicators. An overbought line may be constructed manually by looking at the historic high points on a momentum indicator, or it may be an integral part of the indicator and shown as an indexed number from 0 to 100. When a momentum indicator has risen to a historic or indexed high, it implies an overbought condition where the instrument may be vulnerable to a sell off.

oversold   An oversold line may be constructed manually by looking at the historic low points on a momentum indicator, or it may be an integral part of the indicator and shown as an indexed number from 0 to 100. When a momentum indicator has dropped to a historic or indexed low, it implies an oversold condition where the instrument may be likely to rally.

pattern   A single or a number of separate trading periods that form the data for a defined candlestick formation or other pattern, based on technical analysis.

period   The time increment on a share chart. For example, a daily chart would show each candlestick comprising the open, high, low and close price for a day. The terms session and period are interchangeable.

position size   This shows you how many of a particular instrument to buy or sell. There are several methods to assist in this goal — the equal portions model, the capital allocation model and the volatility-based model, for example.

premium   The dollar amount per share that is paid by the option buyer to the option writer.

pullback   See *retracement*.

put option   A put option gives the buyer the right to sell a given security at a certain price within a given time.

pyramid   To add more to your position as an instrument trends in the expected direction; for example, to buy more of an uptrending share. To do this effectively, you should buy the largest parcel of shares first, and then add increasingly smaller positions to your initial position.

rally   An upward movement of prices.

rate of change (ROC)   A momentum indicator with manually derived overbought and oversold conditions.

real body   The thick part of the candle representing the range between the opening price and the closing price. This is considered to be of more importance than high and low prices for that period.

relative strength index (RSI)   A momentum indicator, typically used on a 14-day timeframe, measured on a scale of 0 to 100, which computes the ratio of higher closes to lower closes and appears as an oscillator.

resistance   A price level where sellers are expected to enter. It appears above the current price action and suggests that the price becomes resistant to making a higher high.

retracement   A less significant version of a correction.

retracement trade   This is where an entry into a position is made, preferably on a candlestick bottom reversal, after the share prices have made a counter-trend reversal.

selling options   See *writing options*.

session   See *period*.

shadow   Shadows are the thin lines above and below the candlestick representing the extreme high and low for that session. The shadow provides an indication of buyer or seller strength. Tails, wicks and shadows are interchangeable terms.

shadow location   If there are long upper shadows at the top of an uptrend, this implies that the buyers have weakened and the sellers have begun to move in. If there are long lower shadows at the bottom of a downtrend, the price has dropped to a low enough level to encourage buyers to purchase the share.

short, or going short   This implies a bearish view where traders short sell the market, or sell to initiate a transaction. Selling shares and then purchasing them at a later date and a lower price can make substantial profits.

sideways trend   A period of lateral price movement within a relatively narrow price band between a level of support and a level of resistance.

slippage   The difference between estimated and actual transaction costs.

smoothed indexed rate of change (SIROC)   A proprietary indicator of www.sharewealthsystems.com.au and is an indexed momentum indicator.

stochastic (STO)   A non-indexed momentum indicator which shows the distance of the current close relative to the center of the high/low range.

stop loss   The predetermined price or set of conditions that prompt a trader to exit the trade and preserve his capital.

strike price   The price at which you can buy or sell the underlying security as an option buyer. For example, you may receive a '30¢ premium' when writing a call option at a '$12.50 strike price'.

support   A price level where buyers are expected to enter. It appears beneath the current market price and signifies that the price is resistant to making a lower low.

system design   Your entry, exit and position-sizing methods that should appear in a written trading plan.

tail   See *shadow*.

technical analysis   The use of price and volume action on a share chart to reach conclusions about the likely direction of future price activity.

trading plan   Your personalised business plan that depicts how you will go about trading the market. Entry, exit and position-sizing procedures should be explicitly addressed and written down before you initiate your first trade.

trigger candle   This is the actual appearance of a reversal or continuation pattern. For a one-line candle, the trigger will be represented by one session only. For more complex two-line patterns, the trigger will comprise two sessions.

true range   Defined by Welles Wilder, this indicator was developed to display the greatest of the following for each period:

- The distance from today's high to today's low.
- The distance from yesterday's close to today's high.
- The distance from yesterday's close to today's low.

uptick   Any upward movement in price action. This upward movement can even be by the smallest available price increment available on the price scale; for example, 1¢.

uptrend   Prices are making consistently higher highs and higher lows.

uptrend line   A straight line is drawn in an upward left slanting angle connecting the troughs of the share price action. Once the prices show evidence of dropping below this line in a sustainable manner, it is likely that the uptrend has been broken.

volatility   Choppy shares with greater distances from the peak to the trough of the share price are more volatile and will produce a greater candle range. For shares with a lower volatility level, the option premiums will also be lower. Shares that are illiquid will usually show heightened levels of volatility.

volume   The level of trading in a particular instrument. If volume increases in the direction of the trend or breakout, this adds to the weight of evidence that the share price movement is sustainable. A volume increase to confirm an uptrend is very important.

warrants   A certificate that gives the holder the right to purchase securities as a stipulated price within a specified time limit. A warrant is essentially a long-dated option. The main difference between warrants and options is that you cannot sell to initiate a warrant transaction (that is, you cannot write a warrant).

weight of evidence   Use more than one indicator to base your decision on the likely share direction. When several chart patterns and indicators point in the same direction, their signals are reinforced. If the weight of evidence of several indicators suggests that the share is uptrending, then the bulls have probably taken control of the market.

white candle   This candle shows a session where the closing price was higher than the opening price. This is inherently bullish.

wick   See *shadow*.

writing options   Option writers collect a premium or fee from an option buyer and, subsequently, they are obligated to fulfil the demands of the option buyer. In relation to call options, the writer must sell his shares or have the shares 'called away' if the buyer decides to exercise the right. A put option writer is under obligation to buy the shares from a put option taker should they be exercised; that is, have the shares 'put to them'.

Macro patterns index

(T) indicates a top reversal pattern.

(B) indicates a bottom reversal pattern.

(C) indicates a continuation pattern.

A blank indicates a particular type of pattern that does not form a continuation or reversal by itself.

Micro patterns index

(T) indicates a top reversal pattern.

(B) indicates a bottom reversal pattern.

(C) indicates a continuation pattern.

A blank indicates a particular type of candle that does not form a continuation or reversal by itself.

Candlestick pattern	Pattern implication	Page reference
The white candle		7
The black candle		8
Bullish dominant candle		202
Bearish dominant candle		202
Shooting star	(T)	288
Doji	(T) (B)	289
Spinning top	(T) (B)	290
Hammer	(B)	291
Inverted hammer	(B)	291
Hanging man	(T)	291
Bearish engulfing pattern	(T)	292
Bullish engulfing pattern	(B)	292
Dark cloud cover	(T)	292
Piercing pattern	(B)	293
Evening star	(T)	293
Morning star	(B)	294
Upside tasuki gap	(C)	296
Downside tasuki gap	(C)	297
Rising three method	(C)	298
Falling three method	(C)	299

Index

Testimonials

Take the first step towards financial freedom — read this book!

You are holding my favourite trading book and reading my testimonial, so please allow me to give you this advice — if you are serious about achieving success in the markets, then take this book home. Read it cover to cover. Do all the exercises that Louise has laid out for you, as I have. At the end, you will close the book feeling that the trading light switch has been turned on.

From this brilliant trader and caring mentor with decades of experience, you will learn what you need to do — and just as importantly, what you must not do — to make money in the markets, and to keep it. With Louise's continued generous mentorship and support I have a defined, mechanical trading system that enables me to trade successfully across different markets and time frames. Take the first step towards financial freedom — read this book!

Verica Cvetkovik, IT business analyst

Louise is a brilliant mentor

Louise is a brilliant mentor who is constantly educating and helping traders with different levels of experience. Once Louise takes you under her wing, you will always have her support. Louise is the type of mentor who is always there when you need her and cares about every mentoree's success. Louise's trading methods work. With Louise's help I was able to develop my own trading plan and I am currently supplementing my income through share trading. As a direct result of reading *Charting Secrets*, now I am able to analyse any chart and interpret the likely movement of any instrument. This helps me to make educated decisions from the moment I get involved in the market. My family and I are very thankful for her help.

Nestor Javier Garcia, mechanical engineer, SA

Louise has a rare mix of experience, patience and honesty

Louise has played a pivotal role in my journey towards becoming a trader. I originally read *Charting Secrets* back in 2006 and it resonated with me to such an extent that I decided to undertake the unique Mentor Program run with her and her business partner Chris Tate. Since then I have observed Louise mentoring hundreds of other traders with a rare mix of experience, patience and honesty. It is clear to me that Louise is passionate about trading and committed to helping those with a similar passion work towards realising their full potential.

Greg Rowney, senior systems analyst, WA

Louise's honesty has made all the difference...

Out of the many trading books I have read, *Charting Secrets* has proven to be the one and only that has provided a stepping stone to further knowledge and trading success. No proprietary system for sale. Just proven and tested, easy-to-understand methods.

For the first time trading CFDs, I find myself in a profitable situation. I'm finally 'in the black'. I have been very impressed with Louise's honesty and willingness to offer straightforward advice.

Sean Lowrey, mining bus driver, WA

I knew that I was onto a winner

When I first picked up *Charting Secrets* off the shelf of the bookstore, I knew that I was onto a winner. It had everything that I had been looking for to kickstart my trading journey. *Charting Secrets* is written in Louise Bedford's trademark simple and easy-to-read style, and her methods have been proven with consistency and longevity in the sharemarket.

Since reading *Charting Secrets*, I have progressed a long way with my trading and still use the timeless principles contained in the book. Louise has been there as a mentor, providing inspiration and constant encouragement to keep me on the right track. Thanks, Louise.

Ben Hinton, electronics technician, QLD

Any chart, across any time frame...

Charting Secrets will help you analyse any chart, across any time frame. It's analysis made clear and simple. Follow everything Louise says and her book will help you become chart savvy and give you the confidence you need to trade effectively.

Brian Carpenter, full-time trader, QLD

Louise sticks by her traders

Louise is passionate about her trader's success and she is passionate about educating. Together, this drive provides a great learning opportunity for anyone willing to seize it.

I wholeheartedly recommend Louise as a committed teacher and successful trader. She has effectively compressed her many years of results-driven experience into an informative, practical and digestible book. Her straight-line approach sets realistic expectations and provides a framework for approaching charts and the market. Having the opportunity to complete the exercises she provided was an effective way to reinforce the lessons. I finished *Charting Secrets* knowing I had gained a lot, and it continues to be a great reference for me.

But what I found, and continue to find, even more important is that Louise is available to provide support and assistance. There is never any risk of being left confused, unsure and feeling alone. She sticks by her traders.

Meisha Synnott, trader in the making, NSW

Louise will guide you through the confusing world of trading

Louise Bedford is the most passionate educator I've come across. She has an infectious enthusiasm, which shows that she cares about the people she teaches and genuinely wants them to succeed. I've found Louise's education to go beyond just learning about the markets and trading—her knowledge and experience can relate to many other areas in my life. Even through difficult times in the markets I've managed to maintain my capital as a direct result of Louise's education in her trading methods. You couldn't ask for a better educator to guide you through the, sometimes confusing, world of trading.

Kym Chilton, telecommunications engineer, QLD

I rediscovered my love for trading

A few years ago I blew up my trading account, AGAIN! I hit rock bottom as I discovered that I had failed at something I truly loved doing. I needed help and as a direct result of reading *Charting Secrets* I not only rediscovered my love for trading but I began to understand how to trade from both a charting and mental perspective.

I also learned that to succeed in the trading game you need a mentor. In Louise Bedford I found someone who was not only happy to share her extensive knowledge acquired over many years trading the markets but a kindred spirit whose generosity and guidance is unparalleled. She truly is the 'mother hen' for all traders in search of an edge to become successful at the craft.

Her trading methods work and she sticks by you through the journey. You can't ask for much more than that.

Matt Forster, bookkeeper, SA

Louise is nothing short of an inspiration

I first read Louise Bedford's books in 2007 and I am glad I did! What I discovered saved me a lot of money trading a risky options trading strategy that I was interested in at the time. Louise showed me that I was totally unprepared for the consequences of that strategy, and I'll be forever grateful.

I contacted Louise shortly after reading her books. From that moment on, she has been nothing short of an inspiration to me. Louise has been a constant source of encouragement and a brilliant mentor.

It's amazing how many of the simple principles I learned from reading her books and studying her material that I have utilised within my own trading system.

If you're interested in learning about trading I can highly recommend reading her books — especially *Charting Secrets*.

Beau Ryan, luxury yacht cruise operator, Seychelles

Not just another boring trading book…

When I opened Louise Bedford's book *Charting Secrets* I was thinking, 'Here we go again. Another book on charting'. But to my surprise, I was totally hooked as I began to realise that all the topics I needed were covered in the one book. I sat down and read it cover to cover. The guidelines Louise uses make total sense to me and really set this book apart from the rest.

Charting Secrets covers everything for beginner traders, advanced and all who's in-between. With easy-to-follow chapters containing screenshots, exercises and space for taking notes as you read, this book offers plenty of useful strategies. I couldn't put it down. What a great and enjoyable book to read!

Erol Andrews, policy and process management officer, VIC

More from Louise...

Charting Secrets is the ideal book for you, whether it is the first book on trading that you've picked up, or if you've read a few other books and you're looking to test your knowledge. You may have even read one of my other titles: *Trading Secrets, The Secret of Candlestick Charting* or *The Secret of Writing Options*, but you're looking for a bit more guidance in relation to charting techniques.

It would probably be logical to start with either this book or my earlier title *Trading Secrets: Killer trading strategies to beat the markets and finally achieve the success you deserve*, 3rd edition. These two books work well together when read as a pair, providing enough information to safely get you started trading or investing. Once you've read these titles, move onto *The Secret of Candlestick Charting*, which will give you more detailed information on this fascinating charting technique. When you've worked out how to trade shares, you may feel ready to apply leverage and read *The Secret of Writing Options*.

The Mentor Program

Louise also runs a six-month Mentor Program. Since the year 2000 this program has continuously booked out every time it opened for bookings. Mentorees love that they can repeat the course as many times as they like for free. Have a look at www.tradingsecrets. com.au and www.tradinggame.com.au for more information. If you're the type of trader who wants to learn how to trade every instrument over every timeframe, safely and confidently, by using your own bulletproof trading plan, then the Mentor Program is just what you've been looking for.

Your free trading pack

Make the best decision of your life. Register now for your trading pack at www.tradingsecrets.com.au...and best of all it's FREE. Here's what you'll get:

- an incredibly valuable trading plan template

- a free monthly email newsletter

- a five-part e-course valued at $99.00 called 'The Sharemarket—Your Unfair Advantage'

- a free month of access to the Trading Game Forum

- the chance to win a home study course.

Why is Louise giving you this pack for free?...

...I'll tell you why. So she can begin a relationship with you. Louise says, 'I'm hoping that after you've used my free resources, one day you'll come to one of my advanced seminars. I love helping people who want to take control of their sharemarket returns. It's my goal to put money into share traders' pockets and make it stick, even if they only have 30 minutes a day available and limited knowledge about trading'.

**Excellent traders are action takers. Don't delay. Go to
www.tradingsecrets.com.au and grab your
FREE trading pack right now.**

Register NOW for your FREE five-part e-course!

Also by Louise Bedford

Trading Secrets,

3rd Edition

Are you sick of watching your hard-earned funds slip away? Can you taste trading success but just don't know how to achieve it? Do you want to discover how to trade consistently and profitably?

Whether you're a novice trader or already in the game, this third edition of *Trading Secrets* is packed with everything you need to get in on the action. Known for her witty and entertaining style, Louise Bedford has demystified the world of share trading for thousands of investors and traders, and you're next!

Inside you'll find fascinating insights into: handling a windfall profit, identifying clear entry and exit signals, understanding the psychological factors that affect trading performance, setting stop losses and managing money.

Full of practical advice from an expert who has figured out the markets for herself, *Trading Secrets* is the book you need to get the most out of the world of trading.

Also by Louise Bedford

THE SECRET OF
Candlestick Charting

Most traders in the Australian stock and futures markets begin by using conventional bar charts to generate buy and sell signals—until they discover the analytical power of candlestick charting.

This Japanese technique dates back over 300 years. Candlestick charts pinpoint trend changes prior to many other methods. Whether you are a beginner or a sophisticated investor, you can learn how to use candlestick charting to trade the markets profitably, beginning with your next trade.

In this book you will discover a technique that has the potential to completely alter the way you view charting, yet is complementary to any of the knowledge you have accumulated so far about technical analysis. Written in easy-to-understand language, these techniques are highly recommended for any traders or investors who wish to develop their technical analysis abilities and enhance their profitability.

Also by Louise Bedford

THE SECRET OF
Writing Options

Once thought to be the domain of highly skilled investors, today more and more private investors and traders are entering the options market. One of the big attractions of options trading is that, unlike a traditional investor, an options trader can still make money in a sideways-trending or falling market.

This book is highly recommended for newcomers to options trading in Australia, and those already trading in the options markets. It starts with the basics, and discusses the discipline and attitude necessary to trade successfully. There is also a cleverly constructed game to play to see if you are ready to enter the options market.

Louise Bedford has degrees in psychology and business from Monash University. She trades full-time from her home in Melbourne and is a regular speaker on trading. She also conducts workshops and seminars throughout Australia.

Trading Secrets, 3rd Edition, *The Secret of Writing Options* and *The Secret of Candlestick Charting* are published by and available from Wrightbooks, an imprint of John Wiley & Sons Australia, Ltd.

"Somewhere inside you there is a brilliant trader wanting to come out."

From the trading desk of Louise Bedford …

**Louise Bedford
Your Trading Mentor**

"Louise Bedford here.

I'm on a quest!

A quest to create as many happy, independent, wealthy and skilled share traders as possible.

Make no mistake——successfully trading the sharemarket is one of the most valuable skills you'll ever learn. Once you know how to trade, **no-one can ever take this ability away from you**.

It's with you for life. The rewards will keep rolling in for you and your entire family.

Register now on my website and I'll give you my free five-part e-course and help you **finally nail the simple trading secrets necessary to make your profits soar.**"

Register NOW for your FREE five-part e-course!

"And just imagine, instead of battling on and struggling to work out the hidden secrets of the market all by yourself, you'll **feel secure and gain the confidence** that every exceptional trader needs to excel.

If you're serious about creating a better life for you and your family, then please don't wait with this one. You have absolutely nothing to lose by getting online right now."

Register at www.tradingsecrets.com.au for your free five-part e-course and you'll never look back.

QUEST-SUNDER-709

Printed in Australia
21 Jan 2019
696206

9 781118 543184